PUBLIC POLICIES

AND

PRIVATE INVESTMENT

PUBLIC POLICIES
AND
PRIVATE INVESTMENT

BY

JOHN F. HELLIWELL

ASSOCIATE PROFESSOR OF ECONOMICS
UNIVERSITY OF BRITISH COLUMBIA

CLARENDON PRESS · OXFORD
1968

Oxford University Press, Ely House, London W. 1

GLASGOW NEW YORK TORONTO MELBOURNE WELLINGTON
CAPE TOWN SALISBURY IBADAN NAIROBI LUSAKA ADDIS ABABA
BOMBAY CALCUTTA MADRAS KARACHI LAHORE DACCA
KUALA LUMPUR HONG KONG TOKYO

PRINTED IN GREAT BRITAIN

ACKNOWLEDGEMENTS

My debts are many, but I count them with pleasure. Nuffield College provided an ideal environment for the research; and I am grateful to all my colleagues and friends there. I think particularly of John Flemming and Martin Feldstein, whose advice was always available and often drawn on from the outset to the completion of the work. At an early stage in the research, David Stout and Philip Andrews, as thesis supervisors, provided many helpful comments. Since that time, I have received advice on matters great and small from many others. At the risk of forgetful exclusion, I would especially like to thank Meyer Bucovetsky, Michael Dempster, Terence Gorman, Sir John Hicks, Marcel Massé, William White, and John Wright. The reader may imagine what Chapter 1 was like before Sir John Hicks persuaded me to set out the argument step by step.

As my research assistant for two years, Elizabeth Warren was responsible for most of the programming and computing involved in the research for this book and for a number of related econometric projects. It was a pleasure to work with her. Susan Darnton helped with the clerical work at the beginning of the project. Jenny Bond, Enid Browne and Irene Roberts cheerfully decoded my left-handed scrawl. Clive Southey did the index.

For the data, I am indebted to the hundreds of business and government officials who devoted hours or days of their time to providing information about investment decisions. I also gained much from discussions with colleagues on the research staffs of the Royal Commission on Banking and Finance and the Royal Commission on Taxation. Both Commissions have kindly allowed me to quote from earlier work published on their behalf. As this book went to the printers in March, 1967, it does not discuss any of the recommendations of the Royal Commission on Taxation, whose *Report* was published in February, 1967.

I would like to acknowledge financial support, for the first years of research, from the Rhodes Trustees and the Canada Council.

To my family I am grateful for any number of things.

Vancouver,
December 1st, 1967

JOHN F. HELLIWELL

CONTENTS

INTRODUCTION

THIS study attempts to develop a coherent view of the investment process in order to analyse the effects of a number of monetary and fiscal policies designed to influence investment by corporations.

The choice of appropriate monetary and fiscal policies requires in the first place an understanding of the general objectives of the economy or country concerned. Given such an understanding, the next step is to find some relationship between the broad general objectives of public policy and particular observable characteristics of the economy. For example, suppose that the general objective was to maximize the present value of real incomes subject to satisfactory distribution of those incomes over time and among individuals. For this objective to provide any help in policy analysis, it must be given some substance. What time horizon should be used? How is income at different points in time to be valued? How can various alternative distributions of income among individuals be ranked as 'better' or 'worse'? However intractable these questions may seem, it is clear that any actual choice of public policies implicitly answers them, even though those making the policy decisions may be (gratefully) unaware of the consequences of their decisions. In part because there has never been much systematic information available about the effects of particular policies, it has been easy for those making the policy decisions to avoid making explicit trade-offs between the well-being of some individuals and that of a group in another region, another country, or another time period. But if we are even to know what is relevant when we are assessing the effects of a particular policy measure, we must make at least some suppositions about what sorts of impact are considered important in a society. And this brings us back to the requirement that we should know what are the relative values attached to alternative distributions of income over time and among regions and individuals.

To get out of this box, and to allow us to get on with the main task, it will be sufficient to assume that the policy-makers wish to have at hand policy instruments whose effects can be roughly fore-told. A distinction between two separate types of policy may help to clarify the criteria by which the policies should be judged. On the one hand, if an economy is to be subjected to unforeseen changes in circumstances which disrupt the process of production and growth, the policy-makers may wish to have instruments which can act in a quick and predictable fashion to mitigate any ill effects of the shocks. Such policies may be referred to as stabilization policies. If the shocks are as likely to be local as general, then the policy-makers may wish to have instruments whose effects are appropriately localized.

The other type of policy is that intended to influence the longer term structure of the economy. Even for this type of policy, the government may wish to know the time pattern of effects, if only to make sure that the measures are initially introduced at a time which is opportune from the point of view of stabilization policy. In general, the difference between the two types of policy is that in the second type the timing of the effects is relatively less important than their regional and industrial distribution. Most policies of the second type are introduced to compensate for differences between social and private costs. If they are to be appropriate policies, it seems clear that the policy-makers must not only have been able to identify the original discrepancy between private and social costs (i.e. those private costs which are not costs for society as a whole, and vice versa) but be able to estimate the extent to which the policies chosen will remedy the situation.

Accepting these vague presumptions about what a good policy might be expected to do, it is possible to ask whether particular policies are likely to be useful instruments. This book will be con-cerned with only some of the monetary and taxation policies which have been used, or suggested, as a means of influencing the invest-ment and growth of corporations. The first four chapters will develop a view of the investment decision process in business firms, and relate this view to the case study and interview evidence on which it is based. The model will then be put to use in three chapters con-cerned mainly with stabilization policies and two chapters about some measures designed to influence the pattern of investment in the longer run.

The raw material for this study was collected over a period of two years devoted to surveys and case studies of decision-making in large

Canadian corporations. The initial project was a survey[1] of the effects of monetary policy on corporations, some of whose results will be presented in Chapter 7. The project was based on a mail and interview survey of all firms with assets over $5 million, and a sample of approximately 1000 firms below that size. Interviews were held with over three hundred firms, including all but two of the eighty-three largest government and non-government corporations. Of special relevance to the present study were the interviews with senior officials of the largest firms. These interviews usually lasted from one to four hours and covered in some detail the procedures used by the firm in making capital expenditure decisions. The second project,[2] based on the seventy largest non-government corporations, drew on the data from the earlier interviews, and from a series of detailed case studies, to analyse decision-making with special reference to the impacts of certain taxation measures.

The more decisions that were studied in depth, the more obvious it became that uncertainty was a pervading influence. This was particularly so in the case of capital expenditures, whose expected profitability depends on a broad range of interlocking guesses and plans. In any group of some size, the collection and communication of information relevant to decisions occupies a considerable portion of the available management resources. Thus the number and nature of estimates of the results of alternative schemes cannot be considered as given to the firm, but must be treated as important intermediate products of the firm. Such an approach implies that uncertainty be given a central role in any framework adequate to explain investment behaviour.

The decision to use a framework based on subjective variables was not taken lightly, for the further we move away from observables when developing a theory, the more difficult it is to test the theory with available data. But the effects of most monetary and fiscal policies, including those discussed in Chapters 5 to 9, cannot be

---

[1] The study was conducted for the Canadian Royal Commission on Banking and Finance. The report of the survey, by John H. Young and John F. Helliwell, with the assistance of W. A. McKay, was published in Ottawa in 1965 by the Queen's Printer, as *The Effects of Monetary Policy on Corporations*. Throughout this book it shall be referred to as *The Effects of Monetary Policy*.

[2] J. F. Helliwell, *Taxation and Investment: A Study of Capital Expenditure Decisions in Large Corporations*, Ottawa, Queen's Printer, 1966. The study, which will hereafter be referred to as *Taxation and Investment*, or *T & I*, was written for the Canadian Royal Commission on Taxation.

described without reference to the mean and variance of forecasts. By explicitly bringing in expectations, we can easily develop a framework which shows why risk and yield are important and interdependent factors influencing the choice of spending and financing plans. We can show clearly the rationale for diversification, and how the best pattern of finance must match the risk and yield characteristics of the chosen set of projects. Such a framework is developed in Chapter 1. Chapter 2 describes the behavioural assumptions and theoretical implications of this view by reference to some other approaches which have been adopted in the literature. Chapter 3 gives references to the studies on which the present work is based, and discusses the links between the formal framework and the available case study evidence. The group of four chapters dealing with investment theory and behaviour is completed by a short chapter discussing the nature of the data on which decisions are based, and emphasizing the importance of decisions about the direction and scale of information-gathering activity.

The policies discussed in Chapters 5 to 9 have been chosen in part because there is some relevant Canadian evidence, and in part because they are policies best analysed with the aid of a model like that described in Chapters 1 to 4. The effects of all the policies depend on their impact on subjective estimates of the risk and yield from alternative sets of projects.

Chapter 5 considers a range of monetary and fiscal policies designed to influence the amount and timing of investment outlays. In that chapter, and in Chapter 6 on taxation allowances for depreciation, the emphasis is on the present value impact of alternative policies, and only casual use is made of the relationship between risk and yield. In both chapters, and also in Chapter 7 on monetary policy, special emphasis is given to the subjectivity of revenue estimates. The reason for the emphasis is that the effects of policy changes depend on their impact on estimates made of future taxes and interest rates. Since the relative importance of this subjective element varies considerably among policies, it must be considered when policies are compared.

Chapter 7 presents a multi-variate analysis of the survey results of the Canadian Royal Commission on Banking and Finance, and uses the analysis of earlier chapters to explain the observed pattern of effects.

Chapters 8 and 9 deal respectively with research and with natural resource development. Special taxation treatment of research and development expenditures, and of natural resource development, has usually been supported on the argument that there are considerable private (rather than social) risks attached to investment of these types. The framework integrating risk and yield allows these arguments to be assessed in some detail. In these chapters, the specific policies are assessed with respect to their effects on the allocation of investment among industries. The effects of a different industrial distribution on the stability as well as the productivity of investment would of course be a necessary part of an overall judgement of alternative sets of policies.

The short concluding chapter attempts to relate the methods used in this book to the appropriate way of choosing the best set of monetary and fiscal policies. It is argued that the present analysis of particular policies, using a detailed view of decision-making by individual firms, provides a useful means of finding suitable policy instruments for various tasks. But public policies, like investment projects, must be assessed finally in alternative sets, by some means which recognizes their interdependence. Policies which pass the initial screening of the type undertaken in Chapters 5 to 9 must then be considered together in the light of their joint effects upon the economy. This last important step goes beyond the scope of this book, since it requires the use of a precise quantitative description of the operation of the entire economy under alternative sets of public policies.

1

THE INVESTMENT DECISION PROCESS

THE effects of public policies influencing investment decisions cannot be studied sensibly without a clear understanding of how investment decisions are made. It is the object of this chapter to develop a framework within which investment behaviour can be described and public policies assessed. Section A of the chapter contains a general description of the investment process. Section B uses a simple one-period model to explain investment decisions in a more systematic way, and then gradually expands the framework, with the help of an appendix, to include all the elements required for the policy analysis in later chapters.

A. A GENERAL VIEW OF THE INVESTMENT PROCESS

If the effects of public policies are to be assessed, it is necessary to examine the links between policy decisions and expenditure decisions. Since this book is concerned with the effects of certain taxation and monetary policies on the gross capital expenditures of business firms, it must depend on a reliable theory of investment behaviour. The right sort of theory will be that which shows how public policies are taken into account by decision-makers, and provides some way of assessing at least the nature and relative sizes of the impacts of these policies. The ideal theory would picture investment decisions in such detail, and with such subtlety, that the consequences of even novel policies could be estimated. For a number of reasons, nothing approaching such a theory is available. For one thing, all decisions are based directly on subjective impressions of the possible consequences, while most of our statistical data refer to the results of past decisions. Even if there were some way of finding out which beliefs had influenced past decisions, there would still be no way of assessing the effects of policies for which no clear precedent existed. And in a rapidly changing economic environment there is only a very short period of history from which valid precedents can be drawn. In the absence of any quantitative measures of expectations we must search for relationships between movements in observable variables. There is some hope that as better statistics become available it will be possible to analyse decisions in terms of observed movements of variables relevant to those decisions.

Quantitative research of this type has been held back for at least three reasons:

(1) There is little statistical information, at the level of the decision-unit (the firm), about the costs and consequences of past decisions.

(2) There has been little analysis of the process by which firms make decisions about the range of past experience to be considered, and the amount of research to be undertaken, before decisions are made which commit resources in the future.

(3) The investment decision process itself is seldom described in terms which take adequate account of the subjective nature of the information on which decisions are based.

Thus it has been that quantitative descriptions of decisions by firms have been forced to rely on makeshift variables as substitutes for those which were really relevant to decisions, and have not been able to explain many important features of investment behaviour. In particular, it has not been possible to derive equations specifying in a satisfactory way the impacts of taxation and monetary policy.

This book provides no statistical series, nor does it present new econometric analysis or review the existing econometric studies of the investment process. But the following chapters do present a description of investment decisions which does account for the subjectivity of the relevant information, and makes some attempt to explain the basis for information gathering. It will be argued that the resultant view of the decision process is applicable in a considerable range of circumstances, and provides a fairly solid base for the analysis of policy alternatives.

To reach this point, which will take several chapters, we must: (1) make generalizations about the goals of management; (2) examine the way in which managers with given goals might rank alternative investment programmes;[1] and (3) find some means of representing public policies in terms relevant to the ranking of investment programmes.

[1] An investment programme contains any number of projects and specifies a related pattern of financing. All the activities of the firm are encompassed by the features of the investment programme.

(1) *The goals of management*

In this study it is assumed that managers prefer, other things being equal, investment programmes which have higher net-cash receipts over time. In the second half of this chapter, and in Chapter 2, it will be shown that there are a number of different interpretations of profit maximization over time, and that different versions lead to the choice of different investment programmes. In this section we are less concerned with a precise formulation of the goals of management, and more concerned with spelling out management preferences to the minimum extent required for conclusions to be drawn about the effects of monetary and taxation policies, as indicated by changes in the ranking of alternative investment programmes. To accomplish this it is only necessary to accept that management groups are encouraged to make efficient use of all factors of production, including capital. In general, such management groups will increase their use of any factors as long as the marginal net present value return to the shareholders is positive, using discount rates reflecting the cost of capital to the firm. The precise definition of these discount rates will be left until the second half of the chapter. For the present introductory view of investment decisions it is sufficient to be able to conclude that there is a positive relation between the present value of an investment programme and its attractiveness to the management group. Where ownership and management are coextensive, the conclusion need only require that managers have a modicum of marginal self-interest. Where ownership and management are separated, there must be some link between the present value of the programme and the security, prestige, or emoluments granted by the owners (or others) to the management group.

(2) *Ranking alternative investment programmes*

Given that present value, other things being equal, is a preferred characteristic of investment programmes, what can be said in general about the ranking of alternatives? Obviously anything that increases the income over time from a set of projects is desirable, as is anything that accelerates the cash inflows or delays cash outflows. Finally, anything that reduces the appropriate discount rates will increase the calculated present values. To put the matter in the language of business finance, the discount rates used in computing present values are representative of the firm's cost of capital. For firms not able or

B

willing to use new outside funds, the implicit 'cost of capital' is the discount rate which serves to ration the available funds among the competing uses. For firms raising new funds, the concept of the cost of capital is more clearly defined, though the analysis of the next section will expose several of the necessary complexities.

Since fixed investment involves the use of funds to purchase capital goods it is important to discover the relationships that exist between the kind of assets that a firm purchases, and the terms on which new funds may be obtained. The return to capital has often been equated with 'the' rate of interest, a fact that has produced as many misleading results as the description of the price of labour services as 'the' wage rate.

The 'cost of capital' is the minimum return that will obtain its use. We must recognize from the outset that the return to capital has more than one dimension. Specifically, the provider of funds has expectations about the money return which he will receive over time, and about what sort of goods and services he will be able to purchase with that money return. To facilitate his expenditure plans, the holder of a financial asset wants to be able to dispose of that asset, on good terms, at a time most suitable to his own plans. A disutility is attached to uncertainty about either the market value of assets or the timing of their income streams, unless the asset holder has reason to suspect that the unpredictable cash inflow from the asset will be positively correlated with his own unpredictable cash requirements. Financial assets have prices, and these prices reflect the various features of the return which that asset is likely to produce. Considering the variety of expenditure plans of asset holders, and the institutional limitations on diversification by managers of several types of portfolio, it is reasonable to suppose that there will be a substantial range of financial claims issued by firms wishing to obtain funds. The relative prices of these claims must be such that there is no incentive (net of transaction costs) for asset holders or issuers to switch the structure of their assets or liabilities. For example, if two ordinary shares are to trade at the same price, the one with the lower (*ex ante*) yield will have to have a more attractive (*ex ante*) probability distribution of that expected yield.

If firms are interested in obtaining capital on favourable terms, they must recognize that shifts in their 'portfolios' of real assets affect the prices of their financial liabilities, and that if they are considering alternative programmes with different mixes of risk and yield, they must evaluate risk and yield in the same way that risk and yield are evaluated in the securities markets in which claims on the firm are traded.

In order to conclude that management groups value investment programmes (of the same expected yield) more highly if the yield is more predictable, it is not necessary to argue that managers are only concerned with the value which the market attaches to the shares of the firm. It is enough to be able to assume that the price of the firm's shares has some influence on management decisions, and that other factors influencing management behaviour do not move systematically so as to upset the presumption that yield has utility and uncertainty a disutility when investment programmes are assessed. Even in this relatively casual description of the investment process we must not assume that all measures of uncertainty will satisfy the presumption that there is a disutility attached to greater uncertainty. In fact, it is quite plausible to assume that one particular aspect of uncertainty—the small chance of a very large gain, coupled with little or no chance of a large loss (positive skewness)—has, for a given level of risk (variance of return) a positive utility to at least some asset holders.

Finally, something should be said about the recurring nature of investment decisions. The ranking and re-ranking of alternative investment programmes is a continual process, since information is continually flowing in to provide a new basis for assessing the probable results of alternative courses of action. It is not necessary to assume that there are daily or weekly changes in the firm's plans, but only to recognize that there are continual flows of new information which accumulate until some change in plans results. It is quite plausible to suppose, in the light of the scarcity of decision-making talent, that information of various types just accumulates without affecting plans until the import of the new information is clear enough to trigger off a reaction, or a date has been reached on which plans are reassessed as a matter of course.

Nothing has been said about the determinants of technological change, about the nature of alternative productive processes available at a particular time, or the whole range of employment, sales, and other plans and commitments involved in the choice of an investment programme. In some of the later chapters (such as Chapter 9 on natural resource development) some such references will be made where necessary to indicate the effects of some special taxation policies. In general, the impact of policies can be adequately described with reference only to the later stages of the investment decision process. It will not be possible to take this short cut when the time comes to make quantitative estimates of the determinants of investment expenditures, but for the present analysis it should serve well. Alternative techniques, products, and markets are, however, implicit in the alternative sets of investment projects. Thus the particular products and markets that are the basis for investment projects are never far from the centre of the stage even though the discussion may refer directly only to the subjective probability distributions of cash flow that are being used to represent investment possibilities for the firm.

It may be useful, now that a preliminary sketch has been made of the investment decision process, to define a few bits of terminology which will be important throughout the book, and then finally to list the key features of the investment process.

There are a few shorthand descriptions, to be presented in detail in the next section, which must be learnt for any reading of the later chapters of the book. The subjective probability distributions of cash flow, which are the basic means of describing any set of investment projects, will be designated by the term 'cash-flow distribution' (or occasionally by the abbreviation CFD).

If there were only one source of finance—equity funds—then the cash-flow distributions would simply refer to the cash flows from the investment projects, with capital expenditures and all taxes being among the outflows. If there are opportunities for borrowing, life becomes more complicated. Since the share market's discount rates will be used to calculate the present market value of an investment programme, the cash-flow distributions must be defined to match. They will represent the net cash flow either coming from, or accruing to the account of, the common shareholders. Funds raised by borrowing are treated as cash inflows, while interest and debt repayments are among the outflows. The cash-flow distributions are therefore net of all debt transactions, but take no account of dividends or other payments to shareholders. For each alternative programme comprising a set of investment projects and a pattern of debt financing there is a separate cash-flow distribution for each time period within the investment horizon.

The cash-flow distributions will be described primarily in terms of their mean values (M_t), their standard deviations (σ_t), and a coefficient of skewness (SK_t). The mean value measures the expected value of the cash flow in period t, while the standard deviation is a measure of the unpredictability of the cash flow, and the coefficient of skewness indicates the relative probabilities of very large and very small cash flows. In order to simplify the computation of present values of investment programmes it is convenient to have a single measure of the attractiveness of a cash-flow distribution. This measure, referred to as a 'risk-standardized' mean value or M_t^*, is obtained by adjusting the mean value to account for non-standard values of the standard deviation and other characteristics of the cash-flow distributions.

There are four intertemporal rates directly relevant to investment decisions. They may loosely be referred to as the marginal and average cost of capital and the marginal and average rate of return on investment. The first section of the appendix to the chapter shows that if the firm chooses the investment programme which maximizes the present market value of the firm, the marginal cost of finance and the marginal rate of return on investment will be equalized. The average rate of return on investment will be above the average cost of finance for any investment programme with a positive present market value. Section B and the Appendix to this chapter define the four intertemporal rates more precisely and establish the relationships between them. In the later chapters assessing the effects of public policies, the average cost of capital (the share market's discount rate) will be used to compare alternative investment programmes, while the marginal cost of finance is appropriate for calculating the present value impact of marginal changes in tax payments.

The key features of the investment process, for the policy analysis purposes to which the model will be put in later chapters, are:

(a) Firms choose programmes rather than projects.
(b) Any programme choice is expected to be changed as new information becomes available. The changes may be expected to occur in the plans for the more distant future, since it is expensive to alter contracts and construction in progress.
(c) The optimum pattern of finance for any programme is dependent upon the risk and yield of the related set of projects.
(d) The discount rates (which may be interpreted as the cost of capital) used in finding the present value of an investment programme increase with increases in the riskiness (dispersion)

in relation to the expected value (mean) of the cash-flow distributions. It will usually also be assumed that, beyond a certain point, the discount rates increase with the size of the programme being financed.

(e) There are substantial costs in collecting information and making decisions, so that the subjective cash-flow distributions may not adjust quickly to changes in circumstances. The number of alternative programmes considered explicitly is likely to be small.

(3) *Describing public policies in terms relevant to investment decisions*

Throughout the study the effects of policies will be dealt with in terms of their impacts on the risk-standardized present values of alternative investment programmes. This frame of reference allows policies affecting the prices of certain financial assets to be treated comparably with policies affecting the prices or net-of-tax earning power of plant, equipment, and inventory stocks.

Ideally, the investment process would be specified in quantitative terms with policy variables explicitly included in the system. Econometric research has not yet reached the point where the structure of the investment process is pictured well enough to allow a variety of monetary and fiscal policies to be represented in the equations. Even if such equations were available, there would still be something to be learned from the *a priori* analysis of policies, especially policies so novel that they cannot be properly assessed using only data from past investment behaviour.

Thus there is scope for *a priori* assessment of any policies whose impacts may be assumed to be related to their influence on present values of alternative investment programmes. To perform this sort of analysis it is necessary to establish the effects of each policy on the size, timing, and predictability of the expected cash flow within the time horizon of each alternative set of investment projects. The policy measures may also affect the cost and availability of various types of funds, which in turn will cause changes in the discount rates appropriate for calculating the present values of investment programmes. In general, any policy measure may be expected to influence estimated cash flows as well as the discount rates appropriate for finding present values.

For those who find the foregoing statements so reasonable as to be commonplace the next section may not be necessary reading. Others who are unconvinced, or would in any case prefer a more rigorous presentation, are invited to concentrate on the remainder of this chapter and its appendix. The reader interested only in a discussion of the effects of particular types of public policy may proceed quickly through the rest of this chapter, omit its appendix, and skim through Chapters 2 to 4 fairly quickly.

B. A MODEL OF INVESTMENT DECISIONS

The firm has a number of opportunities to buy plant and equipment now ($t = 0$) at a cost (assumed to be known with certainty) equal to M_0. The expected return from the project (at $t = 1$), is equal to M_1. The return at the end of the period is uncertain, and the firm has a subjective probability distribution of its possible values. In the simplest case, we shall consider only a single measure of the dispersion of the distribution. The firm wishes to obtain financing for any project undertaken. The simplest assumption to make is that the firm obtains finance by selling a security which entitles the purchaser to receive whatever return may accrue from the project at the end of the period. The return to the entrepreneur is thus the difference between what must be paid for the necessary plant and equipment (M_0) and the present financial market value of the right to receive the total return from the project (M_1) at the end of the period. The present market value of the uncertain return M_1 will depend on the mean value and the standard deviation of its probability distribution. All we need suppose, for a start, is that for any given expected value (= mean value) of return, the security will be worth more in the financial market the lower is the standard deviation of the return. Similarly, for any given standard deviation of return, the market value of the security will be higher, the higher is the expected return M_1. Thus if all the available one-period securities are plotted on a two-dimensional graph according to their values of M_1 and σ_1, lines joining equally valued securities will have a positive slope,[1] as shown in Figure 1. The securities joined by equal-valuation line V' have a lower market value than those joined by equal-valuation line V'', since for a given level of risk they have a lower expected return.

We have already acknowledged that the market value of the one-period security will depend not only on the expected value of return

[1] The curves need not be concave upwards, and may have any number of points of inflexion. It is necessary only that their slopes be positive throughout.

(M_1) and the length of the time period but also on the standard deviation of return (σ_1). If the relationship linking the present market value of the security to the expected value of its return is to hold exactly, then the discount rate r must vary with changes in the standard deviation of return. Thus we can return to the graph showing all possible security returns and add 'equal discount rate' lines as in Figure 2.

If the discount rates depend only on the risk per unit of return (= coefficient of variation = σ_1/M_1), then the equal-discount-rate lines will be rays from the origin, like the dashed lines in Figure 2, since the coefficient of variation is constant along any ray from the origin of the graph. The solid lines in Figure 2 picture the shape of

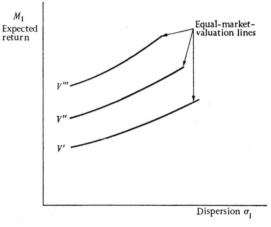

Figure 1

the equal-discount-rate lines which would exist if larger programmes were more expensive to finance than small ones, for a given coefficient of variation. Section (1) of the Appendix discusses the implications of these and other possible assumptions about the cost of finance. For most of our purposes it does not matter which assumptions are made about the shapes of the equal-discount-rate lines.

It is necessary to establish a conventional way of describing the market value of the one-period securities in terms of their expected return and standard deviation. Looking at Figure 3, whose equal-discount-rate lines are drawn on the assumption that the share market's discount rates (r_s) depend on the coefficient of variation, and on the size of the programme, it can be seen that there are two ways of describing the market value of the project $M_1\sigma_1$. There is an equal-discount-rate line and an equal-valuation line passing through each point indicating an available project. The lines drawn through the $M_1\sigma_1$ project are examples. The market value of the security can thus be described either by discounting M_1 by the discount rate r_s', or by moving along the equal-valuation line and discounting the amount M_1^* by the discount rate r_s. The value M_1^* will be described as the risk-standardized mean value of the return distribution with (unadjusted) mean value M_1 and standard deviation σ_1. There are no

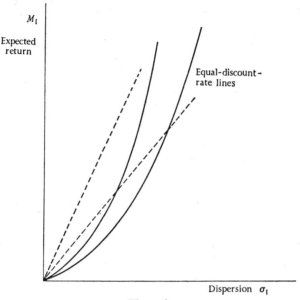

Figure 2

tricks involved in this risk standardization procedure, and it does not tell us anything we did not have to know beforehand in order to construct the equal-valuation and equal-discount-rate lines. What it does provide is a means of bringing risk explicitly, and in a fairly straightforward way, into the analysis of the valuation of financial assets, and, in the next stage, into the evaluation of investment programmes. Since the propriety of the risk-standardization procedure depends on the existence of equal-valuation lines between any particular investment opportunity and the standard-risk line, the standard-risk line should be chosen so as to pass as close as possible to the main group of investment possibilities. It seems reasonable to suppose that some ray from the origin (along any such ray the co-efficient of variation σ_1/M_1 is constant) is likely to provide an appropriate definition of standard risk.

So far it has only been shown that the present market value of a risky asset with a one-period return can be described equivalently as the expected value (M_1) of the return discounted by the discount rate

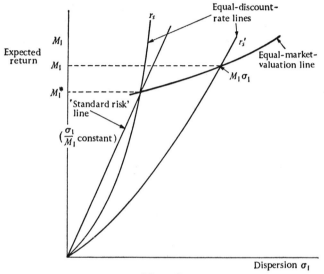

Figure 3

appropriate for a programme of that risk and size, or as the risk-standardized mean value M_1^* discounted by the rate appropriate for a standard-risk programme of that size. That is, in the example shown in Figure 3,

$$\text{Gross Market Value} \equiv G = \frac{M_1}{1 + r_s'} = \frac{M_1^*}{1 + r_s}.$$

Facing a financial market which values securities according to their yield and risk (and, possibly, their total value), how does the firm (the entrepreneur) decide which projects ought to be taken up? To keep the matter as simple as possible, consider that all the M_1 and σ_1 combinations are mutually exclusive, each combination re-presenting a complete and distinct package of activities designed to produce a single return at the end of the time period. The firm plays an entrepreneurial role by having knowledge of the investment projects financed by the sale of securities whose return to the purchaser is equal to the entire return from the investment project. The firm gets an entrepreneurial reward if the present market value of the security issued to finance the investment projects is greater than M_0, the initial cost of the assets (e.g. plant, equipment, raw materials, administration, and labour services) required as inputs to the investment project.

In order that he be able to calculate the present market value of the security related to any particular investment programme the entrepreneur must be able to estimate how the market would value securities with different mixtures of risk and yield, and also to know what estimate the share market would make of the risk and yield of any particular investment programme. In the analysis to follow, the risk and yield characteristics of any particular programme are those which the entrepreneur believes would be attached to the programme by the share market. If the entrepreneur and the share market have the same subjective expectations about the results of any investment programme, then it does not matter whether the analysis is in terms of the entrepreneur's private expectations about the risk and yield of a programme or his views about the share market's expectations about the same characteristics. For convenience of exposition the simple model will assume that the share market and the entrepreneur have the same expectations about the risk and yield of alternative investment programmes; while the consequences of divergent expectations will be considered in Section (3) of the Appendix.

When the entrepreneur is estimating the present market value of a security the appropriate discount rate depends on whether and how the expected return is risk-standardized before discounting, but in any case is a rate reflecting the share market's preferences. The discount rate r_s will be used to represent the share market's discount rate if the risk-standardized return M_1^* is discounted. From the point of view of the entrepreneur the value of any investment programme depends not only on the market value of the security to be sold but also on the cost of the resources required in order to undertake the investment programme. The net present value (N) of any investment programme, from the point of view of the firm, is thus the difference between what the securities can now be sold for and the cost of the necessary inputs.

$$N = \frac{M_1^*}{1 + r_s} - M_0.$$

Any investment programme will be described as 'feasible' if its net present value is positive or zero, i.e. as long as the claim on the return from the investment programme can be sold in the financial market for not less than M_0, the cost of the assets required to undertake the programme.

Now it can be seen, in terms of the simplest case, what is meant by the assertion that the optimum use of capital requires that the firm 'trade-off' risk and yield in the same way as does the financial market. Figure 4 shows the share market's equal valuation line relating to a particular investment programme with expected return M_1 and risk σ_1. The firm can sell a security promising this return for a price equal to $M_1^*/1 + r_s$ (or any lesser amount). What if the firm were to ignore risk altogether when assessing the $M_1\sigma_1$ investment programme? The firm which ignores risk is assuming that the market valuation of securities is unaffected by the standard deviation of the return, and thus that the equal-valuation lines are horizontal on Figure 4. A risk-shy firm, at the other extreme, assumes that the share market charges more for risk than is actually the case, and thus uses an equal-valuation line steeper than the actual one. The actual market value of the project's return is equal to the risk-standardized return M_1^* (using the actual equal valuation line) discounted by the appropriate discount rate r_s. The risk-shy firm underestimates the market value of the security, while the risk-ignoring firm overestimates. Depending on the cost of undertaking the programme (M_0) the risk-shy firm might consider the programme unfeasible if it was actually feasible, i.e. $[M_1^*/(1 + r_s)] - M_0 \geqslant 0$. The risk-ignoring firm might undertake the project even if it were not actually feasible, and be surprised and disappointed that the security was only worth $M_1^*/(1 + r_s)$ in the share market. Neither the risk-shy nor the risk-ignoring firm will choose the programme which maximizes the return to the entrepreneur. Suppose that the only programmes shown on the graph are those with the same initial costs M_0 as the example programme with return M_1 and risk σ_1. All programmes above and to the left of the share market equal-valuation line have a higher market value than does the $M_1\sigma_1$ programme, including all those in the striped and cross-hatched areas of Figure 4. Any firm which does not trade off risk and yield according to the share market's valuations will pass up opportunities to undertake programmes with a higher net market value. In particular, the risk-shy firm would consider all the programmes in the cross-hatched area of Figure 4 to be inferior to the

$M_1\sigma_1$ programme, while in fact they are worth more. In the same way, the risk-ignoring firm will pass up programmes in the striped area even though any one of them would actually produce a higher return to the firm than would the $M_1\sigma_1$ programme. Only the firm which trades-off risk and yield at the market-established rates (as indicated by the slopes of share market's equal-valuation lines) will choose the programme with the maximum net market value. As shown in the Appendix, it is by choosing the programme with the largest net market value that the management of the firm maximizes its own security, by reducing to zero the profits available to a take-over raider.

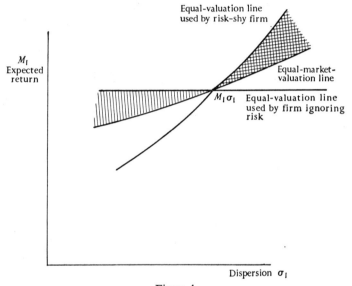

Figure 4

This simple framework will be expanded in stages.

The first complication involves no great difficulty. Higher moments of the probability distributions of returns from the one-period project can be introduced easily. The earlier analysis of the risk-yield trade-off can be extended to cover the coefficient of skewness (or any higher moments). If the diagrams were drawn with skewness (SK) on the horizontal axis (standard deviation σ_1 assumed to be held constant), and if the share market valued positive (or less negative) skewness, then the equal-valuation lines would slope downward rather than upwards to the right, but otherwise the analysis would proceed as before. The simultaneous risk-standardization for co-efficients of variation and of skewness requires another dimension if it is to be drawn, but no other alteration need be made to the simple model.

The next goal of the analysis is to demonstrate exactly how the preferences of managers, the investment opportunities, and the cost of raising funds jointly determine the characteristics of the chosen investment programme. First it is necessary to find a compact way of dealing with the results already obtained. This may be done by means of a simple relationship between the cost (M_0) of an investment pro-gramme and its risk-standardized return (M_1^*). Using the principles already established for the optimal assessment of risk characteristics, the firm can find the appropriate risk-standardized return M_1^* from any initial investment M_0. For any given amount spent on initial in-vestment, there may be a number of different programmes available, each with its own risk-standardized return M_1^*. For each value of M_0, there will be a programme whose expected return M_1^* is equal to or greater than the return from any other programme with the same initial cost. These maximum returns for a given initial cost may be considered as an efficient transformation curve with M_1^* as a function of M_0. Any chosen programme of size M_0 will thus have an expected rate of return of $(M_1^*/M_0) - 1 = r_a$, which shall be referred to as the average rate of return on investment. The slope (dM_1^*/dM_0) of the efficient transformation curve is, correspondingly, equal to one plus the marginal rate of return on investment, $r_f = (dM_1^*/dM_0) - 1$. It is convenient to assume, since it is usually the case, that the marginal rate of return on investment is positive over the interesting section of the transformation possibilities curve, but that the marginal efficiency of investment declines $(d^2M_1^*/dM_0^2) < 0$ as the programme size is increased, since firms may in general be considered to take on the more profitable invest-ment opportunities before the less profitable ones.[1]

The marginal rate of return on investment, $r_f = (dM_1^*/dM_0) - 1$, is therefore likely to vary with the size of the chosen programme.

Just as there are discount rates measuring, respectively, the marginal (r_f) and average (r_a) rates of return on investment, there are marginal and average rates of discount used by the share market when valuing the shares of the firm. Thus r_s is the average discount

---

[1] Indivisibilities of some sorts of inputs may be responsible for the marginal efficiency of investment increasing over some range of programme sizes.

rate employed by the financial market in setting the market value of the claim on the expected return M_1^*. The gross market value of the firm is therefore equal to $G = M_1^*/(1 + r_s)$, and $r_s = (M_1^*/G) - 1$. The net present market value ($\equiv N$) is equal to the gross present value of the expected return less the cost of the assets required to produce the return.

$$N = \frac{M_1^*}{1 + r_s} - M_0.$$

The marginal discount rate (r_m) is defined by the slope of the function relating the expected return M_1^* and the gross market value of the shares of the firm. That is, $r_m = (dM_1^*/dG) - 1$. If r_s does not vary with the gross market value of the programme, then $r_s = r_m$. If larger programmes are more expensive to finance, then r_m will be greater than r_s.

The firm may choose the programme with the largest internal rate of return (= return per share), the programme with the largest size, or the programme with largest present value, where the present value may be calculated in different ways.

Maximizing the average internal rate of return requires choosing the programme with the highest ratio of return (M_1^*) to the initial investment M_0. If there are substantial indivisibilities in the range of available projects, it may be the case that the largest ratio of average returns to investment M_1^*/M_0 requires a programme of substantial size. In general, we may assume that the best projects will be taken up first so that, indivisibilities aside, the marginal efficiency of investment may be expected to decline ($d^2M_1^*/dM_0^2 < 0$) as the programme size is increased. The programme with the largest internal rate of return is that where the average return on investment (r_a) is highest, a programme likely to be small under most assumptions about the available investment opportunities.

At the opposite extreme lies the choice of the largest feasible investment programme. The broadest definition of a feasible investment programme is any programme for which financing can be obtained. This implies that the future return, when discounted by the average share market discount rate, should be equal to or greater than M_0, the cost of the necessary assets ($[M_1^*/(1 + r_s)] - M_0 \geqslant 0$). There may be other restrictions on the choice of a maximum growth[1]

---

[1] In a one-period framework, the largest programme is also the one with the greatest absolute growth. If the firm is considered to have a history, then the

investment programme. For example, a firm which maximizes growth will be subject to take-over bids from other entrepreneurs, who could use the firm's transformation possibilities so as to produce more profit.

Another case, which is used frequently as an example in later chapters, is that in which the firm chooses the investment programme with the maximum present market value, where the present values are calculated using the share market's discount rates. It is shown in Section (1) of the Appendix that the maximum PV programme makes the marginal efficiency of investment (r_f) equal to the marginal share market discount rate (r_m). The maximum PV programme also

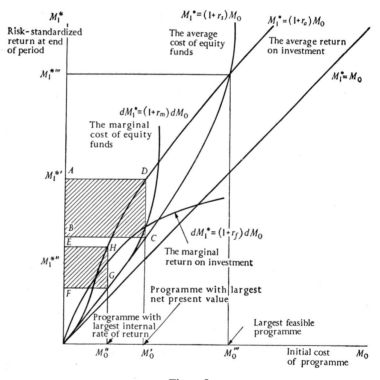

Figure 5

largest programme also maximizes the rate of growth, since the size at the end of the preceding period is a datum not affected by the current choice of an investment programme.

maximizes the security of the existing management, by reducing to zero the profits potentially available to a take-over raider. On most assumptions about the sets of investment possibilities and the supply price of finance, the maximum present value programme is larger than that which maximizes the internal rate of return, but smaller than the maximum growth programme.

Figure 5 illustrates the choice of investment programmes according to the three criteria mentioned. The firm which maximizes the internal rate of return wishes to choose that investment programme which maximizes the ratio of M_1^* to M_0. The investment possibilities open to the firm, as indicated by the curves labelled $1 + r_a$ and $1 + r_f$ in Figure 5, are assumed to be such that the marginal rate of return on investment is higher than the average rate for some range of programme sizes. This permits the existence of a programme of size M_0'' with the largest possible internal rate of return.[1] At the other extreme, the programme of size M_0''' has a zero net present market value. It is the largest feasible programme, since there can be none larger in which $r_a \geqslant r_s$. The programme with the largest net present value is of size M_0', since that is where $r_f = r_m$. The net present value of that programme is equal to the amount represented by the shaded area $ABCD$, discounted by the share market's average discount rate for a programme of size M_0'.[2] Similarly, the net present value of the programme with the largest internal rate of return is equal to amount represented by the area $EFGH$ discounted by the value of $1 + r_s$ at point G.

The next addition to the model is another dimension to the financial markets. It will be sufficient to add only one form of non-share financing, since any further types of financing could be handled in an analogous manner.

The simplest way to bring debt financing into the model is to define the expected return M_1 as being net of interest and debt repayment charges, and M_0 net of the amount of funds to be provided

---

[1] The programme of size M_0'' has the greatest ratio M_1^*/M_0 since a ray from the origin is tangent to the $1 + r_a$ curve at point H.

[2] As shown in Section (1) of the Appendix the net present value (N) of a programme is a function of M_0

$$N = M_0\left(\frac{1 + r_a}{1 + r_s} - 1\right).$$

The shaded area $ABCD$ in Figure 5 equals $M_0(1 + r_a) - M_0(1 + r_s)$. Thus the net present value of the programme equals the amount represented by $ABCD$ divided by the value of $1 + r_s$ at point C.

C

in debt form. The characteristics of the programme can then be extended to include specification of the amount and type of debt financing to be undertaken. The possibilities for debt financing thus enormously increase the number of alternative yield and risk combinations, since every programme involving certain physical assets and activities can be financed with one of a number of debt/equity ratios, each of which constitutes, in conjunction with the specifications of the basic investment projects, a separate alternative programme. Since debt financing typically involves an obligation to repay, at the end of the period, a sum fixed in monetary terms, the effect of increasing borrowing as a proportion of total financing is to increase the ratio of the expected return to the net-of-borrowing cost of the initial assets (as long as the interest rate is less than r_a, the average rate of return on investment), and also to alter[1] the ratio of the standard deviation to the expected value of the end of period return (net of interest and debt repayment). The use of debt finance thus provides one means whereby the firm may alter the mix of risk and yield accruing to the equity shareholders from any particular set of investment projects.

The procedure described above allows full account to be taken of the effects of borrowing, and permits us to continue to identify M_1^* as the risk-standardized return to the shareholders, although the net-of-borrowing definition of M_1 and M_0 does tend to cover up the interactions between debt and equity financing.

An alternative procedure (the one which is adopted briefly in Section (2) of the Appendix), is to define M_1^{*B} as the (net-of-tax) risk-standardized return before payment of interest and redemption of debt, and M_{0B} the total present cost of undertaking the programme. In this case the present value of a programme depends not only, as before, on the risk and yield characteristics of the available projects and the terms on which equity finance is available but also on the amount and nature of the debt financing undertaken. Returning to the simple case in which the best set of alternatives is described by making the (maximum available) expected return M_1^{*B} a function

---

[1] If the money prices of goods are expected to be stable, or if shareholders pay attention only to the dispersion of money returns, then borrowing necessarily increases the risk per unit of return to the equity shareholder. Under the more likely assumptions that shareholders are concerned about the expected value and dispersion of their return in real terms, and money prices are likely to vary, the borrowing need not necessarily increase the coefficient of variation of the shareholders' real return. See Section (2) of the Appendix.

of investment M_{0B}, the discount rates applied by the equity market are related not just to M_1 and σ_1 but also to the nature and cost of debt financing, since the amount of debt financing influences the expected size and variability of the return to the shareholder. The programme which maximizes the net present share-market value of the firm will not only make the share market's marginal discount rate equal to the marginal efficiency of investment but will also make both equal to the marginal cost of debt finance.

This framework is used in Section (2) of the Appendix to examine the relationships between debt and equity financing, and to indicate the conditions under which borrowing is advantageous. Where borrowing is advantageous it increases the net present value of any programme with given project characteristics, and under reasonable assumptions increases the scale of the maximum net present value programme. Except in Section (2) of the Appendix the definition of the cash-flow distributions will be such as to make them net of all interest payments and changes in debt outstanding. To any given set of investment projects there correspond as many different sets of cash-flow distributions as there are alternative patterns of debt financing.

Finally, it is necessary to leave the one-period world and explain the choice of investment programmes by firms which are going concerns, and whose present decisions have consequences spreading over many future time periods. The main analytic feature to be added to the model is that of the investment time horizon, which is the number of future periods whose activities and expected cash flows are relevant to the present choice among alternative programmes. It is assumed that the firm chooses that value for the time horizon (n) which aligns the resulting programme most closely with the preferences of the managers. Thus the time horizon comes to depend, along with everything else in the model, on the characteristics of the investment opportunities and expected conditions in financial markets.

Extending the framework to cover many periods means that M_0, the cost of the assets used in the investment programme, can no longer be assumed to be known with certainty. This being the case, there is no longer any reason for distinguishing the expenditures on assets in one period from the returns on projects operating in the previous period. Investment projects may take any number of periods to build and produce returns for any number of periods. Any set of investment projects may be characterized by a probability distribution of the net cash flow used or provided by the set of projects for each time period. The cash flow in each period will comprise the total returns in that period from all the projects in operation less all expenditures on new assets and current operating costs (including all taxes). It will be convenient to have these distributions refer to the cash flows after allowance is made for interest and changes in indebtedness, but before account is taken of the cash flows relating to dividends or to the issue or redemption of equity securities. These compound subjective probability distributions of cash flow (referred to as cash-flow distributions) thus contain the cash inflows and outflows expected in each period. It is quite possible that among the alternative investment programmes open to an established firm there would be many which do not require any new equity financing. These situations are especially likely to arise if the tax system is such as to make retention of earnings a favoured source of funds. Is it still plausible, in these cases, to assume that firms evaluate risk and calculate present values so as to maximize the share-market value of the firm? This assumption continues to be reasonable as long as the management is interested in the price at which the shares of the firm change hands. The management may continue to have such an interest if they hold any shares themselves, or if their own security of office is subject to shareholder control. Even if shareholders do ultimately have the power to remove a management not acting in the shareholders' interests, it is difficult for a shareholder to know what another management could have done in the same circumstances. Because an established management has access to much information not available to shareholders they may have considerable scope for choosing programmes other than the one which would maximize the market value of the firm, without thereby risking dismissal by dissatisfied shareholders. This is so whether or not an investment programme requires new outside financing, but probably applies to a greater extent to firms with internally financed investment programmes, since external finance usually requires release of more information to those outside the management group.

Bit by bit, the one-factor one-period framework has been developed to the point where most of important features of the investment process have been exposed. The n-period general framework is laid out in more detail in Section (3) of the Appendix. All of the specific conclusions drawn from the one-period model carry over into the larger framework. The programme which maximizes the net market value of the firm is also that which provides the maximum security from take-over bids. If it is further assumed that the share market's discount rate depends only on the total value and riskiness of the shares of the firm, the programme which maximizes the market value of the firm also equates the marginal efficiency of investment and the marginal cost of funds. In the one-period case there is a single discount rate appropriate for evaluating any particular investment programme. The value taken by the share market's discount rate depends upon the yield and risk of the programme, and the conditions in financial markets. Once the appropriate value of this discount rate is found for a particular programme, the net present value of that programme may be calculated. An analogous situation exists in the multi-period model. There is a single discount rate appropriate for linking each pair of adjacent periods within the investment time horizon of a particular programme. These rates may be expected to be different for each pair of periods, since the size and riskiness of the cash flow expected from the programme may vary over time, as will the expected marginal cost of funds. The calculation of the net present value of any n-period programme will thus require the use of n separate discount rates, each linking a separate pair of adjacent time periods.

In the multi-period case, the appropriate discount rates will depend not only on the characteristics of the separate cash-flow distributions for each period, but also on the extent to which these distributions are interdependent. The discount rates appropriate for finding the present value of a multi-period investment programme also depend, as in the one-period case, on the goals of the management group. There is a range of feasible programmes (those for which finance can be obtained), and the choice among these programmes will depend on what the management group is trying to achieve, and on what constraints are placed on their range of choices. The next chapter will be more specific about the relationship between the goals of management and the characteristics of the investment programmes they choose. It can quite easily be seen that even if the management group is not primarily interested in choosing the programme which will maximize the market value of the shares of the firm they will in general prefer a higher present value programme to one with a lower PV (assuming both to be equal with respect to the group's primary objective), since such a programme is likely to ease whatever other constraints there may be on the management's choice of programmes.

This is the justification for measuring the effects of public policies on the present values of alternative investment programmes, and then using these calculations to help indicate the likely effects of the policies.

According to the analysis developed in this chapter there are two discount rates which are used in the chapters dealing with the effects of public policies. The share market's discount rate r_s is used in calculating the present values of alternative investment programmes, while the marginal rate r_m (which equals r_f, the marginal rate of return on investment if the maximum present value programme is chosen) is used to measure the marginal present value impact of policy changes affecting the risk and yield of established investment programmes. Both rates depend on the risk and yield of alternative investment programmes, the objectives of the firm, and conditions in financial markets. Where only a single standard-risk discount rate r is specified, it should be assumed to be r_s if alternative programmes are being assessed, and to be r_m, the marginal discount rate, where the calculations refer to small tax-induced changes in the cash flows from an investment programme.

APPENDIX TO CHAPTER 1

The first section of the Appendix uses the simplest one-period model to show that the programme with the maximum net market value is also the one which equalizes the share market's marginal discount rate and the marginal rate of return on investment. The section also considers the likely shape of the equal valuation and equal discount-rate lines. The second section of the Appendix introduces an additional source of funds into the one-period model, while the third section sketches a multi-period framework.

(1) *The one-period case, using equity finance only*

M_1^* = the risk-standardized expected return at the end of the period.

M_0 = the known cost of undertaking the investment programme.

$G = \dfrac{M_1^*}{1 + r_s}$ = the present market value of the end-of-period return from the investment programme

where
r_s = the share market's discount rate = $\dfrac{M_1^*}{G} - 1$.

r_m = the marginal cost of equity funds = $\dfrac{dM_1^*}{dG} - 1$.

$1 + r_a = \dfrac{M_1^*}{M_0} =$ the ratio of the total expected return to the cost of the programme. Thus r_a, the average rate of return on investment, equals $\dfrac{M_1^*}{M_0} - 1$.

$1 + r_f = \dfrac{dM_1^*}{dM_0} =$ the ratio of the marginal return to the marginal cost. Thus r_f, the marginal rate of return on investment, equals $\dfrac{dM_1^*}{dM_0} - 1$.

$N = \dfrac{M_1^*}{1 + r_s} - M_0 =$ the net market value of the firm, or the present market value of the gross return minus the cost of the required assets.

The objective is to maximize

(1) $$N = \frac{M_1^*}{1 + r_s} - M_0 = M_0\left(\frac{1 + r_a}{1 + r_s} - 1\right).$$

Consider first the relationship which exists between each average discount rate and its marginal counterpart. This may be shown by starting with the definition for the average discount rate

$$r_a = \frac{M_1^*}{M_0} - 1 \text{ and differentiating:}$$

$$dr_a = \frac{dM_1^*}{M_0} - \frac{M_1^* dM_0}{M_0^2},$$

$$M_0 \frac{dr_a}{dM_0} = \frac{dM_1^*}{dM_0} - \frac{M_1^*}{M_0},$$

$$\frac{dM_1^*}{dM_0} = \frac{M_1^*}{M_0} + M_0 \frac{dr_a}{dM_0},$$

but, by definition, $\dfrac{dM_1^*}{dM_0} = 1 + r_f$; and $\dfrac{M_1^*}{M_0} = 1 + r_a$; so that

(2) $$r_f = r_a + M_0 \frac{dr_a}{dM_0},$$

Similarly, since

$$1 + r_s = \frac{M_1^*}{G} \quad \text{and} \quad 1 + r_m = \frac{dM_1^*}{dG},$$

(3) $$r_m = r_s + G \frac{dr_s}{dG}.$$

Proceeding to the main task, a first-order condition for the maximum net market value programme is that $dN/dM_0 = 0$.

Differentiating (1) with respect to M_0,

$$\frac{dN}{dM_0} = \frac{1 + r_a}{1 + r_s} - 1 + M_0 \left(\frac{\dfrac{dr_a}{dM_0}}{1 + r_s}\right) - M_0\left(\frac{1 + r_a}{1 + r_s}\right)\frac{\dfrac{dr_s}{dM_0}}{1 + r_s} = 0;$$

rearranging,

$$1 + r_a - 1 - r_s + M_0 \frac{dr_a}{dM_0} - G \frac{dr_s}{dM_0} = 0,$$

(4)
$$r_a + M_0 \frac{dr_a}{dM_0} = r_s + G \frac{dr_s}{dM_0}.$$

Using relationships (2) and (3) in (4)

$$r_f = r_m + G \left(\frac{dr_s}{dM_0} - \frac{dr_s}{dG} \right)$$

but $\dfrac{dr_s}{dG} = \dfrac{dr_s}{dM_0} \dfrac{dM_0}{dG}$

and $\dfrac{dG}{dM_0} = \dfrac{dN}{dM_0} + 1 = 1 \left(\text{since } N = G - M_0, \text{ and } \dfrac{dN}{dM_0} = 0 \right)$

thus $\dfrac{dr_s}{dM_0} - \dfrac{dr_s}{dG} = 0$

so that $r_f = r_m.$

Thus the investment programme that maximizes the net market value of the firm is one in which the marginal discount rate applied by the share market in valuing the firm (r_m) is equal to the marginal rate of return on investment (r_f). The maximum N programme is also that which, by making most advantageous use of the available investment opportunities, maximizes the security of the entrepreneur against a take-over bid. In the one-period world, it is assumed that the entrepreneur has some stake in the outcome of the project at the end of the period, and thus wishes to stay in the good graces of the initial purchaser of the shares. The stake may most simply be interpreted as a management fee (M_1^* is net of any such fees). If there is any scope for a take-over bid being made to and accepted by the initial purchaser of the shares, and if the bid is made for the purpose of gaining control of the firm, any increase in such an incentive must be interpreted as decreasing the security of the management group.

It may not appear obvious that it is net market value rather than gross market value which the promoter should maximize if he wishes to maximize his security against a take-over bid. Maximizing G involves a larger programme than maximizing N, assuming $dM_1^*/dM_0 > 0$. Suppose the entrepreneur chose the programme maximizing G, involving initial investment in assets costing M_0, and having $N = G - M_0$. The programme maximizing N would have a net market value of $N' = G' - M_0'$ where $N' > N$, $M_0' < M_0$, and $G' < G$. A take-over bidder could buy the gross market value-maximizing programme for G, sell the assets for M_0, buy the assets costing M_0', and sell the new programme for G'. His cash flows would be equal to $G' + M_0 - M_0' - G$. This gain must be positive, since $G - M_0 \equiv N$, $G' - M_0' \equiv N'$, and $N' > N$. This possibility for a profitable take-over exists as long as the chosen programme is not the one which has the maximum net market value, assuming that the assets costing M_0 could be sold for M_0 by the entrepreneur taking over the firm. To the extent that assets are specific to particular programmes, and can only be resold (still at the beginning of the period) for less than their purchase price M_0, the entrepreneur is under less threat of a take-over, since there would be a corresponding reduction in the surplus potentially available to an entrepreneur taking over control of the selection of an investment programme.

The text of the chapter promised some discussion of the effects of alternative assumptions about the shapes of the equal-discount-rate and equal-market-valuation curves. The only necessary assumption about the equal-market-valuation curves is that they should have a positive slope, indicating that a given expected return is worth less if it has a larger standard

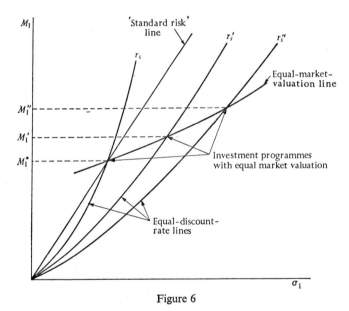

Figure 6

deviation (skewness and higher moments of the probability distribution being held constant). Once a complete set of equal-valuation lines has been drawn on the $M_1 \sigma_1$ graph, and a particular value attached to each line, then the positions of the equal-discount-rate lines are thereby determined. That this is so follows from the original definition of the equal-valuation lines. Each line passes through all programmes which have the same gross market value. Looking at Figure 6, the gross market value is identical for each of the indicated programmes. Thus

$$G = \frac{M_1^*}{1 + r_s} = \frac{M_1'}{1 + r_s'} = \frac{M_1''}{1 + r_s''}.$$

Since G, M_1^*, M_1', and M_1'' are all given, the three discount rates are all determined, and $r_s < r_s' < r_s''$. By mapping in all the market equal-valuation lines, the discount rates could thus be determined for each $M_1\sigma_1$ combination and equal-discount-rate lines could also be drawn joining all programmes whose present values are defined by the same discount rate.

The risk-standardization convention established in the text was no more than a possible way of reducing the number of different discount rates used in evaluating alternative programmes. This reduction will only take place if the 'standard risk' is defined in such a way that the standard-risk line or curve intersects a relatively small number of equal discount-rate lines. If the definition of 'standard risk' is chosen with this requirement in mind, then there may be a relatively small number of 'standard-risk' discount rates required for use in calculating the present values of programmes of different sizes.

What are the likely relationships between the equal-discount-rate lines and the 'standard coefficient of variation' ray from the origin of Figure 6? In the chapter it was assumed that larger programmes (for a given co-efficient of variation) cost more to finance than smaller ones, since large programmes start to play a substantial role in determining the variance of the portfolio returns of the shareholders. Whatever the distribution of portfolio requirements across shareholders, it may be supposed that those having most use in their portfolio for a security with particular risk and yield characteristics will be the intra-marginal shareholders. As the total size of the programme increases, the securities must be sold for a lower average price. The average and marginal discount rates will therefore have to rise to effect the placement. Under these circumstances, the positive slopes of the equal-discount lines will increase as the lines rise, and the lines may even pass through the vertical and thereby acquire negative slopes. Since there may be some fixed minimum cost involved in informing the share market about the characteristics of the firm's programme, the share market's average discount rate may perhaps not rise monotonically, but only after a minimum is reached. This may produce the situation shown in Figure 7, in which the 'standard-risk' line is cut twice by the same equal-discount-rate line. If the marginal share market discount rate rises fast enough with the size of the programme, it is even possible that one or more of the equal valuation lines should cut the standard-risk line at two places, as also illustrated in Figure 7. In such cases there are two 'risk-standardized' returns for any programme cut by the equal-valuation line in question. Since they both have the same gross market value, when dis-counted by their respective discount rates, it does not matter which is used to represent the programme. In situations where the risk standardization does not reduce much the number of relevant discount rates, and when there arises the possibility of multiple risk-standardized expected values of

a single programme, it seems likely that there is available a more appropriate definition of 'standard risk'.

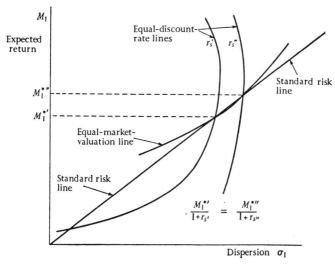

Figure 7

(2) *The single-period model using debt as well as equity finance*

To facilitate the analysis, the cash-flow distributions are defined in this
section as being the cash flows before any allowance is made for the effects
of borrowing. The risk-adjusted mean value of these pre-borrowing end-of-
period distributions will be referred to as M_1^{*B}. The initial cost of the
assets M_{0B} is before any allowance for funds provided by borrowing. In
the case where only equity funds are used (as in Section (1) of this Appendix), M_{0B} is equal to M_0. When borrowing is undertaken in the one-period
model, M_{0B} is greater than M_0 by B, the amount borrowed by the firm. If
borrowing is undertaken, M_0 is the cost of the assets less any funds provided by borrowing, while M_1 is the expected cash return less interest and
repayment of borrowed funds.

In the borrowing case the firm obtains funds by selling both shares and
bonds. A bond gives the purchaser a money return which is fixed in
advance. Lenders as a group buy bonds in the total amount B, and at the
end of the period they are entitled to receive $B(1 + i)$ where i is the (net of
corporation tax) rate of interest on borrowed funds. The rate of interest is
set in advance, and is determined by the amount of bonds which the firm
wishes to sell. In the case of shares, the rising discount rate reflects only

portfolio balance considerations, since the return M_1^{*B} is already risk-standardized. In the case of bonds, however, the interest rate is assumed to rise with the volume of borrowing, not only for portfolio balance reasons but also because a larger bond issue, for any particular expected return M_1^{*B}, means a higher probability that the actual return from the programme will not be adequate to meet the obligation to repay $B(1 + i)$ to the bondholders. The interest rate will also reflect the bond market's expectations about changes during the period in the money price of goods, i being higher if money prices are expected to rise or if there is greater variance of the bond market's estimate of the change in money prices. But even if the interest rate i is defined so as to include payment for the total bondholders' risk, it still does not encompass all the effects of debt financing. The use of debt financing also decreases the amount of funds which must be put up by shareholders, decreases the amount of the shareholders' claim on the expected return M_1^{*B}, and changes the coefficient of variation of the shareholders' return. The impact on the coefficient of variation is accounted for by adjusting the end-of-period return by some proportion b of the total amount borrowed B. The 'cost of borrowed funds' therefore has to be defined in terms not only of the interest rate which covers the lenders' risk and return but also of the impact which debt financing has on the shareholders' return. By including these features explicitly into the one-period model it is possible to determine the optimum debt/equity ratio for the present value-maximizing firm. As previously, the firm is attempting to maximize the net share-market value of the firm

$$(1) \qquad N = \frac{M_1^{*B} - B(1 + i) - bB}{1 + r_s} - M_{0B} + B.$$

The share market's discount rate r_s is assumed to depend on the present value of the risk-standardized return net of borrowing costs. The net market-value expression shows that borrowing has two effects on the risk-standardized end-of-period return to the shareholder. The expected value of the return is lessened by $B(1 + i)$, the original amount borrowed plus the accrued interest. The net market-value expression also shows that the risk-standardized return must be altered by a further amount bB because borrowing changes the coefficient of variation (σ_1/M_1) of the expected return net of direct borrowing costs.

If the expected return and risk are expressed in fixed money terms (i.e. if the positions of programmes on the M_1, σ_1 graph are unaffected by changes in money prices), then any borrowing will increase the coefficient of variation of the shareholders' return. Hence the risk-standardized return will be reduced by more than the amount required to pay the bondholders. On the more likely assumption that the expected return and variance which matter in the valuation of financial assets are in 'real' terms (i.e. the shareholders value the money return for what it will purchase), an expected increase in money prices may increase the risk-standardized return accruing to the shareholders. This is because the real value of the bond repayment is smaller, and may also be because the firm may be able to match the liability fixed in money terms (but risky in real terms) against some expected revenues also fixed in money terms, and thereby reduce the variance of the real return. The increase in risk-standardized return due to the reduction in the expected real value of the bond liability would presumably be offset by a higher nominal interest rate, but the second increase, provided by the opportunity to use bond liabilities to reduce the variance of the return in real terms, may be responsible for the adjustment factor, bB, entering the net market-value expression with a positive sign.

For any given value of M_1^{*B}, this adjustment factor will be some proportion b of the amount of borrowing undertaken.

Borrowing also influences the net market value by reducing (by B) the amount of funds which has to be provided by shareholders.

For any given set of investment projects with risk-standardized return M_1^{*B}, the maximum net market-value programme will involve positive borrowing if $1 + r_s > 1 + i + b$, using expression (1) defining the net market value of a firm using equity and debt finance. Thus borrowing only adds to the net share-market value of the firm if the share market's discount rate is greater than the sum of the (after tax) interest rate and the supplementary risk-adjustment factor b.

The optimum amount of borrowing for a programme with a given M_1^{*B} and M_{0B} is found by differentiating the net present market-value expression with respect to B, and setting the result equal to zero.

$$(2) \quad \frac{\partial N}{\partial B} =$$

$$-\frac{\left[+ M_1^{*B} - B(1 + i) - bB \right]\frac{\partial r_s}{\partial B} - \left(1 + i + B\frac{\partial i}{\partial B} + b\right)}{(1 + r_s)^2} \cdot \frac{}{1 + r_s} + 1 = 0,$$

$$-\left[M_1^{*B} - B(1 + i) - bB \right]\frac{\partial r_s}{\partial B} -$$

$$\left(1 + i + b + B\frac{\partial i}{\partial B}\right)(1 + r_s) + (1 + r_s)^2 = 0,$$

$$B(1 + i + b)\frac{\partial r_s}{\partial B} - \frac{\partial i}{\partial B}(1 + r_s) =$$

$$M_1^{*B}\frac{\partial r_s}{\partial B} + (1 + i + b)(1 + r_s) - (1 + r_s)^2,$$

$$(3) \qquad B = \frac{(1 + r_s)^2 - M_1^{*B}\frac{\partial r_s}{\partial B} - (1 + i + b)(1 + r_s)}{(1 + r_s)\frac{\partial i}{\partial B} - (1 + i + b)\frac{\partial r_s}{\partial B}}.$$

The appropriate way of choosing the optimum amount of borrowing is to maximize net market value (or some other maximand) with respect to changes in the amount of borrowing, as it is only by working with the total expression that the full effects of borrowing can be assessed. The same procedure may be applied if further sources of finance are being considered. If the interest rate (or discount rate) attached to each alternative source of funds is an increasing function of the amount raised from that source, then the probability is increased that the optimum financial plan for any given set of investment projects will involve using more than one source of funds. Under certain quite special assumptions about the valuation of financial assets (equal tax treatment for all forms of payment to holders of financial assets, and freedom for security holders to issue liabilities against themselves, at the bond rate of interest),[1] the net market value of the programme is unaffected by the pattern of financing. In general, given the portfolio balance requirements of the purchaser of financial assets, their limited ability to issue claims against themselves, and the unequal tax treatment of various sorts of financing, the net market value of investment programmes will be influenced by the pattern of finance. In the general case with multiple sources of finance, the marginal costs (i.e. marginal present-value impacts) of all forms of finance employed will be equalized, and the value of r_m, the marginal cost of equity funds, will depend not only on the characteristics of the investment projects, and the conditions in the share market, but also on the terms on which other sources of funds are available.

The analysis in the foregoing paragraphs is partial, in that it considers only the optimal pattern of finance for a particular set of investment projects. It has been seen that the average and marginal share market discount rates are affected by borrowing, since borrowing affects the risk-standardized cash flow to the shareholders, which in turn is assumed to influence the market discount rates. If these rates rise as G rises, then the use of borrowing will reduce r_s for a given M_1^{*B}, since $\partial G/\partial B < 0$. If opportunities for advantageous borrowing are introduced, the programme which had the maximum net market value when only equity was considered will have a higher N and a lower G when debt finance is introduced. If, as assumed previously, the marginal efficiency of investment is declining with increasing programme size, the largest net market-value programme using debt finance will involve a larger M_{0B} and M_1^{*B} than the highest net market-value programme using only equity finance. That this is so follows from the assumptions that $(\partial G/\partial B) < 0$, $(\partial r_m/\partial G) > 0$, $(\partial r_f/\partial M_{0B}) < 0$, and $(\partial r_m/\partial M_{0B}) > 0$. Thus $(\partial r_m/\partial B) < 0$, with M_1^{*B} constant, since $(\partial r_m/\partial B) = (\partial r_m/\partial G)(\partial G/\partial B)$. But in the highest net market-value pro-

---

[1] These are among the assumptions required to prove the Modigliani and Miller [1958] proposition that there is no optimal debt/equity ratio.

gramme using only equity finance $r_m = r_f$. Changing B with M_1^{*B} constant does not alter r_f, so that advantageous debt financing makes $r_m < r_f$. To restore optimality, the programme size must be increased, since, as assumed, $(\partial r_f/\partial M_{0B}) < 0$ and $(\partial r_m/\partial M_{0B}) > 0$.

In this section the relationships between debt and equity finance have been explained by introducing M_1^{*B} to refer to the cash flows before any financing and then introducing the borrowing and debt-repayment terms explicitly into the net market-value expression. In subsequent chapters it will be convenient to have the present value of a programme represented as a simple function of the risk-adjusted means of the cash-flow distributions, discounted by the share market's rate r_s. In order that this form of exposition should be consistent with the use of debt financing, it is necessary that the risk-adjusted mean values should refer to cash flows after all interest charges, debt issues and redemption, and any adjustments for changes in the risk parameters (induced by the use of borrowing). Thus it will be assumed that the risk-adjusted mean value M_1^* is equal to M_1^{*B} adjusted for the effects of borrowing.

$$M_1^* = M_1^{*B} - B(1 + i) - bB$$

and
$$M_0 = M_{0B} - B,$$

so that $N = [M_1^*/(1 + r_s)] - M_0$ holds in the one-period case even if the firm uses debt financing.

(3) The multi-period model

In the stationary case, where investment opportunities and the cost of finance are the same in every period, the multi-period model differs little from the single-period version, and all the same results may be obtained. The real difficulties arise when we allow investment opportunities and financial conditions to vary over time in a way which cannot be predicted. The model becomes much more complex because decisions taken in any one period have consequences spreading over many periods. The importance of these consequences depends on what decisions are taken in subsequent periods, and on the new investment opportunities which arise. In the multi-period case the investment programme is specific about the nature of the expenditures in the first period, but may only indicate the broad nature and expected consequences of the firm's activities in subsequent periods, since some investment programmes are intended to allow future activities to depend heavily on the outcome of events yet to take place. It is in any case possible to describe any particular programme (before any financing) by means of a number of interdependent subjective probability distributions of cash flow, one for each time period.

How does the firm choose a financing plan, and determine the appropriate discount rates for calculating present values in the multi-period case? Since the optimum action in any particular period is conditional upon certain actions in other periods, the choice of appropriate discount rates and types of financing in one period depend upon the choice in other periods.

The model appropriate to describe the evaluation of the multi-period case is therefore likely to be either very vague or very messy, or both.

The basic structure of the problem may be indicated in a general way, and shown to be like that of the two-period case. First it is necessary to derive the relevant discount rates, and then the present value of any particular programme may be calculated. Instead of a single value for B, the amount of borrowing, there is a separate value ΔB_t showing the change during period t in the amount of net debt outstanding. Similarly:

$\Delta S_t =$ the amount of funds raised by sale of shares in period t.

M_t, σ_t, and $SK_t =$ the expected value, standard deviation, and coefficient of skewness of the cash-flow distributions before *any* financing relating to period t.

$i_t =$ the average market interest rate on all new loans in period t.

$i_{st} =$ the average interest rate paid by the firm on new borrowing in period t.

$r_{st} =$ the share market's discount rate applied in period t.

$E_{mt} =$ a general index of share yields in period t.

Where these variables are used without t subscripts, it means that the values of the variable for all periods within the n-period horizon are potentially relevant in the equation.

The following general functions serve to illustrate the basic relationships between the inter-dependent variables:

(1) $\quad\quad\quad \Delta S_t = \phi_{\Delta s} (M, \sigma, SK, r_s, \Delta B)$,
(2) $\quad\quad\quad \Delta B_t = \phi_{\Delta B} (M, \sigma, SK, i, \Delta S)$,
(3) $\quad\quad\quad r_{st} = \phi_s (E_m, M, \sigma, SK, i_s, \Delta S)$,
(4) $\quad\quad\quad i_{st} = \phi_i (M, \sigma, SK, \Delta B, i)$.

There are thus at least four basic equations required for each period to determine the pattern of finance and the appropriate discount rates.[1] Since there is no obvious way of identifying the parameters of all these equations, it is only in a rather vague sense that they can be said to 'determine' the appropriate pattern of finance and the associated discount rates. There may be some recourse to market data in any effort to estimate parameters, particularly of equations (3) and (4). It is sufficient for our

---

[1] A number of definitional equations required to close the system are being ignored in this simple exposition.

purpose to merely sketch the nature of the relationships, and to ignore the problem of finding the parameters which would determine the appropriate values of r_s for particular investment programmes.

In order that the multi-period framework should be consistent with the analysis in Section (2) of this Appendix, the risk-standardized mean values M_t^* are defined as the cash flows net of all interest payments and changes in debt outstanding. Only by having the risk (and debt) standardized mean values refer to the cash flows net of debt financing is it possible to use the share market's discount rates (r_{st}) to find the present value of programmes in a way that allows them to be simply ranked in order of net present value.

For any particular investment programme, with its own set of n cash-flow distributions, and discount rates derived (for each period) from equations (1) to (4), the present value (PV) may be calculated,

$$(5) \qquad PV = \sum_{t=1}^{n} \frac{M_t^*}{(1 + r_{s1})(1 + r_{s2}) \ldots (1 + r_{st})}.$$

In equation (5) net present value is found by discounting the risk-standardized mean values of the cash-flow distributions. By standardizing for risk and debt before discounting, it is possible to limit the required number of discount rates to n, one linking each pair of adjacent periods. To get a present-value expression using the 'raw' mean M_t of each cash-flow distribution, each M_t would have to have its own set of discount rates appropriate to its particular level of risk and pattern of finance. For each time period there would have to be as many discount rates (for a given pattern of finance) as there were time periods beyond that point but within the investment horizon. To find PV by discounting the values of M_t^*, a total of n rates are required; if the values of M_t were discounted a total of $1 + 2 + 3 \ldots + n$ discount rates would be needed for each alternative pattern of finance and for each set of investment projects.

Something must be said about the determination of n, the time horizon of the investment programme. Whatever number of cash-flow distributions may be considered as constituting a particular investment programme, the last one encompasses the probability distribution of the possible sales values of the assets and production rights of the firm as at that date. For any particular set of investment opportunities, the firm may consider a number of different time horizons. The number of time periods considered, n, is therefore one more variable which is free to take different values in different investment programmes. It may be assumed that the chosen value of n is that which is most in line (for given values of the other variables) with the preferences of management. If the management wishes to choose the programme with the maximum present value, then the time horizon will presumably not have to be longer than the period within which the investment plans of the firm are in explicit form. There is presumably nothing to be gained, in present value, by extending the horizon much

D

beyond that point, since the market value of the firm's assets and opportunities at the end of the $n + 1$th period will differ only by the factor $1/(1 + r_{sn})$ from the value at the end of the nth period. Within the period for which the present management can make explicit plans, the choice of a time horizon is more relevant, since the management may be presumed to make use of the transformation possibilities so as to produce different distributions of cash flow than those which would characterize the programme selected by another management group. The time horizon chosen within an optimizing framework might be very short. For example, if the management wished to choose the maximum present-value programme, and could not use the existing assets to produce cash-flow distributions whose present market value was as great as the current market value of the assets themselves, then the optimum programme would involve immediate sale of all the assets (to a firm whose transformation possibilities were such as to make better use of the assets). The time horizon of the preferred programme would thus be zero. In more usual cases, the management of the firm possesses experience and knowledge that gives some programme with a finite time horizon a greater present value than the immediate market value of the assets of the firm. Situations where the management of the firm is not able to use the assets of the firm in a profitable way are likely to be situations where investment programmes are selected on grounds other than their present value, although the present value may always be expected to have some importance, if only as a constraint.

When a multi-period programme is considered, the present value is equal to the gross market value (G) if the cost of the assets (net of borrowing) at $t = 0$ (i.e. the certain cash flow which the shareholders have to provide at $t = 0$) is ignored, or the net share-market value (N) if the cost of all assets is considered. It is the net share market value which is the object of reference in subsequent chapters when the PV of a programme is discussed, since it is N rather than G which is the appropriate maximand for the firm concerned with the shareholders' interests, or with the management's security of tenure.

To add a final touch of realism to the multi-period case, it is necessary to give up the assumption, which was used in the two-period case, that potential share buyers and the management of the firm have the same subjective probability distributions of the cash flow from alternative programmes. This assumption must be replaced by others which state some sort of basis for the share and bond markets' expectations about the consequences of alternative programmes. In the absence of any better information, the financial markets are likely to use the firm's past record (in terms of the amount and variability of profits, dividends, etc.), as a guide to its future prospects. Thus equations (3) and (4) should contain not only the characteristics of the future cash-flow distributions (we may assume that investors still have some idea of future prospects as viewed by the management) but also the recent profit and loss, balance sheet, and share price data for the firm. The hopeful side of this increase in complexity is that it may be possible to use the characteristics of achieved returns as proxy variables for the risk and yield characteristics which the financial markets attribute to the firm's investment programme. But what if firms realize that shareholders watch profits, dividends, and share prices closely, and have no better access to knowledge of the firm's investment opportunities? Would not the firm choose a programme which made the indices watched by the share market have an artificially favourable relationship to the returns actually expected in the future? They might, but if management groups wish to retain the confidence of shareholders over an extended period of time it is in their interests to remove any favourable or unfavourable bias in shareholder expectations. By avoiding deliberate distortion of the *ex post* returns, the management of the firm increases the flow of information to shareholders, usually without increasing the amount of information of direct use to their competitors.

Thus it may be expected that the size and stability of the *ex post* returns to shareholders (the level and stability of dividends, profits, and share prices are presumably all relevant to certain classes of shareholder) will bear some relation to shareholders' beliefs about the size and stability of future returns. If this relation could be presumed to hold over time, the *ex post* returns on various types of financial assets could be used to indicate roughly the shapes of the equal valuation curves applied by the market to securities with different mixes of risk and yield. If the effects of new issues on discount rates could also be determined by recourse to *ex post* experience, then it might be possible to estimate parameters for the equations determining the discount rates and the optimum financial plan for any particular investment programme.

2

ASSUMPTIONS AND IMPLICATIONS
OF THE MODEL

In this chapter the behavioural assumptions of Chapter 1 will be compared with those which have been used in other studies of investment behaviour, and some of the implications of the model will be spelt out. The primary aim will be to compare alternative assumptions by means of the observable behaviour that would serve to indicate their presence.

In Section A we shall deal with alternative ways of treating uncertainty, and alternative goals of investment behaviour. In Section B we shall point out the implications of these behavioural assumptions, and the theory based on them, for the analysis of the effects of monetary and fiscal policies.

A. Behavioural Assumptions

(1) Uncertainty

In Chapter 1 the decisive group is assumed to have estimates of the parameters of subjective probability distributions of cash flow. In Chapter 4 we shall expand the analysis to embrace the possibilities of expenditures on information. There we shall assume that investment programmes based on different amounts of information and information-gathering activity are compared on the basis of the expected values of the estimates of the various parameters of the cash-flow distributions. The trade-offs between the parameter values of different distributions are assumed to be derived from the trade-offs established in the capital market. How does this approach differ from that adopted in other work?

There are at least five different ways of treating uncertainty in the analysis of investment. These different approaches cannot be clearly demarcated, as much writing has involved a combination of approaches, or has left vague the underlying assumptions about the informational basis for decision. We shall consider:

(a) the subjective certainty, or 'certainty equivalent' approach,

(b) decisions made on the basis of a probability distribution whose parameters are estimated with subjective certainty,

(c) decisions made on the basis of a probability distribution whose parameters are estimated with less than complete confidence,

(d) the state preference approach,

(e) rejection of the probabilistic approach.

(a) *Subjective certainty*. One of the most frequent simplifications in the analysis of investment decisions has been the assumption that decisions are made on the basis of subjectively certain estimates of the results. There are three variants of this: the estimates may be certain, the decisions may be made *as if* the estimates were single-valued, or the decisions may be made on the basis of a probability distribution whose parameters are subjectively certain and convertible into a single certainty equivalent expectation value. The first variant fits easily into all analyses of perfectly competitive markets, where information is assumed to be perfect. The second variant implies that the decision-maker makes use only of an unadjusted mean or mathematical expectation, and ignores the values of any other moments of the probability distribution of receipts. This approach may be slightly more realistic than the assumption of perfect knowledge, but does little to help in the analysis of reactions to uncertainty.[1] For example, it cannot cope with interdependent projects, diversification, or any of the other important issues. The third variant goes one step closer to a full explanation, and permits at least the recognition of the effects of predictability on the attractiveness of a receipts stream. The Lutzes' [1951, Chapter XV] analysis is an example of this sort of treatment.[2] They suggest that the choice of investments is the choice between alternative probability distributions of net receipts. Their concern with the dispersion as well as the mean of the probability distribution allows them to analyse the advantages of flexible capital goods, and the effects of different time horizons on

[1] This, may, however, be the optimum procedure in situations where all alternatives have the same riskiness. In Theil's [1961, pp. 414–24] terms, when the stochastic elements in the constraint equations are unaffected by the choice of instruments, the optimum choice will depend only on the expected values of the target variables. Theil's certainty equivalence theorem would of course only be applicable to the choice of investment programmes if alternative cash flow distributions all had the same riskiness, i.e. identical values for all moments higher than the mean.

[2] Others who collapse subjective probability distributions to certainty equivalent approximations include R. Eisner and R. H. Strotz [1963, esp. pp. 88–89], O. Lange [1944], and J. Lintner [1964].

the expected dispersion of receipts. After assuming that the mean and standard deviation adequately represent the interesting characteristics of the probability distribution of net receipts, the Lutzes go on to define indifference curves, each of which shows the various combinations of mean and standard deviation which are equally attractive to the decision-maker. Since these indifference curves are drawn right to the point where the standard deviation is zero, any investment opportunity can be seen to have a higher or lower (or perhaps the same) certainty equivalent return than another investment plan (i.e. be on a higher or lower indifference curve). The analysis suggests that it is the entrepreneur's risk preference that defines the indifference curves, but little is said of the factors governing the shape of the curves. Our model differs markedly from theirs in defining the trade-off between risk and yield in terms of the effects of risk on the cost of capital rather than in terms of subjective risk preference. Our analysis suggests that the trade-off rate is not likely to be valid to the point where the standard deviation is zero; we therefore are not able to speak of 'certainty equivalent' estimates of receipts. (See Subsection (b) below.)

M. J. Gordon [1962], engaged in constructing a normative model of investment behaviour, argues that the Lutzes' analysis is complicated and non-operational. He proceeds to develop a model which defines the allowance for risk in terms of the effects of risk on the cost of capital. His own model of investment behaviour includes an index of uncertainty (derived from share price information) that is to be used to deflate dividend expectations to certainty equivalents. The actual index he uses differs from ours in several respects. The primary difference is that our measure of standard deviation of actual from predicted revenues represents the residual uncertainty remaining after the firm has taken whatever steps it might wish to take to reduce the variability of receipts. Gordon, however, includes variables describing the liquidity of the firm's operating assets, the maturity structure of its debt, and size, in addition to variables measuring the debt/equity ratio and the variability of the earnings yield on ungeared equity. The latter two measures combine to give a measure of the variability of the actual shareholders' return on equity, but it is difficult to know how to interpret the first three variables. Our analysis has assumed that it is the standard deviation itself, or something like it, that measures the risk element in a shareholder's return, while Gordon's implies that the shareholder also takes account of the characteristics of the firm that help to determine the standard deviation.

Despite these difficulties, Gordon's measure of uncertainty goes far beyond the crude assumptions of subjective certainty, and with its focus on the market valuation of risk characteristics provides the most useful of the certainty equivalent approaches to decision-making.

Other approaches which use certainty equivalent approximations, although subjecting them to substantial restrictions, are those of Haring and Smith [1959], Haring [1961], and Egerton [1960]. Since all these authors avoid the use of probability distributions in their analyses, their work will be discussed under (e) below.

(b) *Decisions made on the basis of probability distributions whose parameters are estimated with subjective certainty*. The only difference between this approach and the more sophisticated of those described above is that there is no assumption that the relevant characteristics of the probability distribution can be compressed into a single certainty equivalent measure. There are few examples of this approach, since almost all writers who assume that any trade-off can be established (whether on the basis of entrepreneurs' risk preferences or market prices of securities) between yield and risk also assume that certainty equivalent approximations can be developed.

The importance of the distinction between approaches (a) and (b) depends on the nature of the objections that are made to the certainty equivalent approach. The objections are of two main types. On the one hand, the range of alternative feasible investment programmes ranked by decision-makers may only include programmes with limited ranges of variation in the parameters of the distributions. If so, the function relating, say, risk and yield, can only be measured over that range of variation. Since the alternative investment programmes all have a substantial degree of uncertainty attached, there is no evidence by which to establish an equivalent valuation involving no uncertainty (i.e. zero value of the standard deviation).

The first objection merely recognizes that any sample pattern of achieved returns is going to provide inadequate means of identifying the underlying probability distribution. Since there is no way of knowing the shape of the distribution, let alone what its parameters may be, any assumptions about the characteristics of the distribution should be used cautiously. Since the error involved in assuming the wrong shape for a distribution is likely to increase considerably as the range of prediction is further removed from the range of observed behaviour, it seems sensible to choose 'standard risk' parameter values that are well within the observed range of variation.

The second objection involves a reinforcement of the first. It says that even if some unit of return were suggested such that certain assets had a riskless (zero variance) return, probability distributions constructed using this measure could not be used to derive certainty-equivalent valuations. That is, it is not just that a lack of observations restricts the range of risk and yield variation and so limits the valid range of application of an estimated risk–yield trade-off rate. Rather, it is the case that no future return can be certain (in utility terms) since the utility attached to any particular commodity or means of exchange to be delivered at a future date depends on the complete world endowment and distribution of everything at that date.

For a combination of these two reasons, our model embodies a risk–yield trade-off that is defined only within a certain range of uncertainty.[1] Our procedure does not require that any of the risk-standardized programmes be considered to be equivalent to another hypothetical programme whose value is measured by a single indicator estimated with subjective certainty.

Most of the previous work dealing with the risk and yield combinations provided by alternative portfolios of securities have assumed that there are riskless financial assets available.[2]

(c) *Decisions made on the basis of a probability distribution whose parameters are estimated with less than complete confidence.* The Savage [1954, Chapters 1–7] analysis would suggest that this approach *should* be no different from those described above. Subjective probabilities would be established for each of the possible eventualities, and a decision made on the basis of the utility function showing the trade-off between risk and yield. Given a situation where no further information is obtainable, the best estimates of probabilities (corrected so that the sum of the probabilities of mutually exclusive

---

[1] In a sense any risk–yield trade-off involves the use of 'certainty equivalents' since programmes of differing riskiness are standardized so as to have equivalent risk. The risk standardizing procedure differs from the use of 'certainty equivalents' in that risk standardization requires only that a trade-off be established for a limited range of degrees of uncertainty.

[2] e.g. Farrar [1962], Hicks [1962], Markowitz [1959], and Tobin [1958]. More recently, Tobin [1965] has recognized that there may be no riskless financial assets. It is from there only a short step to our conclusion that for a firm issuing securities the appropriate risk–yield trade-off is not defined to the point of zero risk.

and exhaustive events is equal to 1) are used without regard to the weight of evidence behind them.

Those who object to this approach contend that decisions are affected by the degree of certainty of the decision-maker's estimates of the parameters of his subjective probability distributions. A. G. Hart [1942] has made the point with the aid of F. H. Knight's [1921] overworked distinction between risk and uncertainty. 'Risk,' Hart says, 'is taken to denote the holding of anticipations which are not "single valued" but constitute a probability distribution having known parameters. "Uncertainty" is taken to denote the holding of anticipations under which the parameters of the probability distributions are themselves not single valued.' Hart suggests that in situations where there exists (a) the anticipation of a change in anticipations, and (b) the possibility of deferring decisions, with or without special costs, the 'probabilities' of occurrences in a probability distribution and the 'likelihoods' of various probability distributions occurring cannot be treated in the same way.

A more precise, and stronger, formulation of this objection has been presented by some of those who have tested the Savage axioms with gambling experiments and found that attempts to compound uncertain estimates into subjectively certain probability distributions may produce inconsistent results. Ellsberg [1961] describes situations in which the degree of 'ambiguity' in the available evidence appears to affect decisions. He suggests that there are occasions when a decision-maker has enough information to rule out a number of possible distributions, but not enough to choose (or compound) a distribution as a unique basis for decision. His experiments show, as do those of Fellner [1961], that decision-makers operating in situations when they 'should' make identical estimates of the parameters of two distributions, in fact attach a higher value to the distribution which is less 'ambiguous'.[1]

---

[1] Raiffa [1961], Brewer [1963], and Roberts [1963], have argued that a prime cause of the disutility attached to vagueness in the experiments was the fact that the subjects were faced with asymmetrical bets. If allowed to take either side of the vague bet, and if shown that the expected yield and risk were the same for both the more and the less vague bets, the subjects would not pay more for the less vague bet. Ellsberg [1963] agrees that offering symmetrical bets decreases the premium a subject would charge for accepting the more vague bet, but argues that wherever vagueness remains, even when there are no possibilities for buying information, the subject will pay less for the vague bet. Fellner [1963] argues further that the 'slanting' (downwards) of vague probabilities is a common re-

How would such behaviour manifest itself within the model set out in Chapter 1? The most likely thing would seem to be that greater 'ambiguity' would lead to higher estimates of the standard deviation of the subjective probability distribution. To the extent that there is a disutility attached to vagueness, there will be a trade-off between vagueness and the estimated values of the parameters of the cash-flow distributions, and these trade-off rates can be used to standardize the parameter estimates with respect to their vagueness. Thus we may assume that the estimates of the relevant parameters of the compound probability distributions are adjusted by the decision-maker to account for differences in the 'ambiguity' (in Ellsberg's sense) of his estimates.

(d) *The state preference approach.* A probability distribution of returns may be conceived of as a large number of separate but certain returns, each of which is contingent upon a different state of the world. Each different state of the world has a probability attached to it. Suppose there were a finite number of possible states of the world at the end of the period. Each possible state would therefore have its own finite probability of coming to pass. A security which offers the purchaser a probability distribution of returns can therefore be interpreted as the sum of a finite number of 'primary' securities each promising a certain return if a particular state of the world should obtain. It is possible to analyse decisions under uncertainty in terms of such 'primary' securities, each of which offers a certain return conditional upon a state of the world with a clearly defined probability of occurring. Since the various states of the world are mutually exclusive, the sum of the probabilities of their occurring is equal to 1.

In order that the return from a primary security should be certain, given the state of the world, it must be defined either in terms of some good which enters directly into utility functions, or whose value in terms of such goods is known with certainty.[1]

The approach has been used chiefly to show that optimal allocation under uncertainty requires as many independent securities as there are possible states of the world.[2] When it is applied to the investment decisions[3] of firms financed by shares and bonds of the sort

---

action to asymmetrical bets, and that probabilities must often be estimated for 'bets' that are essentially asymmetrical.

[1] The definition of the state of the world thus implies certainty about the prices and distribution of all goods in that state.

[2] Arrow [1953], Debreu [1959].   [3] Hirshleifer [1965, 1966].

with which we are familiar, the analysis is no longer analytically distinct from one based on probability distributions whose parameters are estimated with certainty. This is because each bond or share promises some sort of return (perhaps negative) in any state of the world, so that there are no longer any primary securities with certain returns; there are only compound securities whose returns are subject to a probability distribution. The problem still remains, whether one starts with the primary securities, or starts right in (as we have done) with the compound securities, that there is no satisfactory *numéraire* for the return distribution, since the compound security may return different primary commodities depending on the state of the world. This is the difficulty always facing our use of cash-flow distributions as a basis for present value calculations, since it must be assumed that the primary commodity-equivalent of the cash flow is independent of the final outcome. This dangerous assumption is necessary if return distributions are to be risk-standardized so as to derive a single measure of their potential market value. One advantage of the state preference approach is that it helps to remind us of the dangers inherent in using any single index (whatever the *numéraire*) for the value of a security producing different returns under different states of the world.

(e) *Rejection of the probabilistic approach.* The common element in theories rejecting the probabilistic approach is a belief that what is of interest to decision-makers cannot be meaningfully represented by the parameters of subjective probability distributions.

The most complete rejection of subjective probabilities occurs in G. L. S. Shackle's [1952, 1955, and 1961] work. His model assumes that a decision-maker is only concerned with a single focus gain and a single focus loss for any project being considered. The decision-maker is assumed to rank mutually exclusive projects on the basis of the ratio of standardized focus gain to standardized focus loss, and to consider combinations of projects by adding together their focus gains, and dividing by the sum of the focus losses.

Critics were quick to notice the shortcomings of Shackle's model, although there was considerable support for it from economists reacting against models which assume the decision-maker to be continually working through a probabilistic calculus. A. D. Roy [1952] has pointed out that Shackle's model cannot explain diversification. This is a consequence of Shackle's assumption that combinations of projects would be assessed by comparing the sum of the focus gains with the sum of the focus losses.[1] Only in the special case where there is a perfect correlation among the fluctuations in the receipts from all the projects can the assumption be justified (and, of course, in this case there *is* no advantage in diversification). Other critics have concerned themselves with the implausibility of the supposition that the decision-maker concerns himself only with two critical values, one a gain and the other a loss. Some have attempted to adapt Shackle's model so as to avoid such criticisms.

R. A. D. Egerton [1960] suggested changes in the shape of the potential surprise function, and brought in a measure of risk to be considered in addition to the focus outcomes. He supposes that there is an appropriate cardinal measure of risk which can be related to the focus-gain/focus-loss ratio by means of indifference curves. Egerton's risk concept is not precisely defined, but appears to include Ellsberg's 'ambiguity' as well as estimates of the likelihood of particular (focus) outcomes. 'The estimate of the riskiness of a project that an investor makes depends on his estimate of the likelihood of its success. . . . A project may be deemed unlikely to succeed for either of two reasons. First, the knowledge which the investor possesses may be such as to lead him to expect the unsuccessful rather than the successful outcome. Second, the investor may have insufficient knowledge to be confident which outcome will be yielded, and because of his lack of knowledge may fear that the unsuccessful outcome will result— although he has insufficient knowledge to expect the unfavourable outcome to be yielded'.[2] In probabilistic terms, Egerton's risk variable is defined so as to encompass the estimates of the parameters of a subjective probability distribution as well as the 'ambiguity' of the evidence on which the parameter estimates are based. It might be suggested that Egerton has introduced into the Shackle framework those elements of probabilistic reasoning that Shackle was most anxious to avoid. The major difference between Egerton's analysis and that based on a subjective probability distribution is that the decision-maker is assumed to concern himself with the ratio between two focus outcomes rather than with a mean value.

Haring [1961] adapts Shackle's model in rather a different way.

---

[1] In his more recent work, Shackle has accepted this criticism, and has agreed that focus gains and losses should refer to portfolios directly without any assumption that focus gains and losses on individual projects should be additive [1961, pp. 180–5].

[2] Egerton [1960, p. 50].

He shares Shackle's desire to avoid cardinal measures of risk, but suggests that decision-makers may be concerned with a central value as well as the two focus outcomes. Haring compares the two focus outcomes (as rates of return) with upper and lower 'range of interest' boundaries. The 'range of interest' boundaries are further apart as the length of the estimating period increases. The maximum focus loss and the minimum focus gain also spread farther apart in the estimates for future years, spreading at a faster rate than do the 'range of interest' boundaries. The time horizon of the decision-maker is 'defined as the point in the future when the focus-loss loci of a specific project crosses the range of interest boundary'.[1] The decision-maker considers only those projects for which the minimum focus gain is greater than the maximum focus loss (within the relevant time horizon), and chooses among such projects on the basis of their 'certainty equivalent approximations' (c.e.a.). Haring differs from Shackle and Egerton by ranking projects on the basis of the c.e.a. rather than the focus-gain/focus-loss ratio. Interpersonal differences in risk preference are accounted for explicitly by variations in the 'range of interest' boundaries. The Haring analysis differs from the model of Chapter 1 on a point whose importance may be greater in principle than in practice. The model of the preceding chapter suggests that any changes in risk or yield affect the attractiveness of a project or programme. Haring's model implies that the riskiness of a project is immaterial, providing the range of interest boundaries are not crossed. In maximizing terms, the Haring decision-maker maximizes the c.e.a. subject to a risk or 'range of interest' constraint.

Both the Haring and Egerton Models, although based on Shackle's focus outcomes, involve several features which are closely analogous to those of a probabilistic treatment.

The probabilistic approach is also rejected by those who use game theory without admitting the presence of mixed strategies. If, on the other hand, mixed strategies are admitted, the game theoretic approach to decisions involving conjectural variation is easily integrated with a probabilistic approach. The use of pure strategies in game theory is often useful as a means of separating the strands of a complex situation,[2] but cannot easily be used as the basis of a descriptive theory.

---

[1] Haring [1961, p. 83].

[2] The game theoretic approach has more often been used to analyse short-term

The behavioural approach to the analysis of decision-making, like the game theoretic approach, does not imply the rejection of subjective probability distributions. On the other hand, the approach need not assume any particular treatment of uncertainty. The behaviourist attempts to build a model which simulates the decision and reaction processes actually witnessed. The models themselves, and the evidence with which they are tested, provide information useful in assessing reactions to uncertainty, although no explicit treatment of risk need be included in the model.[1]

(2) *Managerial preference functions and the goals of business enterprise*

What is the likelihood that managerial preference functions are of such a form as to produce the kind of behaviour that is supposed by the model of Chapter 1? And what are the observable differences in behaviour between a managerial group that acts in accordance with our theory and one acting on some other set of behavioural assumptions?

The model of Chapter 1 shows how the determination of the optimum financing plan for any given set of investment possibilities requires simultaneous solution of the values of the share market's discount rate, the costs of other sorts of finance, and the pattern of financing. Once the pattern of finance has been selected, the set of investment projects becomes an investment programme, with a single risk-standardized present value. No restrictions were placed, in Chapter 1, on the number or nature of alternative programmes which a firm might evaluate; but we did suppose that the chosen programme would be one with a positive present value. In this section we consider the effects of different types of maximizing behaviour. All the programmes with positive present values are feasible ones, since financial markets are expected to be willing, on the basis of unbiased expectations, to provide a continuing flow of funds. The feasible programmes may have different time horizons, stable or unstable growth paths, different capital/output ratios, different profit/sales ratios, and different growth rates. Thus there is room for the application of one of a number of managerial preference functions.

---

competitive reactions to price and output decisions than to deal with the information gathering and investment choices which are our chief concern. See D. R. Luce and H. Raiffa [1957], M. Shubik [1959, 1963], and H. M. Wagner [1958].

[1] For descriptions of the behavioural analysis, see R. M. Cyert, W. R. Dill, and J. G. March [1958], R. M. Cyert and J. G. March [1960, 1963], G. P. E. Clarkson [1962], and H. A. Simon [1962].

By choosing the programme with the largest present value, a firm is not maximizing either the internal rate of return, or the *PV* of profits per existing share. Both the latter maximands have been suggested as appropriate assumptions for a descriptive theory. Of all the alternative versions of profit maximization, the choice of the programme with the maximum present value implies the fastest rate of growth.[1]

The generality of this framework is such that programmes may have different relative rates of growth by one measure than by another. Not only may different programmes have different capital/ output or profit/gross revenue ratios over time but any particular programme may be characterized by different (stable) rates of growth of the various indices. There are also various types of unstable growth path that may be followed. Thus when it is said that the maximization of *PV* leads to faster rates of growth over time, the statement must be interpreted in a general way: that for given sets of investment opportunities and conditions in financial markets the new issue rate will, on average, be higher for a firm choosing the maximum *PV* programme than for a firm maximizing some other definition of profit.[2]

The maximization of gross revenues has on occasion been suggested as an appropriate maximand for a descriptive theory, but usually in a static rather than a growth context.[3] Within our model the maximization of sales revenues might be evidenced by the choice

---

[1] See F. and V. Lutz [1951, Chapter II], for a comparison of several of the interpretations of profit maximization.

Lintner [1964] and Lerner and Carleton [1964] adopt the maximization of the market value of existing shares as an appropriate (normative) maximand, while Alain Barrère [1961] assumes the maximand to be the internal rate of return.

[2] Except for maximands involving undiscounted profits. Over any particular time horizon there may be programmes whose growth rates (of assets, sales, or any other measure) and totals of undiscounted profits are larger than for the maximum *PV* programme.

[3] W. J. Baumol, who gave the sales maximization hypothesis its currency [1959], has since suggested that, in a dynamic context, growth is the equivalent of sales revenues in his earlier analysis. He now suggests [1962] that the firm attempts to maximize growth subject to a constraint that the rate of profit should not fall below a certain level. He analyses a stationary dynamic equilibrium model in which all measures of size grow at the same rate, and so does not consider the possibility presented by our model that different indices of growth would be maximized by different programmes. He also does not consider the possibility that, even within an equilibrium model in which all growth rates were constant, different programmes with the same growth rate might have different levels of sales in the same time period.

of the programme with the highest average sales revenue, the fastest rate of growth of sales, or the maximum *PV* of gross revenues.

More recently Robin Marris has argued [1963, 1964] that the rate of growth is the maximand in most firms, subject to the constraint that a minimum level of security from take-over bids is maintained. Marris analyses only those programmes in which all variables grow at the same rate, so that it does not matter for his purposes which measure of growth is thought to be the one most important to managers.

The relationship between Marris' growth maximization and the behaviour assumed in our model is considerably affected by the nature of the security constraint. The security constraint is likely to affect the choice among feasible programmes (those with positive *PV*'s discounted at the appropriate discount rates) as well as to preclude the choice of programmes with negative *PV*'s. The security constraint exists because the management group requires the confidence of shareholders if they are to avoid dismissal and ward off any attacks by take-over bidders. Dismissal by dissatisfied shareholders is a likely event if management chooses an unfeasible programme when a feasible one is available (or is thought by shareholders to be available). A take-over bid is also a possibility in these circumstances, or more generally, any time the present value of the chosen investment programme is substantially lower than that of an alternative programme thought feasible by the take-over bidder.[1] Thus the management group wishing to choose the feasible programme with the highest growth rate will be constrained to choose a programme with a *PV* high enough that share prices are not driven low enough to attract a potentially successful take-over bid.

Marris states that a management acting in the shareholders' interests will maximize the 'valuation ratio', which is the ratio of the market value (of the shares of the firm) to the book value of its net assets. He describes the resulting situation as one of maximum security for the management, even though the investment programme which maximizes the valuation ratio is not that which maximizes the profit rate. It has been argued in Chapter 1 that it is the maximum *PV* programme which provides maximum security to management,

[1] The problem is not quite as simple as this discussion would indicate, as the *PV* which is important to the potential take-over raider is not the *PV* of the investment programme of the firm but the difference which the control of the firm would make to the risk and yield characteristics of the total operations of the take-over raider.

without there being any conflict between maximum profits (in terms of PV) and maximum security. Since the maximum PV investment programme is in general (i.e. in all cases where the average rate of return is greater than the marginal rate of return in the chosen programme) larger than that which maximizes the valuation ratio (and larger still than that which maximizes the rate of profit), the contrast between growth maximizing and security maximizing behaviour is not as great as is suggested by Marris. If his model is reformulated using PV maximization as a more appropriate definition of the programme which maximizes the security of management, then the security constraint is in terms of the gap between the PV of the chosen programme and that of the maximum PV programme. If the security constraint did not exist, then the growth-maximizing management would choose the feasible programme with the largest rate of growth.[1]

Where there is a security constraint it would limit the range of feasible programmes from among which the managers could choose without facing more than a certain probability of take-over or dismissal.

The difference in behaviour between a growth-maximizing management and one maximizing PV will depend on the supply and quality of take-over bidders. If take-over bidders are enthusiastic, and in elastic supply, the security-conscious firm may be restricted in its choice of investment programmes to those whose present values are near or equal to the maximum. In an environment where there are many firms with large cash flows, but few investment opportunities of their own, the situation is a likely one for take-over bids, especially if the tax regulations, or the costs of reinvesting, are such as to favour retention of profits rather than payment of dividends. Since the existence of a take-over situation presupposes that the potential bidder attaches a higher PV to a feasible joint investment programme than is attached by the shareholders to the firm's present programme, the supply of information on which the three parties (shareholders, management, and bidders) base their PV estimates does much to determine the nature of the security constraint.

[1] In the case where the risk-standardized return M_1^* is assumed to be a twice differentiable function of M_0 such that $(dM_1^*/dM_0) > 0$ and $(d^2M_1/dM_0^2) < 0$, then the largest feasible programme in the one-period model is that where $r_a = r_s$, and the PV is zero, since

$$PV = N = \left(\frac{1 + r_a}{1 + r_s} - 1\right) M_0.$$

E

Once it is recognized that more than one variable can enter explicitly into a managerial preference function, there seems no clear upper limit to the number of variables which should be included. The various items (managerial salaries, number of assistants, good labour relations, public image, etc.) which have been suggested may enter as constraints or as variables in a utility function.[1] We have perhaps taken an extreme view, by treating the PV of the investment programme as a proxy for the actual constituents of the managerial preference function. At the opposite extreme would be those suggesting that so far from maximizing the value taken by a single variable, managerial groups wish only to stay within 'satisfactory' ranges of performance, having no defined preferences among alternative programmes promising to produce results within the acceptable ranges.

There has been a considerable body of literature[2] to the effect that any maximizing theory imposes unrealistic patterns of behaviour on a decision-making group. Many case studies of choices and decisions, particularly those concerned with group decisions, have emphasized that both individuals and groups act according to specific rules and targets rather than maximands.

The aim of this study is to develop an explanation of decision behaviour which is both rigorous and descriptive; so that we must consider seriously the suggestion that group decision behaviour cannot be usefully described on the basis of maximizing assumptions. But does it matter very much whether one starts with a catalogue of rules and conventions that describe behaviour, and specifies the conditions on which the rules have changed from time to time, or with a simple assumption about the decision behaviour which is then made realistic by reference to the attitudes and information of the decision-makers?

Certainly there is much to be gained from detailed studies of the behaviour of groups responsible for making decisions. Only in this way can the most appropriate mix of variables be chosen as elements in a descriptive decision theory.

One of the most valuable contributions of those who describe their theoretical work as 'behavioural' has been their emphasis on the adaptive processes and learning mechanism of managerial groups.

---

[1] e.g. Williamson [1963, 1964] includes certain preferred expenses in his managerial utility functions.

[2] Cyert and March, Clarkson, Simon, works cited; March and Simon [1958], Simon [1959], and Gordon [1961].

Certainly the notion of discontinuous responses to accumulating information has considerable descriptive importance, and it and other aspects of learning theory will undoubtedly be involved in any testable version of the model of Chapter 1, while the idea of investment planning as a process owes something to the many works on adaptive processes.

If it is generally true that management groups respond only to marked changes in their environment, and if the size and direction of their adaptive responses can better be explained by the use of specified targets[1] than by a more general maximizing framework, then a positive version of our model should take more explicit account of such behaviour rules. Even if the rules and the multiple objectives of management defy description by modified maximizing assumptions, these assumptions may continue to be useful in analysing how rules are made and conflicting objectives traded-off against each other.

How are we to decide whether our behavioural assumptions are adequate for our analysis, in later chapters, of the effects of various monetary and fiscal policies?

To a considerable degree, departure from the *PV* maximization assumed by our model would not disturb the direction or general nature of the conclusions about the effects of public policies on the size and timing of capital expenditures. What if we were to assume that managements maximize sales, asset growth, salaries, or relaxation; or that instead of maximizing anything they aspire only to reach levels of performance currently considered acceptable? The choice of maximand or 'zone of acceptable behaviour' in fact affects scarcely any of the basic implications of our model, as long as we continue to be justified in assuming that the firms' choice of programme is restricted to those described as 'feasible' when analysed in terms of the model of Chapter 1.[2] Thus if we are able to judge the

---

[1] See H. A. Simon [1959], for a description of his concept of 'satisficing', which assumes that the goal of behaviour is to reach certain aspiration levels of attainment. His analysis is inconsistent with maximizing behaviour only if the aspiration levels persistently fail to adjust in the direction indicated by the maximizing assumptions. If the aspiration levels are static for a number of independent targets, then there may be defined an 'acceptable range' of behaviour, with the managers presumed not to prefer any one of the acceptable policy combinations over any other. An example of this approach is R. Wright's [1964] 'Zone of Acceptable Performance'.

[2] In closely held corporations, whose shares are either not traded at all, or are in 'firm hands', there is no necessary reason for the choice of investment programmes to be so restricted. Assuming that no new equity funds are required

effect of a particular monetary or fiscal policy on the nature and number of feasible investment programmes, then we can make rough judgements about the nature and direction of changes in investment, even if we are not sure about the preferences governing the selection of a single programme from the range of feasible alternatives. Only if the principles governing the selection of programmes are themselves affected by tax or monetary changes would the conclusions in later chapters be threatened.

Throughout the following chapters, attempts will be made to indicate situations where alternative assumptions about the preferences of managers would make a considerable difference to the conclusions of the analysis.

B. IMPLICATIONS FOR POLICY ANALYSIS

Further development of the model of Chapter 1 as a description of actual investment behaviour requires first and foremost a more definite specification of the process by which subjective cash-flow distributions are generated. In Chapters 3 and 4 some attempts will be made to spell out the principles underlying the process, but the evidence available is not specific enough to permit the dynamic factors to be estimated in quantitative form. If we are therefore not to be able to quantify the subjective cash-flow distributions, and are not in a position to estimate the parameters of the equations determining the relevant discount rates, our analysis of the effects of monetary and fiscal policies will have to be based almost entirely on the qualitative features of the model.

Before we proceed, in the next two chapters, to consider some of the case study evidence on investment behaviour, it would be useful to point out the features of the model that will be most relevant to the policy analysis in Chapters 5 to 9. Monetary and fiscal policies may affect the present values of alternative investment programmes either by influencing estimates of the parameters of any of the cash-flow distributions within the investment horizon, or by influencing other conditions governing the supply of finance. There are a number of respects in which the model of Chapter 1 differs from others which have been used in explaining the effects of tax and monetary policy on investment behaviour. At this early stage we

---

from outsiders, and that the insiders are not concerned with the opportunity cost of the resources they employ, the range of possible investment programmes is greater than the range of 'feasible' programmes.

need point out only three of the basic characteristics of the model which will be found to be of recurring importance in later chapters.

(1) *Projects and programmes*

By taking a global view of the activities of the firm, the model of Chapter 1 makes it very clear that investment projects are not valued for their individual yield and risk characteristics, but for their impact on the risk and yield characteristics of the sets of projects in which they could be included. There are several consequences of this approach. The rationale of diversification over time, space, and products can be dealt with easily. Less easily, but still in a fairly straightforward manner, we can study the extent to which the past of a firm determines its future. If we were restricted to a model that viewed investment as the choice of a series of independent projects, it would be far more difficult to explain inter-industry differences in rates of growth and adaptation, and the whole idea of specialization would have rather shaky foundations.

Finally, the view that firms choose programmes rather than projects does much to explain why assets and opportunities are valued very differently by firms with the same amount of information about the nature of the opportunity. Since the model of Chapter 1 assumes that the return streams of many if not most projects will be interdependent, and risk is related to unpredicted variations in receipts, any particular project may increase the riskiness of one programme and decrease the riskiness of another.

(2) *Discount rates and interest rates*

The model of Chapter 1 draws together investment and financing decisions, and shows that they must be made simultaneously if the optimal programme is to be chosen. Thus the characteristics of cashflow distributions affect not only the values of M_t^* that are discounted to find the PV of a programme but also the terms on which funds are available to finance investment. The optimal mix of debt and equity finance depends on the risk and yield characteristics of the particular set of projects as well as on the relative supply conditions in the financial markets. It is clear from the structure of the model that although the present and expected future interest rates affect the firms' rates of discount, they are by no means the major determinants. In fact, as will be shown in Chapter 7, the primary effects of monetary policy on investment have not been due to the direct impact of market interest rates on firms' discount rates. In a model similar to that we are using, in which risk characteristics of programmes help to determine the pattern of finance, the distinction between rates of interest and rates of discount is simple and obvious. Nevertheless, the distinction should be viewed as an important feature of the model as a tool for policy analysis, since previous works using the marginal efficiency of investment as a tool for assessing the effects of monetary policy have equated the rate of discount with one or more rates of interest, sometimes magnified by an invariant 'risk premium'.[1]

(3) *The formation of cash-flow distributions*

The cash-flow distributions are net of all taxes paid by firms, so that the effects of most tax measures are in the first instance on the estimates of the parameters of the cash-flow distributions. Since these probability distributions are subjective, it is not the tax provisions themselves which affect the *PV*'s of alternative programmes, but what firms think the tax payments will be in the various years within the investment horizon.

To calculate the effects of a tax change on a given subjective cash-flow distribution, it is not enough to know the details of the tax; one must also know whose cash-flow distributions are affected, and what they believe about the tax. This is not an easy task, as we shall see that a firm's 'collective' cash-flow distributions are derived from a variety of sources within and outside the firm, and seldom, if ever, are described in written form. However bereft we may be of solid evidence of the nature of cash-flow distributions, it is perhaps a good thing to use a model in which subjective reactions to policy changes are given a central role. We shall therefore be forced to consider the effects which past tax policies have had on firms' estimates of future tax payments, as well as the speed with which the subjective cash-flow distributions adjust to new tax rates. Much of the analysis of these issues must be impressionistic rather than precise, but there appears to be no substitute for it if we hope to get beyond the formal characteristics of policies towards an understanding of their influence on investment behaviour.

---

[1] e.g. Brockie and Grey [1956], Jorgenson [1963], Shackle [1965], Tarshis [1961], and White [1958].

3

INVESTMENT DECISIONS—SOME EVIDENCE

THIS is a survey of the evidence underlying the model of investment decisions. When looking over the masses of interview evidence collected for the two earlier studies of investment decisions it is all too easy to find enough exceptions to cast dark shadows over almost any generalization about the investment process. In the face of discouraging odds this chapter will attempt to order the evidence so as to reveal whatever relationships there may be between the model and the raw material on which it was based.

The two earlier studies were intended to provide as much detail about investment decisions as was necessary in order to interpret answers to questions about the effects of monetary and fiscal policies. The 1962–3 survey[1] about the effects of monetary policy combined a complete mail survey of all firms with assets over $5 million and a stratified sample of 1000 of the smaller firms. The questionnaires were interpreted with the aid of over 200 follow-up interviews. The 83 largest firms, accounting for over half of total business capital expenditures, were studied by means of 1- to 4-hour interviews with one or more officials in senior financial or general management positions. The usual questionnaire was preceded by a series of questions about the procedures used by the firm in planning capital expenditures. The 1963–4 study[2] of the effects of certain taxation measures relied to a considerable extent on the earlier interview evidence, which was supplemented by case studies of decision-making within eight of the largest firms. From the monetary policy survey it had been apparent that the complexity of investment decisions and of the management group itself was such as to make mail questionnaires a dangerous way of collecting information about the effects of complex or novel policies. In the monetary policy survey we were able to ask direct questions about fairly recent decisions, for there had been quite apparent credit tightness in 1956–7 and 1959–

---

[1] Young and Helliwell [1965], referred to hereafter as *The Effects of Monetary Policy*.

[2] Helliwell [1966], referred to hereafter as *Taxation and Investment*, or *T & I*.

60, and there was a sharp period of credit restraint in the offing in 1962. Even with this recent experience to draw on, officials at one spot in the decision group often found it hard to see and relate the whole picture. It was hard enough for them to recall some of the factors which had been responsible for past decisions; it would have been too much to expect them to predict how the decision group would respond to tax changes quite different from those changes experienced in the recent past. Yet there was obviously much in their corporate experience that was relevant to any assessment of the effects of fiscal policies. It was decided that the best approach might be to make a really intensive study of decision-making within a small sample of the largest firms, with the sample being chosen to represent as far as possible the major types of firm included among the entire group of large firms already interviewed. It would thus be possible to use much of the detailed case study material to shed light on some of the issues still cloudy on the basis of the earlier evidence.

The object of the case studies was to get as clear a picture of the investment decision process as could be gleaned from interviews with all the participants and a comprehensive review of all the documents providing the information on which investment decisions are based. A single case study would have been revealing, and could have achieved considerable depth. The purpose of using eight studies spanning a range of behaviour was to provide the necessary links between the case-study firms and the population of large enterprises. The case-study firms were chosen to cover all the major industrial groups (except utilities), types of management (e.g. centralized and decentralized), ownership (e.g. domestic and foreign controlled, with closely and widely held shares), financial policy, and rates of growth. More than a week was spent in each of the firms, and interviews were held with ten or twenty members of the firm in various areas and at several levels of responsibility.

At last the pieces started to fall into place, and some flesh to appear on the skeleton of the decision process that we had been able to construct from the earlier interviews. In the previous research we had found out a lot about the procedures used for screening ideas for investment expenditures, but all too little about the sources of the investment proposals. To get an accurate impression of the decision process it was necessary to develop an understanding of the factors influencing the behaviour of those responsible for developing and proposing ideas for investment projects. Until we knew how the tentative investment decisions were made at the various corners of the organization, we could not establish the net effects of the policies in which we were interested. As we dug further into the organizations, we found that we needed to make more detailed study not only of the preliminary decisions but also of the sources of information on which all the decisions were based. Our analysis could not be complete unless it involved not just a study of the proposals which do come forward for approval but also of the process by which the prior arrangements are made to collect certain types of information and to analyse the consequences of certain alternatives.

As the study progressed it became obvious that we could not rely on a theoretical framework based merely on the explicit capital-budgeting rules used by the firms. To depart from such a framework, however, was itself a dangerous business. By relying exclusively on the capital-budgeting rules used by firms, we could use the flow of new project proposals as a measure of the available investment opportunities, and assess the effects of public policy by seeing what changes were made, in consequence, in the capital-budgeting criteria, and what impact these changes had on the flow of investment projects receiving approval. Although we were forced, by weight of evidence, to reject this deceptively attractive procedure, there were no simple and acceptable substitutes. It is all very well to recognize that the project proposals represent the results of decisions rather than the raw material on which investment decisions are based, but where may one turn to find better information? In the absence of hard data more representative of the range of investment possibilities, it was decided to adopt an all-embracing explanatory framework which had a place for each of the troublesome complications. The cash-flow distributions so central to the model of Chapter 1 were adopted because they allow all the interactions between projects, between time-periods, and between investment and financing to be admitted, and not because there is any obvious link between the cash-flow distributions and the normal documents used in capital budgeting.

If the model has been designed so as to be all-embracing, what criteria may be used to judge its success? Surely there are any number of vague generalities that may be uttered about the investment process, none of which may be subjected to test. If a model is to offer more, it must have a structure which is clearly enough established that, for example, specific public policies may be seen to have certain implications for investment behaviour. If there are substantial differences in behaviour among firms, the model should suggest ways of explaining these differences in terms of variables directly or indirectly included in the model. If there is certain partial information (such as that contained in capital budgeting proposals) available in written form, the model should suggest ways of relating this information to the unobservable subjective variables of the model itself. The evidence to be considered in this chapter should provide some measure of the extent to which the model of Chapter 1 does manage to explain inter-firm differences in behaviour.

The first step will be to give a general description of investment planning within the large firms. After this brief survey we shall turn to consider what counterparts there are in large firms to the cash-flow distributions and the associated discount rates that are central to the model of Chapter 1.

A. Features of the Investment Process

Large firms are managed by many people, each of whom has his or her own objectives, knowledge, and skills. One advantage of studying decisions in large firms is that there is inevitably a considerable flow of information, much of it in written form, required as a basis for decisions, since the various members of management must coordinate their planning efforts. The first and most striking impression to be gained from the case studies is that the story of each firm is an amalgam of stories (often anecdotal) about persons acting and reacting in an enormous variety of ways. Is it really possible to abstract from this vast diversity of action and experience a single pattern to be christened 'the behaviour of the firm'? If so, it may be only because large firms *are* big, so large that the organization seems to have a character of its own. Decisions made in large organizations often achieve consistency simply because there are so many separate specialists and departments involved that every decision is apt to look a good deal like the one that preceded it. The larger and more complex the organization, the easier does it seem to be to predict the actions of the firm on the basis of its immediate past. In these circumstances, what are the chances that the changes in behaviour that do take place are in accord with what the firm is trying to accomplish? This is the stronger definition of consistent behaviour; that it should not just resemble the behaviour that preceded it, but that decisions and behaviour at all points in time are consistent with some under-

lying goals of the management group. It has already been acknowledged that the most striking feature of the behaviour of the individuals interviewed was its diversity. Is there some process ensuring
that the seal of management approval only falls on those proposals
and actions that are in accord with the goals of the firm?

The difficulty with this question is that the goals of firms cannot
be determined except with reference to how the firms actually react
when placed in certain circumstances. We only have one set of
observations, which we cannot use both to define the goals of the
firm *and* to measure the extent to which their actions are consistent
with the goals. The usual way out of this box is to assume that the
firm has certain goals and then see to what extent the behaviour of
firms is consistent with those goals. This does provide, in some sense,
a test of the appropriateness of the assumed objectives, since different
sets of assumptions about objectives will differ in the extent to which
they appear to accord with behaviour generally observed in firms.
With respect to inter-firm differences in behaviour, however, the
problem remains. These differences may be attributable either to
differences in objectives or differences in the efficiency with which the
firms pursue their objectives.

How, then, are we to interpret the case study evidence? Consider
two examples drawn from the interview reports:

'I think of the conservative firm (our firm may be an example) as one in
which there is more emphasis placed on the continuous integrity of the
company than on immediate increases in the profits accruing to the equity
holder.' The comment was made in response to a specific question about
financial policy, but the same attitudes were seen in subsequent discussions
to apply as well to the provision of new capacity for domestic or export
demand, and ventures into new products (*T & I*, p. 134).

Senior officials in another firm stated that their approach to uncertain
profit opportunities was quite different from that indicated above. 'We
travel in elephant country,' said one executive, and went on to explain that
his firm was always willing to risk major losses in search of very large but
uncertain rewards. He noted that other firms in his industry preferred as a
matter of policy to undertake only projects with a more secure (but
probably smaller) prospect of gain (*T & I*, p. 134).

These two firms apparently differ in their attitudes to risk-taking.
Are we to interpret the conservative firm as one which is 'risk-shy' in

the way discussed in Chapter 1—a firm which uses risk-yield trade-off rates which give too much importance to risk? And is the second firm one which ignores risk at the expense of its equity shareholders? Are risk-avoidance and risk-searching respectively to be considered as objectives of the two firms? Another possibility is that both firms are misinterpreting what is in the long run best interests of their shareholders, and both are 'really' trying to maximize the present market values of their firms. A third possibility is that either firm (or both) may in fact be trading off risk and yield at the market-established trade-off rates, and be attempting (quite successfully) to maximize the market value of the firm's shares. Their announced attitudes towards risk may reflect only the existence of a market preference for shares with mixes of risk and yield that remain stable over time. Such stability would reduce the amount of portfolio switching required to maintain an optimum risk-yield combination.

This sort of difficulty plagues the analysis of almost any sort of decision in firms; there are always several ways of explaining the same behaviour, and often no satisfactory means of choosing a single preferred explanation. All this is by way of an apology for the apparent failure of the case study evidence to provide any clear-cut conclusions about what firms and their managers are trying to achieve. The only claim that can be made to support the model of Chapter 1 as an apt representation of the motives and methods of managements in large firms is that the model itself was a result of the interview research. The model pictures the investment process in the way which the evidence indicated would be most appropriate, although in some areas the emphasis might have been somewhat different without straining the links between the model and the evidence.

There are, however, one or two general features of the investment process which have not received adequate emphasis in the formal model of investment decisions. It might be gathered from the model that the investment programme is chosen at a point in time and then carried out as planned. In fact, the 'investment programme' is no more than a blanket title for the mixed bag of plans, commitments, and forecasts never brought together in a single document, and often never appearing in any written form. So far from being chosen from among alternative programmes at a single point in time, the investment programme is continually subject to change as new information becomes available and market conditions change in unpredicted ways.[1] As information of a detailed sort becomes available within departments responsible for the planning of particular expenditures, the size and nature of the investment projects which make up the investment programme may change quite considerably before final approval is sought.

Finally, the model of Chapter 1 treats as given the subjective probability distributions of cash flow from alternative programmes, as well as the firm's beliefs about the supply conditions for various types of financing. The rest of this chapter examines the investment planning procedures of firms to see to what extent the firms have and use the sort of information underlying the cash-flow distributions so central to the model, and to see if the investment selection procedure has anything in common with calculation and comparison of present values as outlined in Chapter 1. It will become clear that it is a mistake to assume that firms are given all the information in principle available about the consequences of alternative investments. One of the main reasons why few alternatives are explicitly considered is that the preparation and analysis of investment proposals itself is a costly undertaking. Since the collection and analysis of information requires some of the same management skills required for successful current operations, there may be a high shadow price attached to the use of scarce management skills (including the efforts of architects, engineers, etc.) in the collection and analysis of information for decisions. The discussion in the rest of this chapter should make obvious the need for the extension to be made in Chapter 4, when decisions to devote resources to gathering and assessing information will themselves be made part of the general problem of choosing an investment programme.

The remainder of this chapter will be concerned first with the estimates which firms make of future cash flows, and then with the

---

[1] An example may help to indicate the sort of unpredicted change in circumstances which may cause an investment programme to be changed:

Even after one manufacturing firm's budget has been approved in Canada and at the parent's head office, there is still room for some changes to be made, in both the size and timing of particular projects. At the monthly management meeting following the government 'austerity measures' of 1962, the entire capital expenditures programme was reviewed to see whether there were any items which could be postponed, without loss, to a later date. This 'hard second look' at the capital expenditure programme was not related to the availability of funds (the company generates more cash than it currently requires) but to the management's lack of confidence in the sales forecasts prepared before the exchange rate crisis and the related budget measures (*T & I*, p. 94).

implicit or explicit discount rates used in assessing and comparing alternative investment programmes. The estimates of future cash flows will be considered again in Section B of Chapter 4.

B. Estimates of Future Cash Flows

It will already be obvious to readers that the subjective cash-flow distributions assumed to underlie the selection of investment programmes do not have any directly observable counterparts in the planning procedures used by firms. This section canvasses some of the more important types of cash-flow forecast actually used by firms in their investment decisions, and explains how these various sorts of data are conceptually related to the cash-flow distributions underlying the theoretical framework. The main occasions when firms use explicit cash-flow forecasts are when quarterly, annual, or longer-term budgets are prepared, and when approval is granted for specific capital expenditures on the basis of an 'appropriation request'.

(1) Budgets

The detailed statements of sources and uses of funds contained in quarterly, annual, or longer-term budgets provide the closest approximation to a central measure of the cash-flow distributions (for the relevant period(s)) of the chosen investment programme of a firm. A typical statement of the sources and uses of funds contains estimates of each of the major sources and uses of cash, such as product sales, current operating costs, capital expenditures, interest and dividend payments, new external financing, and other changes in non-cash asset and liability accounts. A central measure of the cash-flow distribution could be constructed from the estimates comprising the net cash-flow attributable to the shareholders. This measure is appropriate because the cash-flow distributions are defined as the results of all operations, net of all taxes,[1] interest, and changes in all asset and liability accounts, but before any allowance for dividends or other payments to or from shareholders. In none of the firms studied were there any explicit estimates made of the standard deviation of the expected cash flow, or any other measure of the uncertainty attached to estimates of the aggregate cash flow.

---

[1] This is the appropriate procedure if the usual post-borrowing cash flow distributions (with means M_t^*) are employed. If the pre-borrowing cash flow distributions (with means M_t^{*B}) were used, then the cash flows would be estimated as though there were neither interest payments nor any corporation tax relief for them. See pp. 29–33.

However, officials were always anxious to point out that budget estimates were subject to considerable uncertainty. In most of the firms, officials involved in the planning process had clear ideas about which particular components of the budget were most likely to differ from their forecasts, and which other items could be adjusted in partial compensation. The role of budgets, and the relative importance of budgets with different time horizons, varies considerably from firm to firm. The submission of budget proposals by the various plants and divisions of the firm often is the occasion for the central management of the firm to alter the balance of activity in the various divisions, and to decide on the overall rate of expansion in the immediately following periods. The cash-flow budgets, once approved, often provide a means whereby the central management of the firm controls the operations of the various divisions.

The use of budgets as a means of control was most common in firms with decentralized management. In these firms, it was not unusual for various rules of thumb to be used to guide the divisions of the firm in the preparation of budget proposals. These rules suggested, usually, some sort of balance between the cash generated by current operations and that which can be drawn on by the division for its capital expenditures.[1]

In firms with more centralized management the annual budgets are often less specific, and there is less concern that the actual outcome should be close to the budget forecasts. The annual budgets in these firms do not clearly mark a stage in the decision process, since the forecasts do little to commit the forecasters to particular patterns of sales and capital expenditures. Officials of such firms suggested that the purpose of their cash-flow forecasts was more to give the financial officials some advance warning of the amount of financing likely to be required. At the time of budget approval the financial officials might also expect, and be given, some idea of the likelihood that the actual amount of financing required would be much greater

---

[1] For example:

A diversified manufacturing and processing firm has a policy that allows each of its divisions to spend funds generated by their own depreciation allowances. This policy does not apply in the case of large or special expenditures, or in areas of large growth potential. Annual capital budgets are submitted by each of the operating divisions and approved by the central management. The annual budget is quite specific as to individual projects, and once a project becomes part of an approved capital budget the subsequent appropriation request approval usually follows as a matter of course (*T & I*, p. 73).

or much less than the amount estimated. It is in the process of providing advice of this sort to the financial officials that senior management implicitly makes estimates of the dispersion and skewness of the cash-flow distributions. Once given this sort of advance warning, the financial officials can make arrangements which allow the more likely contingencies to be faced with a minimum of upset.

In all firms, whether their management be centralized or decentralized, the budgets or plans extending more than one or two years into the future seldom contain the best possible estimate of any central value of the cash-flow distributions for the future periods. The annual and quarterly budgets are used as means of both planning and control, and all those officials (except, possibly, at the very highest levels) who are hoping to make expenditures in a certain period are well advised to specify their plans far enough in advance that their expenditures are envisaged by the budget as finally approved. The longer-term budgets, at least in the firms for which detailed information was available, have not provided an instrument of management control, and therefore do not tend to constrain the development of projects differing from those in the approved plan. In several of the firms studied the long-term budgets are prepared in staff departments not responsible for either the selection of projects or the development of annual budgets. In these circumstances the details and even the scale of the investment programme envisaged by the longer-term plan may be quite different from those represented by the cash-flow distributions which would emerge if the responsible officials in the firm were forced to make explicit their estimates of the consequences for several future years of the preferred investment programme. To the extent that planning procedures were being changed within the case-study firms, efforts were being made to improve the quality of the longer-term forecasts, and to tie them in more closely with the regular budgeting procedures. Many of the existing inter-firm differences in the extent and accuracy of longer-term budget projections reflect real inter-industry differences in the ease with which the future of the firm can be foretold. For example, in many utilities, whose facilities must be planned several years in advance, the longer-term budget is often quite specific about the nature of planned expenditures and output several years in the future. On the other extreme, firms in industries characterized by technological and competitive uncertainties, or whose fixed assets can be built relatively quickly, are unable (and unwilling) to be specific about either the scale or the detail of their investment programme, more than one or two years in the future. This situation may be described as one in which the dispersion of the cash-flow distributions increases so sharply with time that no single measure (budget estimate) of the distributions provides much information about what the investment programme will actually entail in future years. These firms face (or think they face) a future of such great intrinsic uncertainty that they see no point in making single-valued estimates of any components of cash-flow distributions in future years, however much such explicit estimates might be desired by those wishing to estimate the future value of the shares of the firm.[1]

Both annual and longer-term budgets provide some measure of the expected cash flow from the entire investment programme, if only for a very few time periods. Firms differ in the extent to which they consider complete alternative budgets before selecting a final approved budget.

(2) *Approval for specific projects*

A different type of cash-flow forecast is provided by the 'Appropriation Requests' which are the basis for the approval of specific capital expenditures. Although the term 'appropriation' is not always used to describe the approval of a certain amount of expenditure on a specified project, all the firms studied had some sort of formal approval procedure which had to be followed for all capital expenditures of substantial size. The appropriation request always authorizes a specified amount of expenditure, an amount which cannot be exceeded unless a 'Supplementary Appropriation Request' is approved authorizing the additional expenditure.[2] Sometimes the appropriation request contains estimates of the cost and revenue consequences of the project in one or all of the relevant future time periods, while in other cases only the original capital costs of the

---

[1] One official noted that long-term projections of earnings were especially popular with financial analysts. He suggested that if his firm were to include a ten-year plan of operations and expected results in their annual report, they would be awarded analysts' prizes for informative statement presentation, regardless of the reliability of the estimates or the underlying quality of management. He prefers to have no formalized plan of activities, since in his industry there are apparently too many unknowns for forecasts beyond a year to be worth anything (*T & I*, p. 84).

[2] Although in some firms the Supplementary Appropriation Requests, and even the Appropriation Requests themselves, were occasionally not formally approved until after the expenditures had been undertaken.

F

project are made explicit. When the appropriation requests contain the cost and revenue consequences of projects for all the relevant future periods, they do not provide an adequate basis for constructing cash-flow distributions for alternative investment programmes, since the appropriation requests for individual projects typically do not make explicit the interdependence between the various projects which the firm might undertake as an investment programme. It is, however, not uncommon for appropriation requests for particular projects to make some sort of estimate of the certainty with which the results of the project may be predicted. These estimates of the dispersion of the net returns from the projects may be made by the use of range estimates, by the use of risk classes, or sometimes merely by a listing of events which would cause the cash flow from the project to be different from that estimated.

If firms use explicit rate of return standards when they assess capital expenditures, they usually apply them at the appropriation request stage, when the costs and some of the consequences of the project come into sharper focus. The actual rate of return criteria used will be discussed in the next section of the chapter, which is concerned with the empirical counterparts to the subjective discount rates used in the theoretical framework. The present section is limited to a discussion of the cost and revenue estimates used in the rate of return calculations, and their relationship to the annual budgets and the subjective cash-flow distributions.

The most general feature of the practices used by firms in dealing with appropriation requests is the much greater attention given to the accuracy of the estimate of the capital cost of the project than to the estimates of the resulting changes in costs and revenues. In part this may be because accounting records have historically not been set up in such a way that the cost and revenue consequences of particular projects could be easily assessed, but there nevertheless remains a striking (and, to me, surprising) difference between the strenuous efforts made to forecast capital expenditures correctly and the rather careless methods used to forecast the cost and revenue consequences of the same projects. The actual costs of a project are always compared with the authorized amounts, and discrepancies have to be explained if they exceed a certain proportion of the authorized expenditure. The estimates of the cost and revenue consequences of the completed project, however, are seldom subject to any check whatsoever. In the relatively few firms where some tentative efforts have been made to assess the accuracy of cost and revenue estimates contained in appropriation requests the impression has been confirmed that the consequences of investment projects have been estimated with far less accuracy than their initial costs. Among the consequences the firms have apparently encountered the greatest difficulty in estimating the costs and revenues of new products or processes.

An analysis of a large number of appropriation requests in several of the case-study firms revealed that estimates of capital cost were more accurate than estimates of the revenue consequences of the projects, although the sample of the latter was restricted to those projects for which 'follow-up' procedures were undertaken to check the accuracy of the revenue forecasts. It is likely that the revenue forecasts are more accurate in these firms where the forecasts are subsequently checked against the actual results.

There is further evidence that the capital cost estimates are treated more seriously than the estimates of the results of investment projects. In some firms there is a two-stage procedure for capital expenditure approval involving a preliminary as well as a final appropriation request.[1] The firms apparently adopted the two-stage procedure so that senior management could get to look over potential projects before the estimates of capital cost had reached the level of precision required for the appropriation request. The accuracy required by the appropriation request was such that it was in the interests of junior management[2] to get most of the engineering done before submitting the proposals.

[1] The firms usually used preliminary appropriation requests for large projects requiring a lot of engineering specifications:

As a senior official in one firm described the relationship between the appropriation request and the preliminary appropriation request, they both amount to an authorization to undertake expenditures, but the preliminary appropriation requests are only expected to be accurate within 20 or 30 per cent., while the final appropriation request is expected to be within 10 per cent. in its estimate of the capital cost. The preliminary request is used to avoid the attribution of blame to those presenting estimates early in order to get a project underway. The official said that the company recognizes that some projects are good enough and important enough that they should be undertaken before there is time to do the detailed final estimation work (the estimation process might take as long as one month). He said that once a preliminary appropriation has been approved, a project is sure of getting final appropriation request approval. There have been only rare occasions when projects have been deferred after a preliminary appropriation (T & I, p. 42).

[2] The following example illustrates the sort of pressures which induce operating officials to make sure that their appropriation requests are accurate:

An engineer noted that one of the chief concerns of management after a project

What is the relationship between the cost and revenue estimates in the appropriation requests, the annual budgets, and the subjective cash-flow distribution of the entire investment programme? The appropriation requests typically provide estimates of the cost and revenue consequences of only those projects which are justified explicitly on rate of return criteria. There are a considerable number of other capital expenditures (usually amounting to more than half of the total) whose revenue effects are not made explicit in the appropriation requests. The sum of all the appropriation requests would therefore fail to provide an adequate central measure of the cash flow distribution, not only because debt transactions and the interrelationships between projects are ignored but also because not all the operations of the firm are referred to by appropriation requests. In practice, too, the revenue consequences of individual projects are estimated for a single 'typical' (unspecified) year, so that it would not be possible to construct the cash-flow distributions for particular time periods.

In the same way, it is not possible to reconcile completely the information contained in the appropriation requests with that found in the annual budgets. In firms which regard approved budgets as binding, the total of current-period capital expenditures under approved appropriation requests will be close in amount to the budget total for capital expenditures. But capital expenditures are only one part of the cash flows of the firm, and it is the total of operating revenues and costs that is not exhausted by the amounts stated on appropriation requests. Only a relatively small fraction of total operating revenues and expenditure could be linked to the cost and revenue forecasts explicitly made on appropriation requests for projects completed and in operation at any particular time. This is because, as already mentioned, cost and revenue forecasts are made

---

has been approved is to make sure that the cost stays within the estimate. One of the chief reasons for this is that only a 5 per cent. discrepancy is allowed before a supplementary appropriation request must be prepared. This 'is a sticky business', requiring substantial effort as well as an analysis of the reasons why the expenditures were more than anticipated. The pressures on officials who overestimate the costs of projects are less severe, but still noticeable. For one thing, high cost estimates reduce the chances of the project showing an acceptable prospective return, and, in addition, if an official frequently spends much less than the anticipated amount, questions may be asked about his estimating skill. One of the ways for officials to avoid this particular problem is to use up left-over funds on related projects, many of which are not even envisaged in the original appropriation (*T & I*, p. 46).

only for a certain proportion of appropriation requests, in general only those which are justified on rate of return criteria (as opposed to being included in some other category—'necessary replacement', 'administration', &c.—of expenditures for which rate of return calculations are not required).

Even when the information in appropriation requests is considered in conjunction with the annual budgets, there is not enough data in suitable form to derive the subjective cash-flow distributions underlying the chosen investment programme. For more than one or two periods beyond the present there are no very useful estimates of any of the parameters of the cash-flow distributions, and even in the periods covered by the full-scale budgeting procedure there are measures only of a central value of the programme's cash-flow distributions. Explicit measures of the uncertainty of cash-flow estimates are only rarely made by firms, and even then just for certain projects and not for the investment programme as a whole.

However imprecise it may be, the relationship between the cash-flow distributions of the chosen investment programme and the data prepared and used by firms is much closer than that between any data used by firms and the cash-flow distributions of alternative investment programmes considered but not approved. For a number of reasons, firms seldom make explicit estimates of the cash-flow consequences of alternative investment programmes, so that there is little in the way of quantitative evidence to use in trying to estimate the relative importance of the various factors influencing managements' choice among alternative investment programmes. The case-study evidence suggested that the major reason why there are few investment projects assessed but not accepted was not that there are no marginal projects available, but that the officials in the various operating divisions do not like their proposals to be rejected. These officials take precautions to ensure that the projects which are sent forward promise a rate of return which is more than adequate to gain approval for the projects. In some firms it was quite noticeable that the officials at lower levels in the firm applied informal discount rates substantially larger than those applied at more senior levels.[1]

[1] For example:

One firm has an established payback rule which varies with the expected life of the asset. A senior operating official was asked what effective rate of return standards were applied at lower levels in the firm. He replied that nobody would bother with anything promising less than a 30 per cent. gross return (which is, under most assumptions about revenue life, a conservative approximation to the

When investments proposals are presented explicitly as alternatives, the alternatives considered are projects (although often very large projects) rather than entire investment programmes. It is these occasions that provide whatever evidence is available about the discount rates used by firms in evaluating capital expenditures.

C. DISCOUNT RATES USED IN ASSESSING CAPITAL EXPENDITURES

This section discusses the rate of return criteria used by large firms in assessing investment projects. An attempt will be made to derive the discount rates implied by the use of particular rate of return rules, and then to explain differences in discount rates within and among firms in terms of the factors influencing the cost of capital for particular investment programmes. Subsection (1) describes the rate of return standards used by large Canadian firms, and attempts to estimate the discount rates implied by these standards. Subsection (2) will present some of the reasons for differences, within and among firms, in these discount rates.

(1) *The formal investment criteria employed by large firms*[1]

The general practice among the Canadian corporations surveyed is to make rate of return calculations when projects are given final authorization. This approval is usually given just before the project is to be undertaken. In only a certain proportion of the seventy large firms could the exact nature of the approved procedures be clearly established. Naturally, if it is not possible to discover how deprecia-

---

formal criterion), having developed a view that higher management would seldom look with pleasure on anything promising a lower return. He noted that there were obvious exceptions to this, particularly in the case of expenditures needed to maintain quality, on which no rate of return requirements were laid. A less senior operating official said that none of *his* subordinates would normally bother submitting a project to him unless it promised a 40 per cent. gross return. An examination was made of the support data for 200 appropriation requests (each over $1000) covering a sample period's operations. More than one quarter of the appropriations were for routine building maintenance. For only 43 of the appropriations were there estimates made of the gross return. For 42 of the 43, the mean estimated gross annual cost saving averaged 150 per cent. of the initial expenditure, while for 30 of them it was over 100 per cent. for each project. In only 4 of the 43 cases was the estimated gross return less than 50 per cent. and in 2 of these there were imperative reasons for the outlay independent of the cost savings (*T & I*, p. 31).

[1] This subsection is adapted from pages 10 to 19 of *Taxation and Investment*.

tion, taxes, variable income streams, working capital, the cost of funds, and other matters are dealt with, it is difficult or impossible to make inter-firm comparisons. In any case, the relationship between the formal procedures and the operative standards is often a loose one.

The study of the investment criteria of seventy large non-government corporations (each with assets, net of depreciation, valued at $90 million or more, as at 31 December 1963) was based on interviews, correspondence, analysis of forms and procedural manuals, and, in a number of cases, a detailed examination of the documents supporting and describing capital expenditure proposals for sample years.[1] The rate of return rules, and the ways in which they are used, vary so much among firms that interviews undertaken with officials of sixty-seven of the firms provided the best guide to the nature of the adopted standards. Even so, the established standards are often so ephemeral or of such little concern within the firm that officials interviewed are not familiar with the techniques employed. Therefore, the rate of return standards listed here do not necessarily provide a reliable guide to the marginal efficiency of investment in the firms which use them. When the rules are put on a more or less comparable basis with respect to their choice of income figures and their treatment of depreciation, the cost of capital and taxes, they can be classified roughly as follows. (Table 3.1 contains definitions and a comparison of the various rate of return measures. Table 3.2 shows the standards adopted in different industries.)

(a) *Gross rate of return or gross payback*

(i) Ten firms regularly use a measure of gross return[2]

$$\left(\frac{\text{gross revenue or cost savings}}{\text{initial expenditure}}\right)$$

or its reciprocal, the gross payback period, as the basic test for proposed expenditures. All ten firms have gross return requirements of 30 per cent. or more for some types of projects, while four mentioned requirements as high as 50 per cent. for some types of projects, and others have requirements much lower than 30 per cent. for long-lived assets. Two-thirds of these firms have a range of

---

[1] See Appendix I of *Taxation and Investment* for an analysis of the procedures used in selecting firms and obtaining information.

[2] No allowance being made for depreciation, taxes, or the cost of funds.

TABLE 3.1

COMPARISON OF FOUR COMMON METHODS OF EVALUATING INVESTMENTS

All figures refer only to the particular project being assessed.

I_t = Cost of fixed assets and inventories in year t. I_t refers to the cost of fixed and working capital for a particular project.

D_t = Depreciation charge in period t, when same charge is made for assessing projects, computing net profit for statement purposes, and estimating the liability for income tax.

T'_t = Expected corporation income taxes payable in period t on income earned in that year.

G_{Rt} = Gross cash receipts from project in period t.

r = Standard-risk rate of discount used to compute the present value of an investment project.

r' = Project's internal rate of return (that discount rate which would make the present value of all related cash receipts and payments equal to zero).

To compare the investment rules in the simplest case, assume that the initial cost of the project is entirely for fixed assets, all of which are subject to the same rate of depreciation (the same rate of depreciation being used in the firm's accounts and for tax purposes). G_{Rt}, D_t, and T'_t are assumed constant for all $t \leqslant n$ and 0 for all $t > n$.

Under these assumptions, simple versions of the four rules may be written as follows:

(a) Gross payback period $= \dfrac{I_F}{G_{Rt}}$, Gross rate of return $= \dfrac{G_{Rt}}{I_F}$.

(b) Net rate of return $= \dfrac{G_{Rt} - D_t - T'_t}{I_F}$.

Net payback period $= \dfrac{I_F}{G_{Rt} - D_t - T'_t}$.

(c) Cash-flow payback period $= \dfrac{I_F}{G_{Rt} - T'_t}$.

(d) Discounted cash-flow methods: $PV = \sum_{t=1}^{n}(G_{Rt} - T'_t)(1 + r)^{-t}$.

   (i) The internal rate of return method ranks projects by the value of r which would make the present value (PV) of cash receipts equal to the original cost of the project.

   (ii) The present value method uses a standard-risk discount rate (r) to find the PV of an investment project. The project is acceptable if the PV of gross revenues is greater than the cost of the project (I_t).

Using these simple formulae and making certain further assumptions about the values of the remaining variables, equivalent standards may be developed for each of the four investment rules.

TABLE 3.1—*continued*

Assumptions	Gross return (%)	Net return (%)	Cash-flow payback period (years)	Discounted cash-flow rate of return (%)
Gross annual cash earnings equal to 25% of the initial cost of the fixed assets ($G_{Rt} = 0.25$, $I_t = 1$). No allowance made for working capital or for interest payments on borrowed funds. Depreciation (for tax and book purposes) equal to 10% straight line ($D_t = 0.10 \, I_t$). Corporation income tax equal to 50% of income after depreciation ($T'_t = 0.50 \, (G_{Rt} - D_t)$).				
Earnings assumed to last for:				
three years ($n = 3$)	25	$7\frac{1}{2}$	$5\frac{2}{3}$	-70
five years ($n = 5$)	25	$7\frac{1}{2}$	$5\frac{2}{3}$	$- 6$
eight years ($n = 8$)	25	$7\frac{1}{2}$	$5\frac{2}{3}$	$+ 8$
fifteen years ($n = 15$)	25	$7\frac{1}{2}$	$5\frac{2}{3}$	$+15$
Assumptions as above, except that $G_{Rt} = 0.40 \, I_t$.				
Earnings assumed to last for:				
three years ($n = 3$)	40	15	4	-25
five years ($n = 5$)	40	15	4	$+ 8$
eight years ($n = 8$)	40	15	4	$+18$
fifteen years ($n = 15$)	40	15	4	$+24$
Assumptions as above, except that $G_{Rt} = 0.50 \, I_t$.				
Earnings assumed to last for:				
three years ($n = 3$)	50	20	$3\frac{1}{4}$	-11
five years ($n = 5$)	50	20	$3\frac{1}{4}$	$+16$
eight years ($n = 8$)	50	20	$3\frac{1}{4}$	$+25$
fifteen years ($n = 15$)	50	20	$3\frac{1}{4}$	$+30$

The four evaluation rules can produce the same accept-or-reject decisions as long as all projects have the same length of life, and tax rates are unchanged. A few complicating factors may be introduced (such as working capital requirements) without losing all comparability between the methods, as long as the additional factors are not treated as variables. That is, working capital may be introduced, and new equivalent standards derived; but the standards will only be equivalent if the ratio of working capital to fixed assets is the same for all projects. More generally, if any of the additional factors are permitted to take different values from project to project, it is impossible to derive a set of targets which would make the four basic types of rate of return rule equivalent to one another.

TABLE 3.2

A COMPARISON OF THE RATE OF RETURN STANDARDS USED BY LARGE FIRMS

(a) Industry group	(b) Number of firms	(c) Type of rate of return standard[1]	(d) Number of firms with majority of voting shares held outside Canada[2]	(e) Mean equivalent discount rates and ranges for each industry[3]
Mining and smelting (iron, copper, silver, lead, zinc, uranium, nickel)	7	2 d.c.f. (10–15% range). 2 net return. 3 gross return or no established standards	4	Mean 9–11%; range 6–16% (3 firms)
Primary metals (steel and aluminium)	6	2 d.c.f. (10–15% range). 2 gross return. 2 net return	3	Mean 11–20%; range 6–15% (4 firms)
Oil	12	6 d.c.f. (8–20% range). 3 net return. 3 gross return or no established standards	10	Mean 13–18%; range 9–16% (4 firms)
Pulp and paper	9	1 d.c.f. 5 net return. 3 gross return or no established procedures	4	Mean 12–13%; range 9–16% (4 firms)
Oil and gas pipelines, and gas distribution / Other utilities	7 } 4 }	1 net return. Most of the rest use a notional rate (often 7½%) as a measure of what they are permitted to earn on assets employed	5	
Retail trade	5	Projects generally evaluated on the basis of sales revenue per sq. ft. or per dollar invested	2	

Manufacturing and other	20	6 d.c.f. (5–10% range). 4 net return. 8 gross or no established procedures. 2 cash-flow payback (2½–4½ year range)	11	Mean 11–15%; range 6–25% (16 firms)
All industry groups	70	17 d.c.f. 17 net return. 19 gross or no established procedures. 2 cash-flow payback	39	Mean 11–15%; range 6–25% (31 firms)

[1] The 'gross return, or no established standards' also includes firms for which only imperfect information was available. This classification change explains the discrepancy between the totals in column (c) and those in the text of the chapter.

[2] See Appendix III of *Taxation and Investment* for further analysis of the investment procedures of these firms.

[3] The figures in this column should be treated with the greatest caution. They do not provide any basis for inter-industry comparisons of the marginal efficiency of investment. The calculation procedure was as follows. The conversion of each firm's announced standard(s) has been made according to the simple formulae presented in Table 1, with the additional (very restrictive) assumptions that each project produces level gross revenue for 10 years, depreciation is 10 per cent. of I_F for all purposes ($D_t = 0.1 I_F$), and income tax is 50 per cent. of gross income minus depreciation ($T'_t = 0.5 (G_{Rt} - D_t)$). The 'mean' figure has more than one value because some firms have more than one minimum standard. The lowest estimate of the 'mean' is the mean of the d.c.f. equivalents (for the project above) for the lowest minimum standards for each firm. The higher estimate is the mean of the highest minimum standard for each firm. The 'range' for each industry is the range between the d.c.f. equivalent of the lowest minimum standard of any firm to the highest minimum for any firm in the industry. Since the industry 'means' and 'ranges' are constructed on the basis of a single project which is not only not typical, but is less typical of investment in some industries than in others, the figures may not be used for meaningful inter-industry comparisons.

payback or gross return standards depending on the degree of risk, the probable length of revenue life, the tax class of the assets, and other factors.

(ii) Seven other firms seldom if ever make estimates of the profitability of proposed expenditures, but use a rough measure of payback or gross rate of return when they do. They have no established rate of return requirements.

(b) *Net return or net payback.* Seventeen firms use the ratio of net income, after tax and depreciation, to some measure of capital employed as their index of the profitability of capital expenditures. Expressing the income of a 'representative year' (net of income tax and depreciation, but before any allowance for the cost of funds) as a fraction of the initial capital expenditure, the required minimum return for nine of the firms averages 10 per cent. One of these nine firms has a 5 per cent. requirement, and one a 20 per cent. requirement for 'quick approval' items, while the remainder fall in the 9–14 per cent. range. Some of the standards were expressed as some form of payback, and have been translated to a rate of return basis for comparison purposes. Of the remaining eight firms, three require that new projects promise to equal or better the rate of return on existing assets, while the remaining five either choose not to reveal their particular standards or have no single rate to represent their standard.

(c) *Cash-flow payback.* Two firms regularly employ a form of payback analysis taking account of all cash inflows and outflows and measuring the time required for the initial cash outlay to be recouped. Their standards range from $2\frac{1}{2}$ to $4\frac{1}{2}$ years.[1]

(d) *Discounted cash flow.* Seventeen firms use either internal rate of return or present value assessment procedures as their principal means of evaluating capital expenditures.[2] The fourteen who indicated the size of their usual required minimum return gave figures ranging from 5 to 15 per cent. The mean figure was approximately 11 per cent., while the mode was 10 per cent. (five firms). Several

---

[1] These procedures were employed by some of the firms classified in groups (*a*) or (*b*) above for the evaluation of large or especially significant projects.

[2] Another fifteen to twenty firms use these methods occasionally when evaluating large projects or projects where the expected time pattern of receipts is uneven. Several firms use a number of different types of calculation, different members of senior management making their separate judgements on the basis of rates of return measures familiar to them.

firms indicated that different cut-off rates were used depending on the type of project, the higher requirements being associated with projects having a greater range of possible outcomes. The calculations are, in general, applied by discounting all associated cash flows, including estimated tax payments. The most common practice is to use these procedures to find the rate which would equate the present value of costs and revenues, although some firms discount using a required rate of return to find a net present value for the project. Virtually all of the seventeen firms have adopted discounted cash-flow techniques within the past decade.

(e) *Special cases.* Nine utilities, five of them pipelines, will make any capital expenditures within their service area which will provide a return on the rate base equal to that approved by their respective regulatory bodies. The most common notional rate adopted by the firms is $7\frac{1}{2}$ per cent. on the asset base.

Four retail firms base their major expenditures on the requirement that a proposed store promise, within a specified period, a certain sales revenue per square foot, or occasionally a certain profit margin on sales. The relationships between these calculations and requirements of a certain rate of return on capital invested are not usually made explicit.

For the remaining four of the seventy firms there was not enough information available to allow classification; in one case because the firm did not wish to reveal anything about its capital expenditure planning, and in the other cases either because the firm was too new for established procedures to have been adopted or because adequate interview and questionnaire evidence was not available.

The foregoing description of procedures refers to the standards in operation when the research was carried out, between June 1962 and September 1963. It may be expected that the number of firms using discounted cash-flow standards will continue to increase. Several officials indicated that discounted cash-flow procedures were being used more and more to supplement or replace other types of rate of return rules. These changes are accompanied in many firms by efforts to improve the quality of the cost and revenue estimates on which the investment decisions are based.

Some mention should be made of the distribution of procedures by industry and ownership of the firm. These comments are intended to supplement the more detailed information contained in Table 3.2. The chief users of discounted cash-flow methods are firms in the petroleum industry, and other firms with parent companies outside Canada. Of the seventy large firms, 55 per cent. are controlled outside Canada, while of the seventeen firms making general use of discounted cash-flow procedures 75 per cent. are foreign-controlled. All of the eight largest oil companies are controlled outside Canada, and six of them use discounted cash-flow techniques. Even if the oil companies are removed, the percentage of foreign-controlled firms using discounted cash-flow techniques remains somewhat higher than that of firms controlled in Canada. There is little remaining relationship between the types of assessment procedures employed and the industry in which a firm operates. There is a slight indication that discounted cash-flow procedures are more intensively used in industries where the duration and time pattern of sales revenues is subject to considerable differences from project to project. Similarly, there is a tendency for some firms with strong or sheltered market positions, making products not subject to rapid obsolescence, to employ gross return or payback standards. An increase in discount rates, or in the strictness with which rate of return standards are applied, has taken place in several firms after periods of what was later thought to be over-expansion, or when market conditions have become more difficult. On the other hand, there were no examples discovered where firms have explicitly lowered their investment standards so as to increase the flow of new project ideas, although several firms have suggested that they have 'had to take a lower return' on some projects when cash generation had been large relative to the anticipated profitability of investment.

Since this study is primarily about decision-making within large firms there has been little data systematically collected referring to the investment procedures in smaller firms. What information there is suggests that fewer of the smaller firms have specific investment criteria. The small firms that do have investment rules apply them to a smaller fraction of their total expenditures. For example, among the responders to the Tax Commission's questionnaire[1] on capital expenditures, 37 per cent. of the sixteen respondents with assets under $25 million said that they employed target rates of return or minimum payback periods, compared with 75 per cent. of the firms with assets between 25 and 90 million, and 80 per cent. of those with assets over $90 million. There was not enough evidence available to allow the

---

[1] A copy of the questionnaire, and a description of the coverage of the survey, are to be found in Appendix I of *Taxation and Investment*.

classification of procedures by types and rates of required return for a representative sample of firms with assets below 90 million. However, it was clear even from the unrepresentative sample of firms surveyed that smaller firms tend to use rougher measures of profitability, and to have less reliable data.

The most obvious danger in using rate of return requirements as measures of the discount rates used by firms to represent their cost of capital is that the established rules may not generally be used in making investment decisions. If many capital expenditures are not subjected to rate of return requirements the possibility arises that the indicated rates of return on the projects for which calculations are made are not at all representative of rates of return on all other expenditures. This possibility that computed rates of return may be misleading is greatest in firms which subject only a small fraction of their expenditure to such assessment. Unfortunately, it is difficult to get reliable information about the proportion of capital expenditures for which the rate of return calculations are made, aside from any difficulties involved in interpreting the calculations themselves. For the few firms whose records were studied in detail it was possible to assess the amount and relative importance of the expenditures which were subjected to rate of return calculations, but for most of the seventy firms the information is far from satisfactory. Many of the officials interviewed had no very clear idea of the prevalence of rate of return calculations,[1] although the executives are generally aware of the types of expenditure for which calculations are made.

(2) *Differences in discount rates over time and across firms*

The wide range of discount rates used by large Canadian firms in assessing projects suggests, at first glance, that there are marked inter-firm differences in the subjective cost of capital. Undoubtedly such differences do exist, but they are not the only reasons for the considerable dispersion of discount rates indicated by Table 3.2. This section will consider first of all why several different discount rates may be used by a firm for different types of project, and then why a firm may use different discount rates in different budget periods, and why there are inter-firm and inter-industry variations in discount rates.

---

[1] Similar evidence was disclosed in a survey of procedures governing the purchase of machine tools in sixty United Kingdom engineering companies. See National Economic Development Council [1965b].

(a) *Different discount rates for different types of project within the same firm.*

(i) *Differences in risk.* It is not always clear, from the evidence, whether firms risk-adjust their estimates of the cash flow from proposed investment projects or use different discount rates to find the present values of projects whose expected cash flows are subject to different degrees of risk. Nor is it always clear what firms mean by 'risk'. Sometimes it apparently refers to a measure of the dispersion of the outcomes, while in other cases it appears to refer only to the probability of outcomes less favourable than the central estimate. It is therefore difficult to know how to interpret the use of higher discount rates for different 'risk classes' of projects. In any event, the use of different discount rates for different categories of project was most often explained in terms of risk differentials, and the projects subject to the highest discount rates were those whose results could be least easily forecast.

(ii) *Interaction between projects.* Some firms use very high discount rates when assessing 'rate of return' projects, and then make a lot of other expenditures which are 'necessary for competitive reasons' and not required to show any rate of return at all. The rationale behind this type of decision procedure is that there is a fairly stable relationship between the two types of investment, a relationship which is not taken account of explicitly in the rate of return calculations. For example, firms making very large replacement or expansion expenditures which are 'necessary for competitive reasons' and not required to show a rate of return may find a large number of related investments, which, when taken by themselves show a very high rate of return.[1] The reverse situation is perhaps more illustrative. Often a large new project is assessed using a high discount rate on the understanding that the project will be directly or indirectly responsible for several subsequent 'non-return' investments whose costs are not taken into account when the cost and revenue estimates are made for the original project. In either of these types of situation an average of the rates of discount used on the rate of return projects will be a misleading guide to the rates of discount appropriate for assessing the entire investment programme.

[1] Similar evidence was found by Erik Lundberg [1959] in his interview study of Swedish firms.

(iii) *Omitted variables.* In many firms the estimates of costs and revenues on which the rate of return calculations are based include only some of the relevant items. Most frequently, especially when time discounting is not used, the calculations do not take account of the speed with which the revenues from the projects build up. If, to take the extreme case, the measures are made using only a single 'typical' value of gross profits, then different standards would be required to achieve the same effective standard if projects differed at all in their capital intensity, time distribution of receipts, length of life, if they were subject to different tax provisions, or if they had different effects on the terms on which finance could be obtained. The omission of so many variables from the rate of return calculations has been one of the chief reasons why the rate of return calculations themselves are not taken seriously in many firms. In other firms it is a reason for applying different standards to different projects, or for exempting certain projects altogether from rate of return tests.

Since in so many firms the formal rate of return measures are very poor indicators of the effective rate of return standards being applied, it is difficult to use the rate of return data to indicate whether the effective standards are applied in a way that is consistent with the analysis of Chapter 1. In general, the effective standards seem to be consistent with the model, although there are enough reasons for inter-project variations in effective standards that it would take an extremely strange set of project standards to establish a *prima facie* case that the standards were not consistent with the model.

(b) *Inter-firm and inter-temporal differences in discount rates.* Over time, and among firms, there are substantial differences in the sets of available investment opportunities. If the theoretical framework of Chapter 1 is appropriate, this should be responsible for inter-firm and inter-temporal differences in the discount rates used in assessing investment projects. Such differences certainly exist, and in many cases it is fairly easy to attribute them to the sort of influence suggested by theory. For example, assuming that the supply prices of various types of external funds rise with the amounts required, it would be expected that discount rates would be higher in periods of low cash inflow. Anything that influenced share market opinion would also affect discount rates, so that low current profits might also

G

increase the cost of finance and hence the required rate of return on new investment. Two examples may help to illustrate these sorts of influence:

At the time the capital budget is presented to the board towards the end of the preceding year, it is accompanied by a *pro forma* profit and loss statement showing the company's anticipated net earnings assuming that all the proposed capital expenditures are undertaken. A statement of anticipated cash flows is submitted at the same time, so that the board knows at once the earnings which are expected to arise in the year in question and also the net amount of new funds which will be required if the proposed capital expenditure programme is carried out. The board also has at hand anticipated net earnings for the current year, a figure which is apparently of great importance when the following year's capital expenditure budget is being considered. The board then examines the proposed capital expenditure programme in the light of the current and prospective earnings. If the current or prospective earnings are 'inadequate', then the capital expenditures programme is reduced. 'Inadequate earnings' are those which are 'not sufficient to support the obtaining of the amount of money required to finance the proposed capital expenditure programme'. Although a case has 'never arisen when funds were not available', the board feels that whenever earnings are below a certain (but undefined) level, there are definite limits to the amounts of capital which the company can expect to get from the capital market during that year. The capital expenditure programme is then trimmed 'to the point where it can be successfully financed, given the company's current earnings position and the state of the capital market'. A board member stated that the particular items cut out are those which are 'least likely to improve the current earnings position'. When asked if there were ever any items cut out of the budget which promised to provide a net improvement in the current earnings position, he said that there were not. However, he did not seem very sure of this statement, and was unable to indicate what calculations were made to determine whether particular projects would or would not provide net increments to current earnings. To the limited extent that calculations are made of the effect of proposed expenditures, procedures are such as to cut heavily expenditures on assets with long lives, and more particularly on those whose early years of operation are unprofitable. Most of the items which are cut out are apparently those whose effect on the current earnings position cannot be easily determined, or at any rate is not determined. The items include such things as new office equipment, replacements, and warehouses (*T & I*, p. 75).

One utility's board of directors feel that they 'must look after the interests of the current shareholders', and do so by not expanding so fast that the current earnings are adversely affected. The reason is that even if the extra expansion is profitable on a long term basis the present share-holders might wish to sell their shares before the cash flow starts to appear, and would therefore be hurt by expenditures so large that current earnings (and share values) were impaired (*T & I*, p. 75).

Other differences over time in the discount rates used may be due to changes in monetary and fiscal policies, or to changes in the volume of investment required by a particular investment programme. The latter reason requires some clarification. Many investment programmes involve lumpy capital expenditures, in that there are sharp year-to-year fluctuations in the amount of expenditure required. Firms with investment programmes of this type were of one view that the discount rates used in assessing marginal projects were higher in years of high expenditure than in years of low expenditure. Sometimes this was simply because the marginal cost of finance was higher in those years, but in other cases the input whose opportunity cost rose most was not credit but the managerial and technical skills necessary to supervise new investment projects.[1] By raising the required rate of return to ration these scarce resources, the firms were acting on the implicit assumption that the amount of resources required to engineer a project is positively related to its initial cost.

Differences in discount rates among firms may occur because the firms are at different stages of a capital expenditure or profit cycle, because the firms have access to rather different sets of investment opportunities, or because their management groups have different objectives. Finally, there may be apparent differences in discount rates among firms due to differences in procedures. For example, if one firm risk-standardized its cash-flow estimate to a lower level of risk than a second firm, the first firm would typically use a lower discount rate when assessing projects. Or if the first firm subjected a smaller proportion of its expenditures to rate of return tests, the discount rate used would probably be higher than that used in a firm

[1] For example:

A division manager described the prime limitation on the amount of capital expenditures done in any particular year as the provision of engineering time. He noted that he ranked the projects in priority for engineering consideration and noted that the length of the priority list of unengineered projects varied from year to year, 1957 and 1963 being two noticeably more crowded years. He stated that there is a substantial incentive not only to cut back some projects in heavy years, but to carry out as much as possible during the lighter years since 'you just can't have the engineering staff loaf around for a year' (*T & I*, p. 80).

which attempted to allocate all overheads to investment projects made subject to a rate of return test. This sort of inter-firm difference in procedures makes it more difficult to use the rate of return rules as measures of the discount rates used by firms in assessing entire investment programmes.

D. Conclusion

As advertised, the foregoing survey of investment selection procedures shows that the subjective cash-flow distributions and discount rates presented in Chapter 1 have no exact counterparts among the data employed by large Canadian firms. Most of the evidence is consistent with the theoretical framework, but there would be obvious difficulties in using data of the kind examined as a basis for deriving either subjective cash-flow distributions or the related discount rates. For the present, all that can be done is to analyse monetary and fiscal policies using only those features of the model that do not require systematic quantitative estimates of the characteristics of the cash-flow distributions of alternative investment programmes.

Before proceeding to the analysis of specific policy measures it is necessary to make a brief attempt to explain how firms come to have estimates of the consequences of certain investment alternatives. This requires some explanation of decisions to gather and assess information. Since these decisions are themselves investment decisions (involving the use of resources in one period in the expectation of some gain at a later date) it will be necessary to recognize that the subjective cash-flow distributions are themselves features of the chosen investment programme. To this the next chapter is devoted.

4

DATA FOR DECISIONS

IF the analysis of Chapter 1 could be extended to treat the amount of information available to the firm as a variable the way would be opened for a discussion of a whole range of decisions that until this point have been more or less ignored. It has already been noted in passing that the subjective probability distributions of receipts that underlie investment programmes are not simply based upon information freely available to the firm but result from a series of prior decisions determining the effort to be expended in discovering, collecting, and analysing information. We saw in the last chapter how firms go about assessing the estimated effects of a proposed project on the risk and yield of the firm's operations; we must now analyse the process by which a firm decides how much information to collect before choosing among the available alternative programmes. In Section A the principles are sketched out. Section B discusses some of the procedures used by firms to control the amount of information available on the risk and yield of particular projects and programmes, while Section C presents some evidence about decisions to maintain or increase information-gathering staff and facilities.

A. THE LOGIC OF INFORMATION GATHERING

A model of decision-making under uncertainty must be able to explain decisions to collect the data on which subsequent decisions are based. The simple analysis presented here considers two main types of information gathering; on the one hand the collection of more information about a preconceived project or programme, and on the other the search for new product and process developments which might provide investment opportunities.

(1) Information about the results of a specific project

Assume that investment decisions are made on the basis of the estimated effects of proposed projects on the present values of alternative investment programmes. These estimates themselves are usually not certain; and the decision-maker's level of confidence in any particular parameter estimate may be related to the amount of information available. How does the firm decide whether or not to purchase more information about the results of an investment before a final decision is made to accept the investment programme of which it is a part?

One obvious rationale for expending funds on investigation is that the expected present value of the chosen investment programme may be increased for one of two reasons:

(a) A more precise knowledge of desired output, costs of inputs, the available technology, and the nature of the risks facing the firm allows more use of specialized equipment, closer scheduling of production, and a reduction in risk by interleaving projects with negatively correlated results.

(b) There is a presumption that more investigation will allow the effects of all potential projects to be more precisely assessed. This may result in a re-ranking of the projects, and the choosing of a different (and potentially better) investment programme than would have been undertaken on the basis of less information.

The amount of information available is a function of the amount of funds spent on information and the time spent either gathering information or awaiting the appearance of trends in markets and technology. The passage of time may be expected to increase the amount of information about how a project would have turned out had it been started at a particular time, but it does not ensure a greater certainty about the result of a project with an unspecified future construction date. Even if the accumulation of available evidence through the passage of time could be expected always to allow more accurate prediction of the parameters of cash-flow distributions, there will be concomitant effects on the investment opportunities themselves which might well reduce the PV of the unstarted projects in the programme. Although all the moments of the cash-flow distributions are likely to be affected by the passage of time, there is no general relationship which is applicable for all types of projects. They will therefore not be included specifically in the analysis.

Although the use of more information is likely to give the decision-maker a greater degree of confidence in his estimates of the parameters of the subjective cash-flow distributions it will be assumed that this level of confidence does not affect his decisions. As explained in Chapter 2, the theoretical framework assumes that it is only the estimated values of the characteristics of the cash-flow distributions (and not the vagueness of these estimates) that determine their attractiveness.

The amount of information which will be collected with respect to a particular project or programme depends upon:

(a) the effects of the passage of time on the investment opportunities themselves and on the amount of information available at no cost,

(b) the costs of gathering additional information. These costs will depend on how busy are those officials in the firm who are able to prepare and co-ordinate the data, and the availability of data which could be directly purchased from outside the firm,

(c) the expected elasticity of PV with respect to changes in information-gathering expenditures. It might be supposed that after some point increases in such expenditures will have less and less effect on the estimates of the parameters of the cash-flow distributions. It must be emphasized that there is no necessary effect of additional information on either the parameter estimates or the decision-maker's degree of confidence in those estimates. It is possible that more information could move any of them in any direction, or not affect them at all.

The general conditions determining the optimum amount of information-gathering expenditure with respect to a particular project are that the risk-standardized present-value contribution of the project to the chosen programme be greater than it would be if any alternative amount were spent on information.

(2) Research and development expenditure

The results of research and development expenditure may be considered as a flow of ideas for investment projects. The value of the results is equal to the difference between the PV of the investment programme involving the R. & D. results and the PV of a programme drawn up without regard to the results. The R. & D. department may therefore be treated as a separate division whose output can be evaluated, and whose decisions can be analysed. The establishment of R. & D. plant, equipment, and skilled staff on a certain scale is comparable to the purchase of manufacturing plant, while decisions about the amount of work to be done by the department in a particular time period have much in common with the short-run output decisions in a manufacturing plant.

In the short run, the R. & D. outlays will have a substantial fixed minimum (rental of facilities and equipment, and salaries of key personnel) and will be expected to show substantial increasing returns just beyond the minimum level. Since the facilities and staff are restricted in size in the short run, decreasing returns to expenditure are expected to set in. In the longer term the function relating R. & D. outlays and the *PV* of the results need not, *a priori*, be subject to decreasing or increasing returns at any stage, given adequate time to build staff and equipment. To give the model any content at all, the 'long-run' analysis must be taken to refer to expenditure within a period short enough for it to make some sense to predict the results of the expenditures in terms of their effects on the present values of alternative investment programmes.

The expected return from R. & D. outlays in the short period will depend on the scale and flexibility of the existing establishment. The difficulties in hiring and integrating new members into a research team suggest that beyond a certain point there are decreasing returns, in the short run, to additional R. & D. outlays. In the longer term, there are fewer spending commitments and the yield on R. & D. is less affected by any capacity constraint. A considerable amount of evidence has been adduced to show that there are economies of scale in R. & D. up to a certain level of outlay, but little indication of the potential yield on still greater expenditures. Since the opportunities for R. & D. in many fields are thought to change more rapidly than the staff and equipment can be adjusted to deal with them, it is not surprising that nothing much is known about the 'equilibrium' optimum scale of R. & D.

A firm has two decisions with respect to the scale of its R. & D. activity: how intensively to use its existing specialized staff and equipment, and how fast to increase the size of the research establishment. In the case of both decisions, the firm has the option of deciding on the basis of existing estimates of the *PV* of R. & D. or spending time and funds obtaining more information about the likely results of R. & D. To keep this piece of the model consistent with the framework of Chapter 1, assume that the firm chooses whether or not to get more information by comparing the expected increase in the *PV* of a given R. & D. outlay with the costs of gaining more information about the results of R. & D.[1] The expectation that more information will increase the *PV* contribution of a given R. & D. outlay exists because more complete knowledge of the R. & D. opportunities should lead to a better allocation of R. & D. facilities among special project areas, and a more appropriate choice of equipment and personnel to co-ordinate the programme.

If the output of the R. & D. is evaluated and treated as a contribution to the cash-flow distributions, the longer-term R. & D. scale decision is completely analogous to an investment in manufacturing plant. The relevance of additional information to this decision can therefore be explained by the analysis of Part (1) of this section.

The two following sections present some of the limited evidence about the ways large Canadian firms go about making the two types of information-gathering decisions whose principles have been described in this section. Section B discusses the ways in which a firm sorts the available information into alternative cash-flow distributions and allocates its efforts among the various ways of finding out more about the consequences of particular programmes. That section deals only with decisions governing the amount of effort to be devoted to finding out more about a particular project or programme, taking as given the basic stock of technological knowledge and investigating capacity. In Section C there will be a discussion of the factors influencing decisions to maintain an investigating staff of a certain size, treating the R. & D. department as the typical source of ideas for new products and processes.

B. Information for Assessing Projects and Programmes

Section A of the chapter considers a rationale for the expending of funds on information gathering. This section goes slightly farther, and considers how investment decisions depend on the joint basis of information available 'free' and that gathered specifically for the decision.[2] In Chapter 3 we did not have at hand a completely

[1] More precisely, the comparison is between *PV*'s of alternative programmes including different R. & D. commitments. It is not strictly legitimate to compare the expected value of the increase in *PV* with the costs of the related R. & D. activity because the estimates of R. & D. outlays are also subjective probability distributions. The appropriate way of assessing the value of any particular R. & D. programme is to compare the present values of alternative sets of cash-flow distributions containing different amounts of information-gathering activity.

[2] Efforts to organize the available information will be treated as expenditures on the collection of information.

adequate explanation of the fact that firms specialize in projects of certain risk and industry characteristics. We are now prepared to provide a more complete explanation based on the availability and costs of information to the firm.

At any point in time there are large numbers of investment opportunities available, but they are opportunities only for those with knowledge of their existence, and ability to obtain and co-ordinate the necessary factors of production. If an opportunity is generated, whether for the introduction of a new product, the provision of additional capacity, or the take-over of an existing firm, knowledge of that opportunity will automatically be available only to some of the existing firms.[1] Firms which operate in a particular product or market area cannot help knowing more about that area than they may know about others. If information about the opportunities for new investment is available free only to those firms already specializing in that area, then any given investment opportunity will be more attractive for the existing firms than for outsiders, by an amount equal to the cost to the outsider of obtaining the relevant information.

Since the outsider's investigation usually costs more and takes longer, the insider has an advantage both in cost and in speed of decision in those industries where changes in products or technology are frequent.[2] Thus although firms may diversify to considerable advantage, the distribution of knowledge about new opportunities among existing firms gives a certain advantage to firms which have existing operations of the type, or in the product or market area, affected by the change in opportunities.[3] Each firm is therefore choosing from a different group of cash-flow distributions. We are concerned in this section with the efforts firms make to clarify the investment opportunities which are in some sense 'their own', while the next section will deal with activities designed to provide the firms with entirely new products and production possibilities.

[1] It may be taken for granted that even if equal knowledge of an opportunity is available (at no cost) to all the existing firms, there may be differences in the firms' ability to call together the necessary productive resources. We are restricting our present analysis to the special role that information plays in making investment opportunities particular rather than general.

[2] There are, of course, many instances where the outsider may have special knowledge or resources which provide an advantage over existing firms in an industry, particularly in industries whose firms are not used to looking for or taking up investment opportunities.

[3] Much of this analysis has been more fully presented by G. B. Richardson [1960, especially Parts I and II]. He is more specifically concerned with the influence of market structure on the availability of information.

In the last chapter there was a listing of some of the various occasions on which written evidence is created which sheds light on the nature of the current investment programme. It is on these same occasions that judgements are frequently made about the adequacy of existing information as a basis for decision. Each time a written document appears indicating the probable future course of growth and expenditure, some evidence can be obtained of the degree of commitment and of the detail in which the capital expenditure plans have been specified. However, since the documents can either exaggerate or understate the degree to which future development has been planned, it is difficult to draw any conclusions. Most of the long-range plans do not reflect any commitment to a particular investment programme; their vagueness about expenditures more than a year to two hence reveals the fact that a final choice has still not been made among the alternative cash-flow distributions with differing levels of outlays in future periods. In the annual budgets, which are usually quite specific about the forecasted amounts, if not the composition, of revenues and outlays, there are often lists of projects pending. Some of these projects require the passage of time to clarify their attractiveness, while others await further investigation, and some are fairly definitely scheduled for construction in the succeeding budget year. The projects listed in the budget and explicitly recognized as requiring further investigation are quite rare; usually by the time a project has advanced to the stage of being included in even a 'pending' section of the budget it is conditional on some factor other than (or in addition to) investigation.

Projects are frequently started later than first predicted because of the time taken to prepare the appropriation request. In cases where a project has clear priority but the precise engineering cost estimates are not available, a preliminary appropriation procedure may be employed to grant authority to proceed. In other cases, more interesting from the point of view of the present analysis, preliminary appropriation procedures are used to authorize substantial investigating and engineering expenditures without there being an implied commitment to undertake any variant of the investigated project.

One of the notable features of the appropriation procedure is that information required for a project to be presented consists of a fairly exact[1] specification of the capital cost of the assets, but only a rough

---

[1] Margins of error greater than 10 per cent. usually mean that a supplementary appropriation has to be submitted and the discrepancy explained.

estimate, or none at all, of the required working capital and the expected operating costs and revenues in future years. In most firms there are certain categories of project that require estimates to be made of related costs and revenues, but in general these estimates are not subject to the same sort of post-appraisal as the estimates of capital cost. In many cases, especially those in which the project affects the cash-flow distributions of the whole programme in a rather complex way, a project will be placed in an 'essential replacement' or similar category for which no explicit estimates need be made of the future revenues.

Thus although the regular flow of data about the progress of investment programmes indicates that projects are on occasion delayed so that their characteristics can be more closely assessed, the investigating activity does not produce written evidence of anything approximating the subjective probability distributions of cash flow that are the basis of our model. However, there was considerable evidence that decisions have been delayed, and branches of programmes held in abeyance, until more data could be obtained about their impact on the total investment programme. It is perhaps not surprising, when the methods of data gathering and processing are in their infancy, that there are no records of the alternative cash-flow distributions, or of the information-gathering effort that is being expended on them. After all, the PV of a programme depends on the number and nature of the underlying cash-flow distributions. If the attractiveness and the number of alternative sets of cash-flow distributions depend on the amount of resources devoted to investigation, there is reason to expect that the special skills of those able to sort good estimates from bad will be treated as scarce factors of production. It is therefore not likely that their time would be spent making records of any cash-flow distributions except those which were likely to be considered seriously by higher management. In view of the obvious disinclination of corporate officials to suggest projects or programmes not likely to obtain higher approval, the number of alternative cash-flow distributions analysed in any detail in written form is likely to be small.[1]

Within the theoretical model itself there are therefore reasons why

[1] This was not true to the same extent when the firms employed outside firms of engineers and consultants for the purpose of preparing a number of alternative proposals, each of which presumably would have become part of an alternative investment programme.

there is not likely to be any recorded evidence of the PV's of alternative investment programmes differing in the amount of investigation they have received. In addition to this lack of information about the yield on information-gathering, the nature of the costs of such activity is such that there can be, or has been, no adequate costing procedure. Since most of the investigation is done by those who have responsibility for executing approved plans as well as for investigation, and since the activity itself may consist mainly of occasional contemplation (rather than full-time investigation) of an idea, it is not easy to suggest what data should be used as a measure of the efforts devoted to analysing alternative investment programmes.

Thus we have the unsatisfactory situation where the model we are trying to test produces reasons why we should not expect to find the evidence by means of which it could be tested. What evidence there is, was derived from discussions with decision-makers rather than obtained directly from corporate records. It is such as to support the general analysis presented in Section A of this chapter, but is not powerful enough to discriminate among similar alternative explanations.

C. RESEARCH AND DEVELOPMENT EXPENDITURES

In this section we consider the decisions governing the establishment and operation of research and development activities. To a certain extent the decisions governing the current operations of such a department are akin to those discussed in the last section. However, it is perhaps worth while to maintain a distinction between activities intended to produce more information about the results of specific programmes (considered in Section B) and those activities essentially designed to produce ideas for new products and processes. The former type of activity allows the characteristics of cash-flow distributions to be assessed more accurately, while the latter type is concerned with deriving new sets of investment possibilities. It is this latter type of investigation which will be discussed in this section.

In Section A of the chapter a further distinction was drawn between short- and longer-term decisions about the desired amount of research and development. The distinction has no very clear logical foundation, as it is not easy to establish just what factors are restricted in supply in the short run, nor what might be the costs of expanding R. & D. activities at different rates. The only reason for making the distinction is to emphasize that there are difficulties in expanding research outlays in a short space of time; since research is concerned with untried ideas and techniques there is little that outside experience can contribute to the process of groping for solutions. Corporate officials, whether directly involved in research or not, were generally of the view that research experience within the firm was the best source of information by which to decide how much to allocate for future research, and how the funds should be spent.[1]

In addition to the often-mentioned difficulties in co-ordinating a rapidly expanding level of research activity, officials interviewed referred to factor supply limitations. Many firms have found the supply of scientists and technologists to be inelastic in at least the short run,[2] while space and equipment limitations have been less noticeable restrictions. Because development is usually more closely tied to particular projects, development expenditures are often increased rapidly, even in the short run, when projects with promising but time-sensitive profit prospects reach the development stage.[3]

The short-term allocation of research effort is really a variant of the general research and development decision. In the short term there are more constraints on the rate of change of the size and composition of research effort, and the problem of choice is thereby simplified, but the general principles are the same.

(1) Types of research and development expenditure

Knowledge of products and techniques may be purchased from outside or created entirely within the firm. The choice depends on the way in which the knowledge in question creates investment opportunities for the firm. An analysis of the opportunities will help to unravel the complex nature of research decisions. Knowledge adds to productive opportunities by changing the input requirements for a

---

[1] Officials within research departments were more likely to view their function as one of 'selling' senior management on the value of an expanded research programme. Some traced their enthusiasm to the research potential that had been indicated to them by the results of previous research, although recognizing that they were not in a position to provide objective evidence with which the *ex ante* (or the *ex post*) rate of return on research could be compared to the rate of return on other parts of the investment programme.

[2] Recent Canadian experience is that it has been harder to fill the senior scientific positions than those of technicians. For United Kingdom and United States evidence, see Carter and Williams [1959, Chapter 4], and Machlup [1962].

[3] Too much depends on the particular type of development for fruitful generalizations to be possible. The flexibility of development expenditure in the short run obviously depends on the nature of the required facilities. Some pilot plants take as long to build as full-size production units.

given set of outputs, or by changing the nature or range of the output and sales possibilities. The total gain from a given piece of information depends on the relative advantage which it confers on the firm over other firms in the industry, and on the industry over other industries. The relative sizes of these advantages largely determine the research strategy of a firm or industry. The more easily can access to the knowledge be restricted, and the greater the number of present and potential substitutes for the product, the greater is the incentive for a firm to have its own private research programme.[1]

More generally, it appears that research activity tends to be concentrated at the level of the largest group that can derive substantial benefits relative to its competitors. For example, the plywood manufacturers of Western Canada have the view that there is more collective advantage in improving the characteristics of plywood in relation to those of competitive building products than in trying to achieve a temporary technical advantage over competitors within the industry. The firms therefore trade technical information freely and have a collective research programme.

On the other hand, firms producing chemicals, electrical products, and most consumer goods in Canada seldom have co-operative research activities, since the value of research by these firms depends on the competitive advantage which the results confer on the investigating firm.

Further generalization requires clarification of the types of research activity. Research and development may be classified according to its relationship to the current products and processes of the firm. In general, the more fundamental the research (and the less concerned it is with the costs and characteristics of current output) the more likely are the benefits to have general rather than specific application, and the more likely are firms to enter co-operative schemes.[2] For example, all the major Canadian producers or potential producers of sulphur (often as a by-product) have a joint research venture attempting to discover potential end-use compounds of sulphur.

---

[1] The chemical industry is a good example. The information may not be kept very securely within the firm, as close substitutes may be made without infringing patents. This is the main cause of the short life cycle of the special chemical products of innovating firms. The private (and substantial) research programmes are justified on the basis of the substantial return that goes to the innovating firm during the period before close substitutes have been introduced.

[2] See Edwards [1950, Chapter II].

This does not mean that the more 'fundamental' types of research are never undertaken by individual firms, for in some cases the prospects of gains to the firm are substantial enough to justify them. Furthermore, it is the view of some research directors that any large industrial research programme must contain a substantial element of relatively undirected research if the firm is to get and keep the highest grade of research personnel.

A variant of the distinction between more and less 'fundamental' research is that which contrasts research intended to produce ideas for new products with that intended to discover improvements in existing techniques. One version of this distinction approximates the shadowy line separating research expenditure from development expenditure. Although this latter distinction will be of concern in Chapter 8, it is not necessary here. The distinction between research for new products and that for improvement of existing processes is one that was mentioned frequently in firms with parent companies in other countries. In many of these firms the Canadian research activities are concentrated on the particular problems of production in Canada, while the search for new products is primarily located in the central research laboratories of the parent company. Since various national divisions of an international firm are co-operating rather than competing, the research benefits for the group are frequently maximized by centralizing the research effort.[1] There are relatively few instances of this type of international pooling of industrial research except where the firms involved are under common ownership and control.

The foregoing discussion refers only to product and process research, as it is these types with which research and development departments are primarily concerned. Since our concern is more general—the sources of the subjective cash-flow distributions—the type of research studied in this section must be treated as only an example of the kind of information gathering activity which produces alternative investment programmes. The present discussion is concerned with technological research (rather than market research or other investigating activity) because there is more information avail-

---

[1] This assumes that there are economies of scale in conducting research activities. Otherwise, the research operations could be divided among several centres and only the results centralized. In fact, it may be the greater speed with which information travels within a laboratory that makes a single large unit more productive than co-operating groups of smaller laboratories.

able about it, and because these expenditures are the major elements in the research activity of most firms.

(2) *The scale of research and development expenditures*

The preceding section dealt with the factors limiting the immediate expansion of research activity, and those determining the appropriate mix of co-operative and internal research. Given that the firm has a strategy that involves the use of an internal research staff, how is the optimum size of the staff determined?

In principle, the matter is fairly straightforward; the choice depends on the characteristics of alternative sets of cash-flow distributions, each of which includes a different amount of research expenditure, and estimates of the likely results of the efforts. Is there evidence that the actual choices follow this pattern? It is difficult to know what to count as evidence that the scale of research activity is determined in this way. Certainly none of the recorded decisions are analysed by the firms in such explicit terms; in fact, the observed decision process has so little related written evidence that almost any subjective interpretation of the decision could not be confuted by reference to corporate records.

In the case of the more usual types of investment decisions, *ex ante* rates of return are often only tenuously related to the actual basis for the decision, but at least they provide some evidence of the characteristics of the expected returns. There is apparently no such body of data supporting decisions to expand or contract the scale of research.[1] Sometimes research budgets are supported by qualitative judgements of the chances of successful results, and sometimes by comparison with the research expenditures of other firms in the industry. Beyond the rules of thumb that research outlays in some industries should bear a certain relation to the sales revenues or profits of the firm,[2] there do not seem to be any explicit methods used for choosing the appropriate scale of research. There are extreme difficulties in making

[1] For example, a senior executive responsible for research reported: 'Research is like motherhood; you just have to believe in it' [*T & I*, p. 131]. While this kind of explanation of the basis for budget decisions on research was evident in several firms, it was usually impossible to gain approval for plant and equipment investment without a rather more precisely stated expectation of return.

[2] Officials of firms in several different industries noted that among the firms in their industry there was a common view of the 'appropriate' scale of research outlays, usually expressed as a percentage of gross revenues. None of the officials interviewed were anxious to suggest that the amount so chosen would be optimal [*T & I*, p. 131].

H

suppositions about what sort of return a firm might expect to receive from its research activity. Aside from the fact that the most important factor in the investment is research talent whose productivity is difficult to measure either *ex ante* or *ex post*, there is little basis for predicting what will be the result of a research programme. Even if the experience of other firms, or the same firm in earlier years, were thought to be relevant to a current decision, there is no clear way, even after the event, of measuring the elasticity of PV with respect to the scale of research outlays.[1]

Within firms, the setting of research budgets is often seen as a 'political matter', with the persuasiveness or prestige of the research director being the key factor determining the scale of activity. Our explanatory framework would have us treat the board's evaluation of the talent of the research director as their best measure of the improvement in investment opportunities likely to result from research. In principle, the use of personality as a proxy for profit expectations would only last until the research could be assumed to have produced its results, and thus the influence of personalities might be thought to be temporary. But if it is true, as the interview evidence indicates, that it is usually easy to show enough advantages achieved by past research to justify the maintenance of a department of a given size, then whatever influences act to increase the size of outlays in a particular year also have effects on annual outlays thereafter.

Chapter 8 will deal in more detail with the nature of the information used by firms to compare alternative sets of cash-flow distributions involving different amounts of R. & D. outlays. In particular there will be an analysis of the effects of tax measures and government cost-sharing schemes on the attractiveness of alternative research budgets.

[1] In the light of the rules of thumb used to establish research budgets, it is dangerous to use correlations between sales or profits and research outlays as a measure of the yield. For example, when D. B. Hertz [1961] obtains a close fit with a regression (for a firm) of market share on research and development expenditure, the relationship may be one of research expenditures as a function of gross profits, with market share being a proxy for gross profits.

5

MONETARY AND FISCAL POLICIES TO INFLUENCE INVESTMENT

THIS is the only chapter in which an attempt will be made to compare in detail the effects of particular tax and monetary measures on the present value of investment projects. The four subsequent chapters will analyse the effects of different types of policy on the capital expenditures of large Canadian corporations. The concluding chapter will deal briefly with the factors governing the choice of an appropriate set of monetary and fiscal policies. The scope of the present chapter will be restricted to a comparison of the direct effects of particular tax and monetary measures on the present value of investment programmes.

The method of attack will be as follows: First we shall make suppositions about the reasons why one policy might be preferred over another, and then we shall use these criteria to assess several specific types of monetary and taxation policies.

A. POLICY REQUIREMENTS

Without explicit reference to the macro-economic system, one cannot specify the optimal characteristics of policies to influence investment. Nevertheless, in the light of the view of investment presented in Chapters 1 to 4 it is possible to indicate roughly the characteristics that policy measures ought to have if they are to influence the size or timing of investment outlays in a predictable manner. Assuming that the policy-makers are concerned with the amount, timing, regional and industrial distribution, and marginal efficiency of investment expenditures, they will wish to have at least some policies whose influence on investment can be specified in advance.

It is not enough that policies should have differential effects among industries, regions, and time periods; these differentials must be at least roughly predictable by the policy-maker if they are to be of any help in the choice of optimum policies. Thus one need know not just that some cash-flow distributions and discount rates are altered, but that the present values of certain programmes are altered to a roughly measurable extent. To get very far in such an analysis, it is necessary to know the characteristics of the cash-flow distributions and the parameters governing the values of the market discount rates for firms in different regions and industries, and the factors causing changes over time in their investment opportunities. There are many factors influencing the cash-flow distributions in ways that cannot be predicted in advance. The factors may be either exogenous or endogenous variables whose distributions have substantial variances, so that particular changes in the cash-flow distributions cannot be predicted with great confidence. In these circumstances, given that the policy-makers wish to counteract some of the unpredicted shifts in cash-flow distributions or market discount rates, there will be a preference for policies whose effects may be felt quickly, and whose duration can be altered to suit the immediate policy requirements.

Tax and monetary measures affect investment by altering the *PV*'s of alternative programmes, thus changing their ranking and leading to the substitution of one programme for another. The *PV* of a programme may be altered by a change in any of the parameters of the cash-flow distributions for one or more time periods, or in the external factors influencing the discount rates used by the market in evaluating the firm.

The most flexible policies are those which can alter the cash-flow distributions (operating on any of the parameters) and the market discount rates in specific time periods so as to make the programmes with the most appropriate time patterns of investment outlays (as well as other characteristics) have higher *PV*'s than the alternative programmes. We need make no distinction in principle between measures which are designed to stabilize investment and those intended to alter its structure over time, since the basis for choosing policies is the same. If there is an important difference between stabilization policies and other policies affecting investment, it is that the former are designed primarily to offset unpredicted changes in other factors influencing the ranking of investment programmes. In so far as the policy-makers are not concerned with stabilizing investment, they will try less to affect expenditures in particular years, and try more to see that the programmes chosen have the desired technological, industrial, and regional distribution of employment and growth. However, we may assume at least that the policy-maker wishes to know the time pattern of reactions to a policy, even if the reaction times are only relevant when the measure is first introduced. In general, therefore, the choice of a particular policy to influence investment will depend on its ability to produce the desired results, which will in turn depend on the degree to which the following characteristics can be predicted:

(1) *Differential effects on the cash-flow distributions of investment programmes with different time patterns of investment outlays*
The closer the link between the cash flows (after tax) and the investment outlays in particular years, the more effectively can a policy be used to influence the timing of investment.

(2) *Effects on the cash-flow distributions of firms in different regions and different industries*
If differential effects are desired then the policy should be flexible enough to produce them.

(3) *Effects on the predictability of cash flows*
In general, greater dispersion (σ) of the cash-flow distributions reduces the present value of any programme. Assuming that the marginal efficiency of investment declines as the size of the investment programme increases, greater dispersion of the cash-flow distributions will reduce the volume of investment undertaken. Some tax measures may increase the predictability of cash flows for certain periods while decreasing it for others.

(4) *Effects on current and estimated future interest rates*
Interest rates affect the cash-flow distributions, and also the set of discount rates used to find the *PV* of a programme. Although the model of Chapter 1 does not specify more than one market interest rate for each period, there is, of course, a spectrum of interest rates, so that the optimum borrowing policy may involve borrowing on short term when rates are high, and on long term when rates are low, depending on the shapes of the yield curves in the two cases. Thus the effects of monetary policy depend on its influence on expected long- and short-term interest rates in the various periods within the investment horizon.

(5) *Changes in the share market's discount rate*
Changes in particular periods may be due either to measures affecting the flow of new investible funds, or to taxes influencing the division

of the stock of investible funds among the available securities. In addition, the announcement effects of policy changes, as well as beliefs that a tax rate or the tax structure will be changed, may influence the general level of expectations in the share markets, and hence the values of the share market's discount rates.

We may now examine the basic types of taxation and monetary measures which have been used, or suggested for use, in influencing investment. The characteristics of the policies will be briefly assessed to see to what extent they are likely to be effective in attaining policy goals.

B. Specific Measures Used to Influence Investment

(1) *Changes in the rate of corporation income tax*

Effects on the present value of net revenues:

$$\Delta PV = \sum_{t=1}^{j} (G_{Rt} - D_t)(\tau_t - \tau_t^*)(1 + r)^{-t}$$

where

j = the number of periods for which the changed rate of tax is expected to apply,

$G_{Rt} = M_t^* + I_t + T_t$ = cash revenues, before tax and capital expenditures, in period t,

D_t = the amount of depreciation allowances permitted for tax purposes in period t,

τ_t = previously expected rate of corporation income tax in period t,

τ_t^* = the new rate of tax,

r = a standard-risk discount rate. There may be separate rates linking each pair of adjacent future periods within the time horizon of the investment programme. For convenience, the time and firm subscripts will be ignored in this chapter, since only infrequent references are made to inter-firm and inter-period differences in discount rates.

The effect of a change in the tax rate on the inducement to invest depends on investors' expectations about the length of time for which the new rate will apply. If there is a temporary increase in the corporate income-tax rate, firms will attempt to reduce taxable income by maximizing current tax deductions, hoping that the rate will be reduced at a later date. If a firm has fairly certain expectations that the rate will fall again in, say, two years, there will be an incentive to invest heavily in projects with high current depreciation allowances and low initial earnings. Thus a temporary increase in the tax rate may actually increase the current volume of investment outlays.

On the other hand, if the tax rate is reduced below its normal level for a short period, firms will delay making allowable charges against current income, and will be less attracted by slow-yielding investments with large initial depreciation charges. In times of abnormally low tax rates, firms will try to maximize their income from current operations, and may even reduce the volume of renovation and replacement investment so as to avoid disrupting the current flow of production. Thus we see that a temporary cut in the corporation income tax, intended as a stimulus to investment, may very well have the opposite effect. A general cut in taxes would, however, tend to lower the cost of funds to some firms, and hence to exert some upward pressure on investment. This lowering of the cost of funds occurs because the flow of internally generated funds will be greater, and because the higher recorded profits may increase the prices of the shares of the firms involved, thereby reducing for them the cost of new equity funds. The higher earnings would provide a larger cover for any given burden of interest payments, and would thereby increase the firm's ability to borrow.

The smaller the group of firms receiving the tax cut, the greater would be the decrease of the cost of funds for these firms. If the tax cut were extended to all corporate enterprise, and if the supply of funds available to corporate enterprise were inelastic, the effect of the tax cut on the cost of capital (i.e. on the values of the share market's discount rate) might be negligible. The shorter the period for which the tax change is expected to apply, the more likely are the effects on the cost of capital to be negligible.

Shifts in the corporation tax rate, unless the changes in the rate are specified well in advance, are likely to increase the dispersion of the cash-flow distributions, because of uncertainty about the future rates of tax, unless the tax rate changes were thought likely to be positively correlated with unpredicted changes in pre-tax cash flow.

Finally, some mention should be made of the distribution of the effects of a general change in the tax rate. Firms not expecting to pay taxes within the period for which the new tax rate is expected to remain will be affected only indirectly by the rate change. Firms which are subsidiaries of firms controlled abroad may or may not be affected. If a firm controlled abroad is in a position to offset the entire domestic tax paid against taxes otherwise payable in the parent company's country, then a change in the domestic tax rate should not affect their behaviour. If, on the other hand, the parent company has made use of all the foreign tax credits available to it, then marginal changes in the domestic taxes would have corresponding effects on the total taxes paid by the firm.

(2) *Open-market operations designed to affect the cost and availability of credit*

Effects on the *PV* of net revenues

$$\Delta PV = \sum_{t=1}^{j} B_t(1 - \tau_t)(i_t - i_t')(1 + r)^{-t}$$

where

j = the number of years for which the higher or lower interest rates are expected to be paid (or received, if the firm is a net lender),
τ_t = corporation income tax rate,
B_t = the amount of outstanding open-market borrowing (lending) by the firm in year t,
i_t = the interest rate expected in the absence of open-market operations,
i_t' = the expected interest rate in year t after open-market operations.

We shall discuss first the results of official buying or selling of securities of several maturities, affecting the whole spectrum of interest rates. Monetary policy designed to stabilize investment relies on movements of interest rates having certain effects on the inducement to invest. Movements in interest rates have something in common with general changes in the corporate income tax in that their effects are very dependent on expectations about the length of time for which the new rates are expected to last, and about the existence and height of expected average rates about which the short-term fluctuations are taking place. For firms whose financing has some degrees of flexibility, an upward movement of interest rates affects estimates of the cost of funds for those years during which interest rates are expected to be high.[1] A decline below the average rate might be expected to have a slightly greater long-term effect on the cost of funds since corporations might be able to lengthen the term structure of their borrowing during the low-interest periods. In any event,

[1] Unless the firm is forced to borrow for a term longer than the period during which interest rates are expected to be abnormally high.

temporary upward or downward movements in rates for firms with flexible debt policies do not have substantial effects on either the cost of funds, or on the advisability of changing the timing of investment outlays. The main effects of monetary policy on the cost and availability of funds are on firms whose expenditures require current borrowing of a certain type. If the borrowing must be long term, then the firm will find changes in interest rates having a substantial effect on the marginal cost of funds. If the firm is primarily dependent upon short-term borrowing (e.g. on bank loans), then open-market operations may lead to quantitative limitations which make additional funds unobtainable. In a system where rates, rather than availability, ration short-term funds this channel of influence would not apply.

Except to the extent that some firms feel compelled to finance long-term assets with long-term debt and short-term assets with short-term debt, short-term changes in interest rates have no more effect on an investment programme comprising short-lived assets than on a programme containing long-lived assets. The frequently made comment that monetary policy affects long-lived assets rather than short-lived assets is based on the far-fetched assumptions that all borrowing is for the lifetime of the related assets,[1] and that all projects must be wholly financed by borrowing at current market rates. An alternative, and slightly more acceptable, assumption would permit the conclusion that changes in current interest rates have greater effects on the PV's of programmes containing long-lived assets. The required assumption is that current movements in short- and long-term interest rates are not thought by investors to be movements about an unchanged expected value, but are taken as evidence of a substantial movement, in the same direction, of the expected average of future interest rates. If this were true, (if the elasticity of expectations of future interest rates with respect to changes in current rates were positive, and close to 1), then increases in current interest rates would raise the values of expected interest rates, and thus discount rates, in future periods, and hence would favour programmes with

---

[1] Even this is not a sufficient assumption, for any open-market operation may be expected to affect the term structure of interest rates so that long- and short-term rates will not normally change to the same degree, whether the changes are measured in absolute or in relative terms. If open-market operations are likely to alter the term structure of interest rates, it is not possible to conclude *a priori* that monetary policy will have a greater impact on assets with longer lives even if assets are always financed by fixed-interest debt to be paid off at the rate at which the assets are depreciated.

less capital investment (which would presumably include programmes containing assets of less than average durability). But the assumption that expected future interest rates are elastic with respect to changes in current interest rates is not very acceptable, since we are specifically concerned with the effects of countercyclical interest rate movements. However, the assumption is often made, though seldom justified, in discussions directly concerned with the effects of cyclical movements in interest rates.[1]

We can therefore see that only certain types of firms are likely to find that cyclical movements in interest rates affect materially either the cost or the availability of funds. There is one further important group of firms whose cost of funds is not likely to be affected at all by changes in domestic credit conditions; those firms which rely as a matter of course on funds obtained from outside the national economy, whether from foreign markets or from associated firms in foreign countries. For these firms the relevant values of current and future interest rates are the rates in foreign markets, or the required payments to the parent company. The direct effects of domestic credit conditions on investment are therefore restricted to those firms which are at least marginally reliant on domestic sources of funds.[2]

The same kind of analysis applies if we consider the effects of official purchases or sales of securities of a particular maturity. The only difference is that action thus concentrated on debt of a certain term will alter the term structure of interest rates, and thereby tend to cause flexible firms to change the term structure of their borrowing or lending, and to redistribute some direct effects to some of the firms whose borrowings are always of a certain type and term.

Although both open-market operations and general changes in the corporate income tax rate share the short-coming that they cannot influence substantially the inducement to invest without formally committing the authorities to maintain the new rate of interest or rate of tax for a number of years, they differ considerably in the scope of their application and effects. Many firms are completely unreliant on domestic sources of funds, and are therefore unaffected by changes in domestic credit conditions. On the other hand, the influence of national taxes on foreign-owned firms depends on the regulations governing foreign tax credits as well as the circumstances of indi-

---

[1] For example, see Tarshis [1961] and Shackle [1965].
[2] Evidence on this point is to be found in Chapter 7.

vidual firms. The firms affected by tax changes are not likely to be even approximately the same firms as those affected by changes in interest rates.

(3) *Subsidized loans*

Effects on present value of net revenues:

$$\Delta PV = \sum_{t=1}^{j} B_{ts}(1 - \tau_t)(i_t - i_t^*)(1 + r)^{-t}$$

where

j = the duration of the subsidized loan,
τ_t = corporation tax rate,
B_{ts} = the amount of the subsidized loan,
i_t = expected market-interest rate in year t,
i_t^* = subsidized loan rate.

This kind of measure can be implemented by tax legislation, although it is more usually done either through direct government lending, or government guarantees of private loans. Although the effects of this kind of policy on the inducement to invest can often best be expressed in terms of an interest rate, the effects of such schemes differ considerably from those of interest rate changes induced by open-market operations.

Since the terms of a subsidized loan agreement can deal with the time pattern of construction outlays, as well as with the industrial and regional composition of the aggregate investment programme, a subsidized loan scheme can provide far more selective encouragement or discouragement to investment than can general changes in interest rates.[1] The use of subsidized loans to provide selective stimulation to investment is in principle quite straightforward; it is a matter primarily of choosing an interest rate sufficiently low to provide the necessary degree of incentive. To use such a policy to restrict investment is rather more difficult. If the curtailment of subsidized lending is to cut back investment, it is necessary that there currently is

---

[1] See, for example, pages 267–89 and 440–1 of the R.C.B.F. *Report*, for a description of the effects of National Housing Act (N.H.A.) mortgages, and direct lending by the Central Mortgage and Housing Corporation (C.M.H.C.). An example of the approach was provided by the Swedish government in 1960 and 1961, when the firms using the investment reserve system were offered tax reductions whose value was equivalent to 10 per cent. per annum interest (on the additional funds deposited) for making extra deposits in the central bank for the required period. See Canarp [1963].

a substantial amount of investment which would not be feasible if financed from any of the available alternative sources. Thus there has to be a regular continuing flow of subsidized loans if there is to be scope for selective cuts in investment induced by reductions in the number of subsidized loans. Another way of using the interest incentive effect in reverse might be to allow tax concessions to be made to firms freezing liquid assets by depositing them in the central bank. Such a scheme would be much less selective than the subsidized loan plans, and would seem in many ways to be less efficient for influencing investment than are open-market operations, since firms could borrow sufficient funds in domestic or foreign financial markets to deposit at favourable rates with the central bank, and to continue as well with their planned investment programmes.

The value to firms of a subsidized loan scheme, and hence its effects on the inducement to invest, depends not only on the interest rate on the subsidized loans but also on the firms' expectations about the costs of alternative sources of funds. The most definite expectations about the value of the subsidy would be created by a scheme wherein the interest rate on the subsidized borrowing would be a specified amount below some selected market rate. In such circumstances the value of the subsidy could be clearly demonstrated, so that the firms might be better able to compare the extra costs of undertaking construction at the officially specified date with the benefits of the loan subsidy.

The chief advantage of subsidized loans as an instrument of economic policy is that they can be used to alter the amount of investment of a chosen type in a specified time period. In this respect they are considerably superior to general movements in interest rates, to the extent that investment plans can feasibly be altered within the specified time period.

(4) *Accelerated or deferred depreciation*

The regulations governing the speed at which capital expenditures may be charged off against taxable income[1] affect the size and timing of income-tax payments. Most tax changes involving either an acceleration or deferment of depreciation allowances affect the timing rather than the total amount of taxes payable with respect to a given asset, so that the incentive or disincentive to investment depends on

---

[1] Depreciation changes are the subject of Chapter 6.

the value to the firm of faster internal generation of funds. The effects of depreciation changes also depend on whether the change is of a 'marginal' or of an 'average' type. An 'average' measure changes the depreciation allowances for all assets not yet fully written off, while a 'marginal' measure alters the speed of write-off only for assets (usually only new assets, lest firms trade assets back and forth to gain a tax advantage) purchased during a specified period. 'Average' measures rely for their power chiefly on their effects on the cost and availability of funds, while 'marginal' measures also increase (or decrease) the marginal efficiency of investment by making new assets more (or less) attractive substitutes for existing ones. The 'average' measures lack power for two reasons. First, the new rate cannot be assumed to apply for the length of life of the assets being considered, since all depreciation rates must be expected to be changed when economic conditions change. Second, since the depreciation allowances change for existing as well as new assets, the change does little to affect the rate of return on investment to replace existing assets. Marginal measures have therefore a much stronger influence on the marginal efficiency of investment, and also produce more widespread capital gains and losses among the owners of existing assets.[1]

Both marginal and average changes in depreciation affect the cost and availability of funds, by increasing or decreasing the volume of internally generated funds. The effects of these changes are greater for average than for marginal measures, and for both types of measure depend upon the price elasticity of the supply of funds to the firms affected. For fast-growing firms who feel that their expansion is constrained by the cost of getting new funds in sufficient quantities (i.e. the new issue rate is at a point where it has a substantial positive effect on the share market's discount rate), a postponement of tax payments may cause a substantial drop in the marginal cost of funds for an investment programme of a certain size. On the other hand, for those firms with substantial stocks of liquid assets and untouched borrowing power, the acceleration or deferment of depreciation may have no effect at all on the marginal cost of financing the planned level of investment.

There are several forms which an acceleration or deferment of depreciation may take.

---

[1] The pattern of capital losses on existing assets when a 'marginal' depreciation incentive is introduced is similar to that caused by an unexpected increase in the rate of embodied technological progress. Cf. Chapter 8.

(a) *Initial allowances and deferments.* Effects of an initial allowance on present value of net revenues

$$\Delta PV = \tau_t A(1 + r)^{-1} - A\left(\frac{\tau_t d_t}{r + d_t}\right)$$

where

τ_t = the corporation income-tax rate,
A = the amount of the initial allowance (available at the end of the year of purchase),
I = the cost of the asset on which the initial allowance is granted,
d_t = the declining balance depreciation rate used for tax purposes,
r = the standard-risk discount rate.

Effects of a depreciation deferment

$$\Delta PV = -I\left(\frac{\tau_t d_t}{r + d_t}\right) + I\left(\frac{\tau_t d_t}{r + d_t}\right)(1 + r)^{-m}$$

when m is the number of years before any depreciation may be claimed, and the other variables are as defined above.

This kind of provision stipulates that assets purchased in a particular period (the coverage is usually restricted to new assets) be allowed a high initial depreciation charge (initial allowance) or else a diminished initial charge (deferment) in the year of purchase. After the period covered by the initial allowance or deferment, the normal depreciation rates are applied to the undepreciated capital cost of the asset. Initial allowances have been used from time to time in the United Kingdom,[1] Austria,[2] and Canada.[3] The deferment of depreciation was a feature of Canadian anti-inflationary policy during the Korean War period,[4] and again in 1966.

The value of an initial allowance depends on the present value of the tax deferment, which in turn depends on the marginal value of internal funds and the time profile of both the regular and the accelerated depreciation allowances. An initial allowance of a given size (as a percentage of the capital cost of the asset) obviously has a larger present value (as a percentage of the capital cost of the asset)

[1] For an analysis of the specific provisions and their effects, see Bird [1963b], Corner and Williams [1965], and Dow [1964].
[2] For an indication of depreciation rules in European countries, see Moore [1963].
[3] Income Tax Regulations 1108 and 1109 of 1961 offered what was in effect an initial allowance, as they increased the depreciation allowance only in the first year of the lives of the qualifying assets. See Chapter 6 for further discussion.
[4] For a description, see Goode [1957] or Sharp [1953].

the slower is the normal rate of depreciation. Thus initial allowances of a given size have a different value to the firm depending on the tax class to which the assets belong. For assets within the same depreciation class, the value of the initial allowance is not dependent on the length of life of the asset.[1]

(b) *Exaggerated or reduced depreciation.* Effect on present value of net revenues

$$\Delta PV = (I^* - I)\left(\frac{\tau_t d_t}{r + d_t}\right)$$

where

τ_t = corporation income-tax rate,
d_t = declining balance depreciation rate,
r = standard-risk discount rate,
I = the cost of the asset,
I^* = the amount which is deemed to be the cost of the asset for the purposes of computing depreciation allowances for tax purposes.

This type of measure differs from the other depreciation changes described, since it alters the total amount as well as the timing of depreciation allowances. It may equally well be viewed as an investment allowance (or tax) spread over time.

Under a system of this type the regular depreciation rates are kept stable over time, but assets are put into the pool of depreciable assets at either more or less than their actual cost, depending on the timing of the investment. As an example, in a time of underemployment, firms might be allowed to enter assets into their books, for the purposes of computing depreciation deductions, at 120 per cent. of their actual costs. By the same token, only 80 per cent. of actual cost might be allowed as depreciation charges over the lifetime of assets purchased in times of excess demand. As with initial allowances, the value of this kind of measure to the firms depends on the appropriate discount rate, since the tax advantages are spread over time. Like the initial allowance, exaggerated or reduced depreciation is essentially a marginal type of measure since it is specifically aimed at the taxes relating to new investment. It differs from the initial allowance in that the total amount (as well as the timing) of depreciation allowances attributable to a particular asset varies with changes in the depreciation regulations.

[1] Except for assets which are scrapped or sold before they are fully written off for tax purposes. The present value of an initial allowance is less for an asset of this type than for other assets in the same depreciation class.

(c) *Faster or slower write-off over the lifetime of the asset.* Effect on present value of net revenues

$$\Delta PV = I\left[\frac{\tau_t r(d_t{}^* - d_t)}{(r + d_t{}^*)(r + d_t)}\right]$$

where $d_t{}^*$ is the new rate of depreciation, and the other variables are as defined previously.

This kind of measure is like the initial allowance in that it changes the timing rather than the total amount of depreciation claimed with respect to a particular asset.

It shares with scheme (b) above the characteristic that the depreciation allowances under the special provisions are either larger or smaller in each early year of the asset's life than the allowances under the regular rates.[1] If such measures are announced as applying to investments made within a certain period, and to none made before that time, they are of the type described earlier as 'marginal'.

(d) *Faster or slower rate of depreciation for an unspecified length of time.* Effect on present value of net revenues

$$\Delta PV = I\left[\frac{\tau_t r(d_t{}^* - d_t)}{(r + d_t{}^*)(r + d_t)}\right]\left[1 - \left(\frac{1 - d_t{}^*}{1 + r}\right)^m\right]$$

where

$m =$ the number of years for which the new declining balance depreciation rate $(d_t{}^*)$ is expected to apply,

$I =$ the undepreciated capital cost, at the time of change from d_t to $d_t{}^*$, of all the assets to which $d_t{}^*$ is to apply,

$\tau_t =$ corporation income-tax rate,

$r =$ standard-risk discount rate.

This may be either a 'marginal' or an 'average' type of measure. If it is of the 'average' type, applying to existing as well as new assets, it is essentially a means of altering the amount of liquid funds in the hands of firms, as it has relatively small effects on the demand for investment funds, unless the change in the rate of depreciation allowance is expected to apply for some time. The use of this kind of measure is likely to increase the uncertainty of estimates of the

---

[1] Examples of this kind of measure are the Canadian 1963 acceleration of depreciation for Class 8 assets purchased by manufacturing or processing businesses and for buildings and equipment purchased by new enterprises in depressed areas. Under these provisions a declining balance rate was changed to a much larger straight line rate, making depreciation allowances larger for each year until the asset is completely written off. See Chapter 6 for details.

present value of depreciation allowances for particular assets, since the rates are liable to change any time there is a change in economic conditions.

(5) *Investment allowances or taxes*

Effect on present value of net revenues

$$\Delta PV = I \propto_t \tau_t (1 + r)^{-1}$$

where $\propto_t$ is the rate of investment allowance or (if negative) taxation. It is assumed to be paid at the end of the period in which the asset is purchased.

Since these measures relate specifically to investment, they are of the type we have been describing as 'marginal', since their direct effects are on the rates of return of only new assets.[1] In their usual form they involve a tax credit which is a certain percentage of the investment outlays during a specified period. An investment tax has been used less frequently, but might be expected to involve an additional tax equal to a certain fraction of the investment outlays made within a prescribed time period.[2] Because they can be dated and because they change the relative rates of return on new as compared to existing assets, investment allowances or taxes have substantial effects on the marginal efficiency of investment outlays in a particular period. The effect of an investment allowance on the present value of a project does not depend on the length of life of the assets.

It has on occasion been suggested that investment allowances, relative to initial allowances, discriminate in favour of short-lived assets.[3] Since its present value is unrelated to the length of life of the project, the investment allowance cannot be said to discriminate in favour of short-lived assets. It would only be correct to say that an investment allowance provides *relative* discrimination in favour of short-lived assets by comparing it with another measure (such as an initial allowance whose rate does not vary with the assets' allowable

---

[1] Most legislation governing investment allowances specifies that the assets purchased must be new, presumably so that firms will not create inter-firm sales of existing assets to increase the amount of investment earning an investment allowance.

[2] The Swedish investment tax of 1951–2 and 1955–7 is one of the few examples of the use of an investment tax as a disincentive to investment. See Wickman [1963].

[3] Bird [1963a], Black [1959].

I

rate of depreciation) whose value does increase with the length of life of the asset. If it is compared with an initial allowance with different rates for the various tax classes of assets (which can, for any given discount rate, effectively remove the initial allowance's discrimination in favour of long-lived assets) the investment allowance has not even any relative discrimination in favour of short-lived assets. The matter can be put somewhat more explicitly. From the fact that the partial derivative of PV of an investment allowance with respect to the length of life of the related assets is zero, it follows that at least in some sense the introduction of an investment allowance (compared with the situation where there is no investment incentive) discriminates neither for nor against longer-lived projects. Can we not go farther? The PV of investment allowances, for any given discount rate is proportional to the PV of investment outlays. An increased rate of investment allowances leads firms to expand investment outlays. Firms will:

(a) prefer programmes which use up more fixed assets over time. The preferred programmes may involve either
    (i) substituting fixed assets for current inputs, or
    (ii) scrapping fixed assets sooner, i.e. making them less durable, and
(b) for a given use of capital over time, increase the present value of investment, and therefore of investment allowances, by buying larger (and therefore more durable, given the total of expenditures over time) assets.

Can we say anything about the relative sizes of the offsetting tendencies towards greater and less durability? In cases where internal funds constraints are binding, or the discount rates are high for some other reason, there will be less scope for substitution of capital inputs for current inputs. The scope is least in the case where long-lived assets are to be substituted for current inputs; so that in firms with high implicit discount rates the increased capital expenditures will be more concentrated (than in firms with lower discount rates) in short-lived capital assets (i.e. those requiring smaller initial capital outlays). We still do not know whether the average durability of fixed assets will decrease, but it is more likely to do so in these firms than in firms with easier access to outside funds.

The effects of investment allowances on the cost and availability of funds are slight, in part because the size of the tax reduction or increase is only a fraction of the investment outlays themselves, and in part because the changes in tax payments are delayed for one or more years. There will be some effect on the cost of equity capital produced by the pattern of capital gains and losses which accompanies any marginal measure. For example, an investment allowance for the purchase of new assets will cause the capital value of existing assets to drop, which in turn will tend to decrease the share prices of those firms with recently purchased facilities.[1] Therefore the cost of equity capital for those firms will rise, at least temporarily, in relation to the cost for firms with few existing assets but substantial opportunities for new investment. These effects are not likely to be substantial unless the rate of investment allowance were very large.

Investment allowances or taxes may be made to apply to all or some fraction of capital expenditures made during the prescribed period. One way which has been used to make the measure as powerful as possible for a given current tax loss or gain has been to apply it only to investment in excess of all[2] or some fraction of depreciation allowances. The net investment allowance can provide a greater inducement to invest at the margin than can an equal amount of tax reduction applied to gross investment.

Investment allowances and taxes are much better adapted for stabilization policy than are corporate tax rate changes since the effects of an investment allowance or tax on the marginal efficiency of investment are greater if the allowance or tax is only expected to be in force for a limited time. This is in contrast with a change in the corporate income tax, which has a smaller effect on the marginal efficiency of investment the shorter is the period for which the tax rate is expected to apply. The temporary investment allowance has more power than a permanent one because it makes current investment more attractive in relation to investment in a later period when the allowance might not be available.

The permanence of the allowance or tax also affects the choice between a gross and a net credit or tax. It has been pointed out that the greater power of a net investment tax credit is substantially reduced (in relation to that of a gross investment tax credit) if the allowance is expected to be permanent, since this year's investment

---

[1] Unless these firms also have investment programmes involving exceptionally large additional capital expenditures.

[2] As in the case of the Belgian investment-tax credit brought in during 1959, and the Italian investment allowance of 1956, cf. Nortcliffe [1960].

will increase the depreciation allowances and hence decrease the base for the investment credit in subsequent years.[1] This point only applies to the extent that the investment allowance or tax is assumed to be permanent. In any event, predictions about the future size of the tax credit are likely to be less certain than estimates of income and the general level of taxation,[2] but if the investment allowance or tax is assumed to be an intermittent stabilization measure, the net investment subsidy or tax maintains its power relative to the gross measure. In fact, if the net investment subsidy or tax is expected to be periodically applicable for a short period of time, then firms will have a considerable incentive to concentrate their investment in those years when the investment credit is available (or the tax suspended), and to spend no more than their depreciation allowances in those time periods when an investment tax must be paid (or when the subsidy is not available). Finally, it should be noted that investment allowances have been made available only to those firms with current taxable income, and thus have discriminated against firms whose operations are not (yet) producing taxable profits.[3]

(6) The investment reserve systems

Effect on present value of net revenues

$$\Delta PV = I\tau_t\left(1 - \frac{\alpha_t}{r + d_t} + \frac{\alpha_t}{1 + r}\right)$$

where α_t is the rate of investment allowance, available at the end of the year of purchase, and the non-interest-bearing deposit at the central bank is equal to $I\tau_t$ and is released at the time the asset is purchased ($t = 0$).

Although there are several alternative forms for an investment reserve system, we will base our discussion on the Swedish scheme, since it has been the one which has received the most attention in

---

This point was emphasized by White [1962].

[2] This suggestion is supported by Brown [1962], who emphasizes the fact that the certainty with which a tax reduction is expected as well as the expected value of the deduction must be taken into account when the benefits to the firm are being assessed.

[3] The example calculations in the National Economic Development Council pamphlet [1965a], p. 5, demonstrate clearly the greater PV of allowances for firms currently paying taxes. The same situation exists, of course, for all incentives or disincentives which are related to current taxes, as will be seen from the examples in Chapters 6, 8, and 9.

other countries.[1] Firms which take part in the scheme place any fraction they choose[2] of their pre-tax profits into an investment reserve. Instead of paying tax, they pay an amount almost equivalent[3] to the tax into a non-interest-bearing account with the central bank. If the firm subsequently invests when advised to do so by the Labour Market Board, the entire cost of the investment can be charged to the reserve, the fraction deposited with the central bank being released at the same time. In addition, the firms get a further 10 per cent. investment credit which can be charged against taxable income. The assets purchased and charged against the investment reserve are not eligible for depreciation allowances. The net effect, from the point of view of the firm, of the opportunity to invest out of the investment reserve is equivalent to a 100 per cent. initial allowance plus a 10 per cent. investment allowance. The principal difference between the investment reserve scheme and a combination of investment and initial allowances is that the investment reserve is released at the time the investment is made, and is in effect a remission of taxes that have been paid in prior years. The initial and investment allowances, by contrast, only result in a reduction in taxes at the end of the current year, and do nothing even at that time to increase the cash flow of firms not currently paying taxes.[4] There are additional features of the Swedish system that make it attractive for firms to take part and reduce the possibility of withdrawal of funds from the reserve at times other than those recommended by the Labour Market Board.[5]

Since firms must join the investment reserve scheme in advance of making investments out of the reserve, the policy authorities have a better idea of the identity and capacity of the participating firms than they would under the other tax incentive measures described in

[1] Other Western countries which have an investment reserve system include Finland and Norway. See Moore [1963], pp. 40–1, for a brief description of their schemes. For analysis of the Swedish scheme and its effects, see Canarp [1963], Mildner and Scott [1962], and Sandberg [1963].

[2] Forty per cent. of the year's profits was the maximum allowed allocation to the reserve in the years prior to 1961. The restriction was removed in 1961.

[3] As of 1964, the marginal tax rate was 49 per cent., while only 46 per cent. of the reserve allocation had to be deposited with the central bank. This meant that participating firms received an interest-free loan of 3 per cent. of the amount deposited in the reserve.

[4] It would, of course, be possible, as suggested in Subsection (5) above, to design a system of investment allowances and taxes applicable to all firms at the time the investment outlays were made, but it would thereby differ from those systems which have actually been used.

[5] For example, unauthorized withdrawals may be subject to a 10 per cent. tax.

this chapter. In addition, since firms cannot draw from the reserves without making application for specific projects, those directing policy can be kept continuously informed of changes in the expected volume and composition of capital expenditures. If only certain sectors are expected to operate at less than capacity, withdrawals from the reserves may be restricted to projects of a particular type.

Because the value of an initial allowance of a given size is relatively greater for projects whose normal allowable depreciation is small, the bulk (over 80 per cent.) of the applications for use of the Swedish reserves have been for the construction of buildings. This, of course, is not a necessary feature of the reserve system, since the benefits could be altered so as to establish rough equivalence between assets subject to different depreciation allowances.

In general, the investment reserve system provides a more flexible and more powerful means of influencing investment than do any of the existing systems of initial allowances, investment allowances and taxes. It can apparently provide a pattern of investment incentives and disincentives that is specifically related to the regional, industrial, and cyclical distribution of investment and employment.

(7) Measures to influence investment in inventories

Since inventory investment has been perhaps the least stable component of total investment, we should pay some attention to policies which might have a steadying influence. In Sweden there is a modified form of a subsidy for investment in inventories in times of less than full employment, inasmuch as inventory write-downs can be charged to investment reserves. However, since the reserves can more advantageously be used for the purchase of buildings than for writing down inventories,[1] the impact on inventories has been slight.

An inventory tax or subsidy would affect the marginal efficiency of investment in inventories in the same way as an investment allowance or tax affects the profitability of investment in plant and equipment. The object of such measures would presumably be to offset artificially exaggerated changes in expectations that lead to destabilizing fluctuations in inventories. Current knowledge of the expectations governing inventory decisions is not thorough enough to allow the

---

[1] The advantage in favour of buildings arises because the normal depreciation process for buildings is a slow one, while inventory write-downs can normally be expensed in the year they occur. Both uses of the investment reserve receive the 10 per cent. investment credit.

conclusion that there is a recurring pattern of destabilizing changes in desired inventories which could be offset by a pattern of taxes and subsidies.

Perhaps the greatest difficulties with measures to affect inventory investment are administrative rather than conceptual. Among related firms operating in different countries the ownership of raw materials, work in process, or finished goods may often be arranged as a matter of convenience. It is to be expected that measures designed to encourage inventory investment in one country would lead to stocks of goods being transferred to the control and ownership of that firm without there being any related changes in the volume of production and employment. For the majority of firms whose dealings with foreign parent companies or affiliates are not at arm's length, it is difficult to see how measures to influence inventory investment could be designed so as to accomplish their purposes.

We have examined several of the measures of economic policy which may be used to affect the aggregate level of investment, and assessed their suitability in conditions where there is imperfect knowledge of the future requirements of economic policy.

The next four chapters deal in more detail with specific policy measures, and attempt to assess evidence of their effects on the behaviour of large Canadian corporations.

6

TAX ALLOWANCES FOR DEPRECIATION

CHANGES in the tax regulations governing depreciation allowances have been suggested for two rather separate reasons. On the one hand, it has been suggested that periodic alterations may be useful in stabilizing investment, and on the other that the acceleration of depreciation allowances as a long-term measure would be a reform likely to increase the volume of investment over time.

We shall consider these two types of depreciation change as quite separate issues. Section A will deal with temporary changes in depreciation provisions done either on a regular countercyclical basis or to give a temporary fillip to investment in a particular region or industry. Section B considers the arguments that have been advanced for making a once-for-all change in the income-tax law to permit a faster write-off of capital expenditures against taxable income. The two types of change are treated independently, although there are some points where the issues merge. For example, Section B discusses long-run changes in depreciation provisions. Although such discussions seldom refer to countercyclical changes in depreciation rules, the nature of the basic depreciation rules does affect the scope that exists for influencing the timing of investment by making periodic changes in depreciation allowances.

A. COUNTERCYCLICAL CHANGES IN DEPRECIATION RULES

This section considers separately two sorts of countercyclical depreciation measure that have been used in Canada since 1950. One sort of change is deferment of depreciation, as used in 1951 and 1966. The other is temporary acceleration of depreciation, as evidenced by several separate policy changes in 1961 and 1963. Both types of change took place within the general depreciation system which has been in use in Canada since 1949. The basic system uses various declining balance depreciation rates to determine the maximum depreciation expense allowed to be set against income for the purposes of calculating the amount of corporation income tax payable. Fixed assets are entered in the firm's accounts (for tax purposes) at their actual cost to the firm, and each year a specified percentage of the undepreciated cost of the assets in each asset 'pool' may be charged against income. When assets are sold, the amount received for the asset on disposal or the original cost of the asset to the firm (whichever is the lesser) is removed from the appropriate fixed-asset pool. Firms are allowed to claim less than the maximum allowable depreciation, since the regulations only set an upper limit to the amount of depreciation which may be claimed in a particular year. There are many different asset classes, each with its own maximum rate of depreciation. The most important classes, and the basic declining balance depreciation rates which have applied to them since 1949 are as follows:

		Maximum rate
Class 2	—Oil and gas pipelines, electrical generating equipment	6%
Class 3	—Buildings (except frame buildings, for which the rate is 10%)	5%
Class 8	—Machinery and equipment, furniture and fixtures	20%
Class 10	—Motor vehicles, mining and logging equipment, oil and gas well equipment	30%

On several occasions since 1950, these rates have been altered temporarily for some classes of assets purchased by certain firms. In assessing the relative importance of the various changes, it is necessary to make assumptions about the ways in which the changes would impinge upon decisions; in particular, about the methods used to assess investment projects and the assumptions made by firms about future tax rates and about the duration of the measures. The main effect of taxation changes related to depreciation allowances is to alter the timing rather than the total amount of taxes paid, assuming that the changes are temporary. (Section B will discuss long-term changes in depreciation rules.) The present value of a depreciation acceleration or deferment is therefore heavily dependent upon the discount rate used in evaluating investment projects. In the extreme case, firms which do not use any form of time discounting when evaluating investment projects attach no explicit value to a change in the timing of tax payments. *Taxation and Investment* [pp. 152–8] contains comparisons of various depreciation policies according to discounted present value, internal rate of return, and other means of evaluating investment projects. In this chapter only present value comparison of the various depreciation policies is presented, in Table 6.1. The argument of earlier chapters suggests that, if the appropriate discount rates are used, a present-value expression indicates reasonably well the relative power of the various depreciation policies. It is still necessary to realize that the actual decision rules used by firms do influence the impacts of policy changes. This fact became obvious during the course of the interviews with large firms, and was useful in interpreting the answers to the Royal Commission on Taxation questionnaire dealing with the 1961 depreciation changes. The results of that survey are reported in some detail in *Taxation and Investment* [pp. 159–66]; this chapter will merely allude to the evidence.

(1) *Deferment of depreciation*

(a) *1951 deferment.* Included in the 1951 budget was a provision that certain classes of capital expenditures, after April 1951, were not to be eligible for any depreciation until four years had passed. By late 1951 there was some easing of inflationary pressure and additional exemptions were granted; by the end of 1952 regular depreciation allowances were again available for all assets, including those purchased during the deferment period. The survey conducted in 1963 for the Taxation Commission did not ask about the effects of these provisions, and executives interviewed in 1963 were often surprised to find that depreciation had been deferred in post-war times, and were in no cases prepared to provide reliable evidence about the effects. The reliability of the available data depends on the nature of the definition of the classes of assets made subject to deferred depreciation. If the asset class definitions were not altered by firms to any significant extent (it is likely that they were), the evidence from an investment intentions survey indicated a 22 per cent. decline from 1951 to 1952 in the volume of investment not eligible for depreciation allowances compared to a 27 per cent. increase in the volume of investment made on the basis of certificates of eligibility for depreciation.[1] There is little that can be done to interpret this evidence. Table 6.1[2] shows the present value effect of the deferment on the assumption that those making decisions about 1951 expenditures believed that 1951 investment (of the sort not eligible for certificates of exemption) would not receive any depreciation allowance until the specified four year period had passed. As it turned out, such a belief was mistaken,

---

[1] For a fuller account of 1951 deferment and its effects, see Richard Goode [1957], Benjamin Higgins [1954], and M. W. Sharp [1953].

[2] See pp. 126–7.

as even the assets purchased when the deferment was in effect received depreciation allowances by the end of 1952.

(b) *1966 deferment*. In his 1966 budget speech, the Minister of Finance announced that certain classes of fixed assets purchased between 29 March 1966 and 1 October 1967 would receive restricted depreciation allowances in the three-year period following acquisition. Among the asset classes listed above, the rates on buildings, machinery, and equipment (classes 3 and 8) were reduced by one-half, while the rate on class 10 assets was changed from 30 per cent. to 20 per cent. for each of the three years in the deferment period. The calculations in Table 6.1 have been made on the assumption that the 1951 experience was remote enough that firms believed that the three-year deferment period would be applied as announced in the Budget Address. The 1966 deferment has an extra feature which presumably gives it more impact on the timing of expenditures. In 1951 the period of application of the measure was not announced, while the 1966 change was said in advance to apply only to expenditures made between 29 March 1966 and 1 October 1967.[1] Assuming that decision-makers believed that the deferment would apply to all and only expenditures made before October 1967, the power of the measure to induce postponement of expenditures was greater than it would have been if firms had expected the deferment to apply to expenditures made over a longer period of time. The calculations in Table 6.1 take no account of this particular feature of the 1966 deferment, as they only compare the present value of depreciation allowances for a given asset purchased in the deferment period with the present value of the normal depreciation allowances.

(2) *Accelerated depreciation*

(a) *1961 changes*. Regulation 1108, which became operative on 1 January 1961, provided for depreciation at double the usual rates in the year of purchase, with the normal rate being applicable in subsequent years. The provision was in force until 1 January 1964, and applied to all depreciable assets required to produce goods new to Canada or to one of the specified surplus manpower areas. The second change, Regulation 1109, was designed to encourage re-equipment and modernization by providing a 50 per cent. increase of depreciation in the year of purchase. The measure was in force

[1] In March 1967, the deferment was removed for all assets purchased after 31 March 1967.

TABLE 6.1

Change in depreciation provision	Present value of the acceleration (+) or deferment (−), expressed as a percentage of the initial cost of the depreciable assets. A 50% corporation income-tax rate is assumed in all the examples		
	If the target rate of return used for discounting is:		
	(a) 5%	(b) 10%	(c) 15%
Effect on Class 8 assets of the 1951 deferment, had the measure been anticipated by firms to be carried out as originally announced. Depreciation rate of 20% on the declining balance deferred for four years and then started on the same basis	−7·1%	−10·6%	−12·2%
Effect of 1966 deferment on Class 3 assets. Depreciation rate of 5% on the declining balance deferred for 3 years and then started again on the same basis	−3·4%	−4·1%	−4·3%
Effect of 1966 deferment on Class 8 assets. Depreciation rate of 20% on the declining balance deferred for 3 years and then started again on the same basis	−5·5%	−8·3%	−9·8%
Effect of 1966 measure on Class 8 assets which were eligible for the 1963 acceleration. Depreciation rate 50% straight line changed to 25% straight line	−4·3%	−6·3%	−7·1%
Depreciation rate of 5% on the declining balance doubled to 10%	+8·3%	+8·3%	+7·5%
Effect of Regulation 1108, 1961, on Class 3 assets, including most buildings. (See Section A (2) (a) for details.) Depreciation rate of 5% raised to 10% for the first year only, thereafter reverting to 5% on the declining balance	+1·2%	+1·5%	+1·6%
Effect of Regulation 1109, 1961, on Class 3 assets. (See Section A (2) (a) for details.) Depreciation rate of 5% raised to 7½% for the first year only, thereafter reverting to 5% on the declining balance	+0·6%	+0·7%	+0·8%

TABLE 6.1—*continued*

Change in depreciation provision	*Present value of the acceleration (+) or deferment (−), expressed as a percentage of the initial cost of the depreciable assets. A 50% corporation income-tax rate is assumed in all the examples*		
	If the target rate of return used for discounting is:		
	(a) 5%	(b) 10%	(c) 15%
Effect on Class 3 assets of 1963 measures providing accelerated depreciation for new manufacturing or processing businesses in areas of slower growth. (See Section A (2) (b) for details.)			
Depreciation rate of 5% on the declining balance changed to 20% straight line	+18·3%	+21·3%	+21·0%
Depreciation rate of 20% on the declining balance raised to 40%	+4·4%	+6·7%	+7·8%
Effect of Regulation 1108, 1961, on Class 8 assets, including most machinery and equipment. (See Section A (2) (a) for details.)			
Depreciation rate of 20% on the declining balance raised to 40% for the first year, and 20% on the declining balance thereafter	+1·9%	+3·0%	+3·7%
Effect of Regulation 1109, 1961, on Class 8 assets. (See Section A (2) (a) for details.)			
Depreciation rate of 20% on the declining balance changed to 30% for the first year and 20% on the declining balance thereafter	+1·0%	+1·5%	+1·9%
Effect of 1963 measures to provide accelerated depreciation for all Class 8 assets purchased by corporations with the necessary degree of Canadian ownership and control. (See Section A (2) (b) for details.)			
Depreciation rate of 20% on the declining balance changed to 50% straight line	+6·5%	+10·1%	+12·0%
Depreciation rate of 20% on the declining balance raised to 100%	+7·6%	+12·1%	+14·9%

between 21 June 1961 and 1 April 1964. Although available for all classes of fixed assets, Regulation 1109 only applied to the amount by which the current year's expenditures exceeded (the lesser of) those of the previous year or the average outlays of the three preceding years. The effects of both provisions on the discounted cash flow profitability of buildings and equipment are outlined in Table 6.1. Since the higher rates applied only to the first year's depreciation allowance, the present value impact of these measures was substantially smaller than that of either of the deferments. Despite the difficulties in interpreting mail surveys not subject to follow-up interviews, the answers to a Taxation Commission mail questionnaire supported the case study evidence that neither of the 1961 measures was thought by firms to have had a noticeable influence on their investment expenditures.

(b) *1963 changes.* The 1963 budget proposed that machinery and equipment (class 8 assets only) purchased, by certain firms, in the two years commencing 14 June 1963, should receive 50 per cent. straight-line depreciation and also that new manufacturing and processing businesses in designated areas of slower growth should be allowed 50 per cent. straight-line depreciation on machinery and equipment, and 20 per cent. straight line on buildings (class 3). There was considerable controversy about both measures, since the first was originally to be available only to corporations having a 25 per cent. beneficial Canadian ownership and a proportionate number of Canadian directors, while the second was available only for new businesses in specified localities. In both cases there were difficulties in establishing workable definitions of the classes of eligible firms; to such an extent that many firms were not sure whether or not the proposals would ever become law (they were introduced by a minority government) and, if so, whether or not they would apply to a particular firm. This should serve as a reminder of the primary difficulty standing in the way of accurate econometric assessment of the effects of this sort of new policy—even if a rough measure of the power of the policy can be derived from calculations such as those in Table 6.1, there is no general way of allowing for special factors influencing the expectations which firms have about the probability that a policy will be carried out as originally announced. And it is equally difficult to estimate the extent to which firms have on various occasions anticipated policies similar to those eventually announced.

The class of firms eligible for the accelerated depreciation granted to firms with a degree of Canadian ownership and control was, on

8 July 1963, broadened to include any firm whose shares were listed for sale on a Canadian stock exchange, as long as not more than 75 per cent. of the shares were owned by a single foreign shareholder and his associates. As revealed by the case-study evidence [*Taxation and Investment* pp. 169–72], the primary impact of the measure appeared to be on the timing of investment outlays; since firms were accelerating expenditures so as to get machinery and equipment in place before the scheduled expiration of the incentive in June 1965. However, the April 1965 budget extended the deadline until the end of December 1966. The March 1966 budget announced that the incentive would be allowed to expire at the end of 1966. Business officials interviewed in 1963 were generally of the opinion that the announced two year duration of the incentive was likely to be the actual duration. After the 1965 extension of the expiry date, it is likely that firms increased the subjective probabilities which they attached to a further extension of the incentive, and hence reduced the extent to which expenditures were accelerated so as to fall within the announced period.

Although the March 1966 budget did not explicitly cancel the 1963 measure, the reaffirmation of the December 1966 expiry date was coupled with the announcement of a depreciation deferment to apply to all assets purchased after March 1966. Thus machinery and equipment, which is normally subject to depreciation at a rate of 20 per cent. on the declining balance, received 25 per cent. straight line depreciation if purchased between March and December 1966, and 10 per cent. on the declining balance (for the first four years) if purchased between January and October 1967. These cycles in permitted depreciation rates are marginal in that changes in the rules are applicable only for new assets purchased in the period for which the rates apply. The effective size of the incentive on the timing and amount of expenditures made under a particular set of rules depends on current expectations about the rates which are likely to apply in the future.

B. LONG TERM CHANGES IN DEPRECIATION RULES

In this section we shall assess the likely effects of a permanent depreciation change on the ranking of alternative investment programmes. For illustrative purposes we shall assume that the reform is an acceleration of depreciation, although a postponement, magnification, or any other alteration could be analysed in the same way.

First, we shall examine the effects of permanent acceleration on investment programmes with different characteristics, and then briefly mention the possible effects of the reform on the cyclical distribution of investment outlays.

Depreciation allowances govern the timing of tax payments. The two extremes of cost depreciation are immediate write-off, which makes before- and after-tax project rates of return identical,[1] and 'final reckoning' depreciation, under which no depreciation could be claimed until the asset was sold or scrapped. By postponing tax payments, any acceleration of depreciation reduces the PV of tax payments, and increases the PV of investment programmes to an extent governed by the degree of acceleration, the cost of the relevant assets, and the appropriate discount rate. Since the increase in the PV of investment programmes varies with the amount of expenditure on fixed assets, the reform would tend to alter the PV ranking of programmes in favour of programmes with larger amounts of expenditure on those assets whose depreciation is accelerated. Thus, if the discount rates are constant, the acceleration of depreciation will lead to higher ranking for the more capital intensive programmes. But we must also consider the effects of the reform on the discount rates. If the reform changes the relevant values of the cost of new funds or the riskiness of the programme, then a simple discounting of non-risk-standardized cash flow estimates by standard-risk discount rates will not measure the relevant present value of the investment programme. What effect is the reform likely to have on riskiness and on the share market's discount rates? The effects on the variability of earnings depend crucially on which definition of risk is relevant to investment decisions. The alternatives include:

(1) Risk measured by the deviations of realized cash flows from their expected values

With this measure of risk, there is no *a priori* reason to suppose that the cash flows net of the tax will be either more or less predictable after the tax reform. Naturally, if there was uncertainty about either the nature or the duration of the reform, then the estimates of the standard deviations of the distributions would be higher.

---

[1] To ensure the equality of before- and after-tax rates of return it is necessary that all cash outlays, whether on capital or current account, lead to an immediate reduction in tax payments (or, where the net cash flow is negative, a cash payment from the government).

(2) *Risk measured by the deviations of cash flows from their trend values*

In this case the acceleration would decrease the relevant estimates of risk if it were true that the firm's capital expenditures were large enough and lumpy enough that the years of heavy capital expenditures were also the years of the lowest positive values of cash flows. These circumstances are plausible, as the cash generated by operations minus capital outlays is lowest in periods of greatest capital expenditures. Thus, the reform is likely, if anything, to decrease the riskiness of investment programmes whose riskiness is measured in this way.

(3) *Risk measured by variations in accounting profits about their trend values*

Since this measure of risk depends entirely on the accounting conventions adopted by the firm, it may not reflect the risk assessments of the management group. But in circumstances where the share market has little information about the subjective profit expectations of the management group, the market valuation of shares often depends heavily on the profit history of firms as revealed by their accounting records. The effects of depreciation reform on the variability of accounting profits depends on the exact accounting procedures adopted by firms. There are at least three distinct possibilities:

(*a*) Accounting profits using actual taxes paid as the tax-expense item, and calculating depreciation for accounting purposes on some basis not affected by the tax reform. In these cases the effect of the reform is to alter accounting profits by the amount of the change in actual tax payments. To the extent that capital expenditures take place in years of abnormally high profits, and are low in years of low profits, the reform acts to increase the variability of accounting profits.

(*b*) Accounting profits based on depreciation and tax-expense figures calculated without regard to the accelerated depreciation. The reduction in cash outflow for tax payments is thus accounted for not by a reduction in the tax-expense item in the profit-and-loss statement, but by a credit to a balance-sheet account 'tax reductions applicable to future years'. In these cases the acceleration has no effect on a measure of risk based on accounting profits. Of course, the reform's effects on cash

K

flow may reduce the effective cost of external funds. (See (4) below.)

(c) Accounting profits based on actual taxes paid, and on tax depreciation allowances. In these cases the reform decreases accounting profits in years of abnormally high capital expenditures. To the extent that these years would otherwise be the years of highest accounting profits, the reform would reduce the variability of profits about their trend. This case is just the reverse of (a) above.

(4) *Present value affected by changes in cost of external funds not related to risk*

Most of the movements in discount rates which are not independent of the actions of a particular firm are functions of the parameters of the cash-flow distributions, and therefore have already been considered above. There is one possible further factor affecting discount rates which might be mentioned. It may be the case that institutional rigidities in the financial system are such that there are substantial differences between borrowing and lending rates on funds with the same risk characteristics, or that the cost of raising new funds is a sharply increasing function of the amounts being raised in a particular time period. Either or both of these situations can exist because outsiders have less optimistic cash-flow estimates than do the members of management, discussed under (3) above. Here we are concerned with rising costs of new external funds which are independent of anyone's estimates of the characteristics of the firm's investment programme. If there are such limitations on the quantity of new external funds which the firm can obtain in any particular period, and differences between borrowing and lending rates are large enough to make financing in advance of need a costly procedure, then if the depreciation reform stabilizes the net cash requirements of a programme, the appropriate discount rates are lowered, and the *PV* of the programme correspondingly raised. The depreciation reform is likely to stabilize the cash requirement of a programme if the years of greatest capital expenditures are also the years of greatest net cash requirements (as in (2) above), assuming that the acceleration involves at least some increase in the depreciation allowance available in the year the assets are purchased.

In the light of the variety of possible effects of the tax reform on cash flows and discount rates, we cannot easily reach categorical conclusions about the net effects on *PV*. However, since risk was not necessarily increased according to any of the measures of risk examined, and was probably decreased according to most of them, the net effects of the reform are probably to decrease the riskiness of programmes with larger and more variable capital expenditures. Under certain assumptions about the correlation between accounting profits and capital expenditures, there may be downward pressures on discount rates, in certain types of capital markets, for reasons not connected with characteristics of the firm's alternative cash-flow distributions.

Thus, under most assumptions about the effects of the reform on the cash-flow distributions and discount rates, the acceleration of depreciation allowances will affect the rankings of alternative programmes in favour of those with greater investment in depreciable assets. What qualifications are necessary to this conclusion if we take some account of the conditions of the aggregate supply of finance? Whether the tax deferment was financed by government borrowing or taxation, the immediate effect would be to increase interest rates and market discount rates. Would these effects be sufficient to cancel out the positive effects outlined previously? Apparently not, as the positive effects served to re-rank programmes in favour of those with more outlays on depreciable assets, while the increases in interest and market discount rates would apply to all programmes (and the borrowings of individuals and governments) without discrimination against those with more capital expenditures. Thus, the programmes chosen are likely to be more capital intensive,[1] although it is within the realm of possibility that the effects of the market supply price of funds would be so marked that the chosen programmes were so reduced in size as to contain a smaller total of capital expenditures.[2]

Finally, some mention should be made of the likely effects of depreciation reform on the stability of investment. If we suppose that

---

[1] These conclusions are more definite than those of Hall [1960, Chapter VI] because they admit the possibility of alternative production techniques with different capital intensities, and take account of the effects of the tax reform on the measures of risk. Hall [1960, p. 127] assumes that the riskiness of a programme depends only on the fraction that is in capital goods.

[2] The possibility is very slight, as the government would have to be a borrower regarded as so much inferior to private borrowers that the increment of public debt was considered a more risky element in private portfolios than the private debt it would be replacing.

firms do face a rising supply price of external funds in any given year, and that the years of largest capital expenditures are also the years of greatest demand for external funds, then the rising supply price of funds serves to encourage the smoothing of investment outlays over time (assuming, once again, that borrowing and lending rates differ enough that financing in advance of need has a net cost). Since the acceleration of depreciation allowances decreases tax payments in the years of peak investment, it thereby reduces the smoothing effects of the rising supply price of funds. Thus the reform provides relatively greater relief for firms with lumpy capital expenditure programmes. To the extent that the lumps in individual firms' expenditures are correlated, the reform likewise tends to increase the magnitude of fluctuations in aggregate investment outlays. In common with several of the other tax provisions analysed in Chapter 5, long-term acceleration of depreciation increases the *PV* only of those programmes that have currently taxable income against which to write off the depreciation allowances. In a dynamic context, where much industrial growth is generated by small and fast-growing firms, the acceleration of depreciation is an investment incentive whose advantages accrue primarily to those firms with stable flows of taxable income.

Since its effects are unevenly distributed, and it is likely to increase the cyclical instability of investment, accelerated depreciation is probably less appropriate as a permanent investment incentive than would be an investment credit or investment reserve scheme, particularly as the reserve systems are more easily adapted for stabilizing investment.

7

MONETARY POLICY

THIS chapter continues the analysis, started in Chapter 5, of the effects of monetary policy on the selection of investment programmes. The outline, in Section A, of the ways in which monetary policy may impinge on investment behaviour is followed, in Section B, by material describing the changes which took place in Canada, between 1954 and 1963, in various aspects of credit conditions. These sections provide the necessary background for the presentation and interpretation of the Royal Commission on Banking and Finance (R.C.B.F.) survey results in Sections C and D.

A. EFFECTS OF MONETARY POLICY ON INVESTMENT BEHAVIOUR

Monetary policy influences investment decisions by altering the characteristics of the feasible investment programmes so as to change their relative attractiveness. If the attractiveness of an investment programme is determined (at least in part) by its present value, then monetary policy influences investment by altering the number and present value ranking of feasible investment programmes. The present value of a programme is the sum of risk-standardized cash flows discounted by the share market's discount rates. How does monetary policy affect these components?

The cash-flow distributions, as defined in Chapter 1, are net of all payments to and from lenders; they are thus the cash flows to the equity shareholders, so that their present value can be found by using the share market's discount rates. The cash-flow distributions of investment programmes may therefore be affected by monetary policy influencing either the returns from investment projects, or by altering the cost of debt finance. The returns from the investment projects may be affected if credit conditions influence or are expected to influence the demand for the firm's products. In some cases, firms anticipate that monetary policy will affect the demand for their products, and revise sales estimates accordingly. These explicitly recognized demand effects are likely to be detected by surveys such as the one reported in this chapter. Another way that monetary policy can alter cash-flow distributions is by affecting the current flow of orders for the firm's products; changes in current sales may then lead to revisions of sales forecasts without the firm ever attributing the changes to monetary policy. These unrecognized impacts of monetary policy cannot be measured by survey techniques of the type employed by the R.C.B.F.

Since the cash-flow distributions are net of payments to and from lenders they will be affected by changes in the costs of various sorts of borrowed funds. If current interest rates rise, the net cash inflow from any investment programme will decline to the extent that the programme involves net borrowing at the current rate of interest. The cash-flow distributions for future periods will be influenced if the programme involves long-term borrowing at the current rates. If the programme involves net borrowing in future periods, the expected cash flows will be altered to the extent that the current change in interest rates affects the firm's expectations about rates of interest in future periods. An increase in interest rates leads to an increase in the expected cash inflows from those investment pro- grammes involving net lending by the firm at higher current or ex- pected interest rates. As was shown in Section (2) of the Appendix to Chapter 1, higher current and expected future interest rates reduce the amount of borrowing that is optimal for any given set of investment projects, and reduces (on certain assumptions) the optimal amount of capital expenditures. That discussion was couched entirely in a one- period framework involving no costs of adjustment to new informa- tion.

These conclusions are less clear-cut when the investment process is recognized as a continuing movement towards an ever-changing set of goals. The firm is always altering plans as price and market expectations change; but the extent of the alterations is affected by the costs of chopping and changing, and the likelihood of further new information becoming available in the future. The effects of any particular change in a current interest rate will depend on its impact on expectations about future values; thus a movement of rates to a new level which is thought to have some permanence will affect the cash-flow distributions far more than any movement thought to be a temporary deviation from the expected average of future interest rates.

Interest rates are not the only important aspect of monetary policy. Quantitative restrictions on the amounts of funds available from particular sources exist whenever there is an excess demand for loans at the market rate of interest. The effects of credit rationing on the present values of alternative investment programmes depend upon the types of credit rationed, the nature of the available investment projects, and the range of alternative sources of funds. If no alternative sources of funds are available, and the sole source of funds is restricted by monetary policy, the effect of the credit restriction is to make unfeasible those programmes requiring more cash outlays than can be financed within the budget constraint.

If the existence of a quantitative restriction on the amount of funds available is only apparent when the constraint is a binding one, we should expect to find that the easing of credit restriction would be less noticed by firms than the previous tightening. If firms expect funds to be available at the market rates, as a matter of course, then if funds are not available a reason will be sought; while the fact that they are available would be treated as the normal situation rather than evidence of credit ease.

Quantitative restrictions on the amounts of debt finance available may be regarded as ruling out all those investment programmes whose cash-flow distributions assume more than the permitted amount of borrowing. The other impacts of monetary policy described above may be regarded as acting on the estimates of the characteristics of the cash-flow distributions of alternative investment programmes, each with its own set of projects and pattern of debt financing. Finally, we must consider the effects which credit conditions may have on the discount rates used to calculate the present values of alternative investment programmes.

The discount rates which are used to establish the share-market valuation of an investment programme are assumed to depend on the characteristics of the subjective probability distributions of cash flow. But we must not ignore the relationship between the share market and the markets for other financial assets. Just as the optimum financing for a given set of projects involves less borrowing (and more equity financing) when interest rates are high relative to share market discount rates, so there may be expected to be some switching on the other side of the market. Holders of financial asset portfolios may be expected to increase their demand for bonds relative to shares if interest rates rise relative to share market discount rates. These possibilities for switching on both sides of the market suggest that any changes in credit conditions will be reflected in the prices of all financial assets. The extent (and direction) of the effects of monetary policy on equity prices will depend on the extent to which bonds and equities are substitutes in various portfolios. It is not easy to distinguish these general effects from the particular impacts already described.

That they are separate is easy to see, for the changes in cash-flow distributions would affect the present values (and PV ranking) of investment programmes even if the discount rates applied to a given (risk-standardized) cash flow were unchanged. The general changes in equity prices that may be expected to accompany general changes in bond prices may not have substantial impact on the PV ranking of alternative investment programmes. It may be recalled from the multi-period framework in Chapter 1 that there is a separate discount rate linking each pair of adjacent periods within the investment horizon. Cyclical variations in equity prices (like cyclical variations in interest rates) may not change much the expected values of share market discount rates linking future periods. The correct subjective interpretation of temporary shifts in equity prices may be either that all subjective cash-flow distributions have shifted (more or less uniformly) for each period, or that the discount rate linking the current period to the first future period has changed markedly. In neither case are there likely to be important changes in the PV ranking of alternative investment programmes, although the number of feasible programmes may be altered. In particular, programmes involving the current issue of equities for the purchase of capital assets with future returns may have present values which drop below zero as equity prices generally fall. However, the majority of preferred investment programmes would not shift into or out of the feasible region as equity prices vary in a cyclical manner. If the ranking of programmes is not markedly influenced by cyclical variations in share prices, then such variations are not likely to have effects on investment decisions. It is difficult to sort out these cyclical variations in the general demand for equities from the changes in share prices brought about by changes in cash-flow distributions, such as those described in the first paragraphs of this section. Thus the evidence, including that from the interviews, is difficult to interpret. Since the share market's implicit discount rates are not related in an easily explicable way to the cost and availability of debt finance, the R.C.B.F. questionnaire and interview survey concentrated on asking about the effects of the more recognizable features of credit conditions. The next section describes these aspects in more detail, so as to illuminate the subsequent discussion of the survey and its results.

B. CHANGES IN CREDIT CONDITIONS BETWEEN 1954 AND 1962

Since the various aspects of credit conditions[1] have different effects on the ranking of alternative investment programmes, analysis of the effects of monetary policy depends on our being able to specify the changes which have taken place in the relevant measures of the cost and availability of funds. By the same token, when evidence is collected about the effects of monetary policy, we should try to establish which were the important dimensions of credit conditions in particular cases.

The most important sources[2] of outside funds for corporations include borrowing from the chartered banks, bonds, commercial paper,[3] trade credit, and equity issues. Credit conditions, broadly defined, are affected by the price and availability of all these types of funds. Monetary policy may affect them in different ways, depending on the nature of open-market operations, and the efforts made to control various types of lending. The price of funds in foreign markets cannot be directly controlled by domestic monetary policy, but spot and forward exchange-rate policy, as well as exchange control and fiscal measures are possible supplements to domestic monetary policy.

Figures 8 to 11 indicate the movements between 1954 and 1962 in the prices of different types of finance available to corporations. As indices of the tightness of credit conditions, no set of price series is likely to be fully appropriate, as research has shown clearly that in

[1] The usage of 'credit conditions' as a term descriptive of the various aspects of monetary policy follows that of the Bank of Canada [1962] in submissions to the R.C.B.F. The approach was subsequently adopted by the Commission, and is discussed in Chapter 21 of their *Report*. The credit conditions approach is compared to its alternatives in Chapter II of *The Effects of Monetary Policy*.

[2] Table 7.6 in this chapter indicates the likelihood that firms in different size and industry groups used external funds of certain types between 1954 and 1962. See Table V.I of *Taxation and Investment* for an analysis of the quantities of funds obtained by a sample of large corporations, 1955–62. See also Chapter 2 of the R.C.B.F. *Report* for a discussion of the pattern of business financing during the period.

[3] As the term is used here, commercial paper refers to notes of a duration of one year or less issued in the firm's own name. This type of borrowing (and lending) by large firms has grown dramatically since 1958. The time series may be found on page 103 of the Bank of Canada *Statistical Summary-Supplement 1965*.

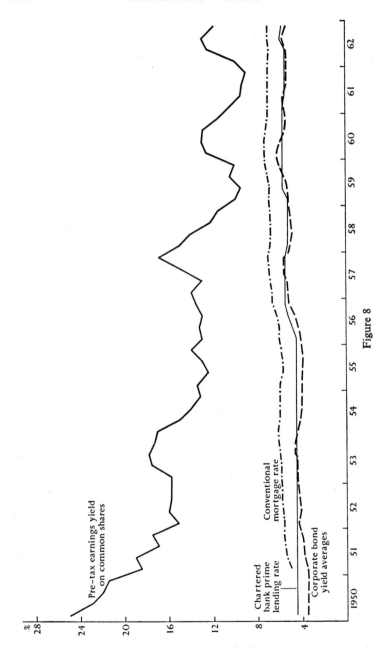

Figure 8

many cases funds were not available at the indicated prices. The treasury bill rate (Figure 9) is highly correlated with commercial paper rates; and the commercial paper rates usually move so as to leave no fringe of unsatisfied borrowers. The chartered bank prime lending rate (Figure 8), however, is not at all representative of the implicit cost of bank loans, as the degree of bank credit rationing varied considerably 1954–62. Since the liquid asset ratios of the chartered banks, during the 1954–62 period, were never as low as the agreed minimum, while their cash ratios have seldom been above the 8 per cent. minimum, there is no reliable excess reserves figure to use as an index of the availability of bank loans. The bank liquid assets series in Figure 9[1] does help to show the shifts during the period in the composition of the banks' portfolios. It may be presumed that, at any given level of interest rates, the banks were more likely to have rationed credit in periods when their liquid asset ratios were relatively low. In addition to putting pressure on bank reserves through open-market operations, the Bank of Canada also influences chartered bank lending by means of informal agreements.

The stickiness of bank deposit rates and the ceiling on bank-lending rates put limits on the powers of the chartered banks to expand their loans and deposits in times of high interest rates. The combination of open-market operations and informal agreements was responsible for quantitative restrictions on bank lending three times between 1954 and 1963. The following excerpts from the *Report* of the Royal Commission on Banking and Finance indicate roughly the extent and timing of the restraint during each of the three periods.

Either at the suggestion of the Bank of Canada or as a result of consultation among themselves, the banks have in each period of monetary restraint adopted a common loan policy and informed branches of the change at about the same time. The Bank of Canada can shorten the delay between the onset of monetary restraint and a move to effective restriction on loans either by pursuing its policies with unmistakable vigour or by bringing the banks together for discussions out of which a generally accepted policy emerges. A combination of the two methods is likely to bring the quickest results, as events in 1962 showed. In November 1955, the banks were called together very shortly after restraint on total bank assets began, and the first restrictive circulars went out almost immediately.

---

[1] The series shown in Figure 9 includes Government of Canada bonds and net foreign assets, while the post-1956 15 per cent. minimum liquidity ratio referred only to cash, day loans, and treasury bills.

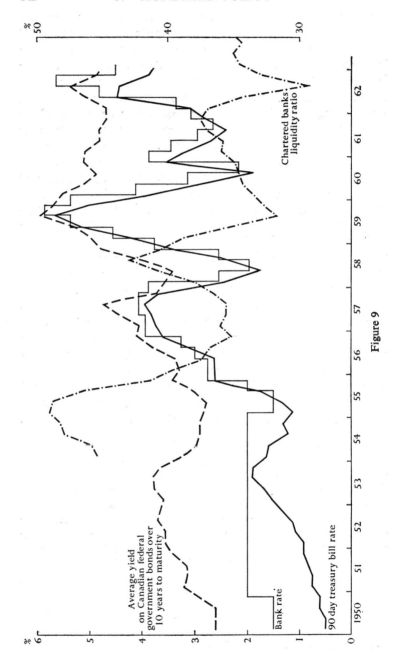

Figure 9

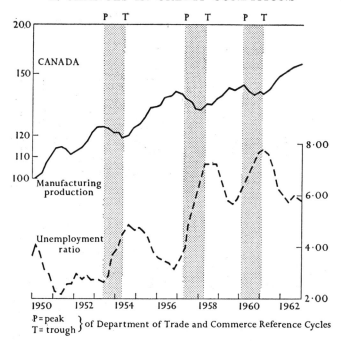

P = peak   } of Department of Trade and Commerce Reference Cycles
T = trough

Figure 10

However, central bank policy was not sufficiently restrictive to bring about an early or complete stop to loan increases. In 1959, on the other hand, the Bank of Canada restrained total bank assets with determination but did not take the lead in discussion with the banks and a full six months elapsed between the end of increases in the money supply at the end of 1958 and the banks' decision in May 1959 to adopt a more stringent lending policy. Loan increases came to a halt fairly shortly thereafter, in part because the banks' liquidity positions were by then seriously impaired.

Once the banks are brought to an alteration of course in their lending policy, they issue circulars urging managers to scrutinize credit applications more carefully and to do their best to persuade borrowers to keep their calls on lines of credit to a minimum. In the recent bouts of restraint the managers were also told to follow a freer policy in dealing with small accounts—personal borrowers and other accounts with lines of credit below $100,000. In addition to quite general lines of policy such as these, the banks have entered into specific agreements to restrict certain types of lending, sometimes at the suggestion of the Bank of Canada. . . .[1]

[1] R.C.B.F. *Report*, pp. 133–4.

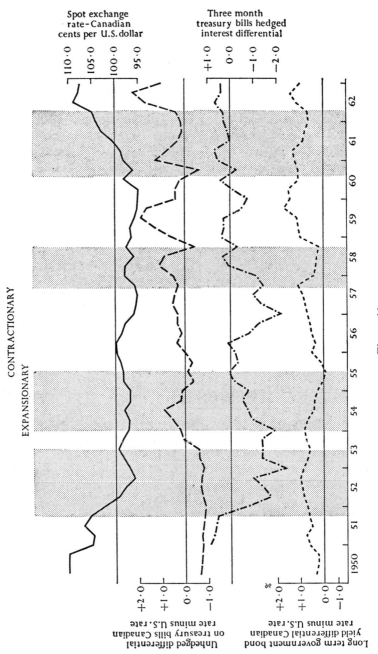

Figure 11

To provide a quantitative index of monetary policy as a whole, Johnson and Winder [1962] have proposed grouping months with similar rates of increase in either the money supply (currency plus demand deposits) or net chartered bank reserves. If the money supply version of their index is used to divide monetary policy into contractionary and expansionary phases, the results are as shown in Figure 11. Although the above excerpts from the R.C.B.F. *Report* indicate that Bank of Canada pressures on bank assets are not a uniformly reliable measure of central bank policy towards bank lending, the money supply index is a useful adjunct to the other measures of credit conditions. Either it or the bank liquid assets ratio in Figure 9 may provide the best measure of the availability of bank credit, although it should be possible to improve such an index by specific reference to bank circulars.

The attractiveness of foreign funds as a substitute for domestic borrowing is indicated in part by the interest differentials shown in Figure 11. Neither the short- nor the long-term interest differential tells the whole story. Short-term borrowing is generally fully hedged in the forward exchange market, so that the hedged short-term differential is the best measure of the incentive for short-term international capital movements. The willingness of firms to borrow abroad on a long-term basis is affected by exchange-rate expectations, which varied substantially during the period.

The availability of equity funds is not as closely linked with monetary policy, although Figure 8 does indicate a positive correlation in the quarter-to-quarter shifts in earnings yields on equity and interest yields on bonds. However, the contrary trends are responsible for a negative correlation of the year-to-year first differences in the two series.[1]

C. The Survey: Procedure and Results

One of the largest of the R.C.B.F. research studies was a survey, by mail and interview, of the effects of monetary policy on corporations. Since a full report of the survey has already been published, it is not necessary to present again the detailed interview results. The published report of the survey did not, however, analyse fully the results

[1] For one thing, the price of equities moves up in relation to that of bonds whenever there are more widespread expectations of inflation. In addition, both series are imperfect measures of the purchaser's expected yield on the asset, since the true yield is in the one case from dividends and capital gain, and in the other from interest plus changes in capital value.

of the mail questionnaire and follow-up interviews, a job which we shall undertake in this chapter. The mail survey included all firms with assets $5–90 million and a stratified random sample of 1076 firms in smaller size groups.[1] The 83 firms with assets over $90 million as at 31 December 1961 were interviewed without a prior mail survey. Interviews were also held with 231 firms which had responded to the mail questionnaire and approximately 100 which had not. The tables at the end of this chapter (pp. 160–72 ff.) refer to two groups of firms, Tables 7.2, 5, and 6 referring to the 1221 completed mail questionnaires, and Tables 7.1, 3, 4, and 7 including also the 83 interviewed firms with assets over $90 million. Tables 7.5 and 7.6, and part of Table 7.2 record the responses as they were shown on the questionnaires originally submitted. On the basis of an extensive programme of follow-up interviews designed to get more details about the questionnaire answers, Tables 7.1, 3, 4, and 7 were prepared showing the responses on a 'verified' basis. That is, adjustments were made to reflect the interviewer's judgement about the actual effects of changes in credit conditions on the behaviour of the interviewed firms.[2] It is only when the questionnaire evidence is converted to a 'verified' basis that information about the firms with assets over $90 million can be included, since the large firms were interviewed in the first instance. As is emphasized in *The Effects of Monetary Policy*, it is difficult to isolate the specific effects of changes in credit conditions on particular firms, and hence to classify, even after interviews, groups of firms whose behaviour was or was not influenced.[3] The

[1] The design of the survey is described in Chapter IV of *The Effects of Monetary Policy*, and in Appendix I of *Taxation and Investment*.

[2] The Tables to be found in Chapter VII of *The Effects of Monetary Policy* indicate the size class and industry distribution of follow-up interviews.

[3] The problems of interpreting the answers to a mail questionnaire, with special reference to the R.C.B.F. survey, are discussed in Appendix I of *Taxation and Investment* and in W. H. White [1966]. The importance of the follow-up interviews (and of the earlier pilot surveys) cannot be over-emphasized. William White [1966] has compiled a large list of ways in which the responders could have misinterpreted the mail questionnaire so as to bias downwards the number of answers indicating that monetary policy had influenced the firm's expenditures. Without a comprehensive programme of follow-up interviews (which revealed that the net bias caused by misinterpretation of the questions was actually the opposite of that suggested by White), there would have been no way of deciding what the survey evidence meant. The interviews (more than 400 in all) revealed that it is extremely difficult to use subjective interpretations of past decisions as a means of quantifying the impacts of monetary policy; but they also allowed us to find out exactly what the responders thought was meant by each of the queries on the mail questionnaire. Although the extended series of interviews helped to

same is true, perhaps to an even greater extent, of the estimates of the amount of capital expenditure postponed.

Tables 7.1 to 6 show some of the questionnaire responses analysed to show separately the industry, size group, and foreign ownership differentials. Tables 7.1, 2, 4, 5, and 6 show the percentage probability that a firm with particular size and industry characteristics was affected in the indicated way.

Table 7.3 estimates the expected amount of expenditures postponed by firms with different size industry, and ownership characteristics. Finally, Table 7.7 contains aggregate estimates, classified by industry, of the total amount of expenditure reduction by corporations in 1959 and 1962.

Table 7.7 was compiled directly from the survey data, while the other tables are derived from multivariate regressions allowing the influences of size, industry, and ownership to be separated. The coefficients were first estimated on the assumption that size, industry, and ownership influences were additive. That is, in the initial set of equations there were 13 industry dummy variables (1 less than the number of industries), 9 or 11 size variables (1 less than the number of size classes, which was 10 for the 1221 firms with assets below $90 million, and 12 for the 1304 firms covering all size classes), one ownership variable (which took the value 1 for each firm controlled outside Canada), and a constant term. If the regression equation is written

$$y = X\beta + u$$

the X matrix has 24 or 26 columns ($13 + 1 + 1 + 9$ or 11) and as many rows as there were firms in the sample (1221 or 1304). Any row of the matrix contained between one and four 1's; one in the constant term column, and possibly one in one of the industry columns, one of the size columns, and the foreign ownership column. A row with only a single 1 (which would, of course, be in the constant term column) identified a firm which is in the 'wholesale and retail trade' industry, of 'unknown' size, and 'controlled in Canada'. It was necessary to associate the constant term with firms having particular size, industry, and ownership characteristics so that the number of dummy variables would be less than the number of sub-classes. If each sub-class (i.e. each industry, and each size class) were given its own

eliminate most of the possible misinterpretations of the results, nothing much can be done, using the survey approach, to determine the extent to which monetary policy has had impacts which have not been recognized by decision makers.

L

dummy variable, the $X'X$ matrix would be singular, and the regression could not have been estimated.

Since the X matrix was composed entirely of 1's and 0's, the $X'X$ matrix was 24 × 24 or 26 × 26, its diagonal elements showing the number of firms in each size or industry group; and the off-diagonal elements showing the number of firms in each cross classification.

In each regression shown in Tables 7.1, 2, 4, 5, and 6, the y vector contains either 1221 or 1304 elements, each of which takes the value 0 if the firm was not affected, and 1 if it was. The constant terms in the original regression thus indicated the probability that firms in wholesale and retail trade, owned in Canada, and of unknown size, were affected in the specified way. The other β coefficients showed the effect of being in some other industry and size group on the probability of giving an affirmative answer to a particular question. The estimated probability for any particular firm was found by taking the constant term and then adding or subtracting industry, size group, and ownership components where appropriate.[1]

For the regressions whose results are shown in Table 7.3 the 1304 elements of the y vector took the value 0 if the firm did not alter its expenditures. If the firm did alter its expenditures, y indicates the number of thousands of dollars by which the firm's expenditures were reduced (because of the change in credit conditions) during the nine months following August 1959 or June 1962. The high values of $\bar{R}^2$ in these two regressions are due primarily to a few large expenditure changes concentrated in small industry and size groups.

Two refinements were made to this initial analysis, one to make the results more easily interpreted, and the other to improve the logic and explanatory power of the regressions.

The first change was made by converting the coefficients into

---

[1] It may be noted that the use of dichotomous dependent variables (i.e. all of the y's are either 0 or 1) means that the disturbances will be heteroscedastic. The estimated $\hat{y}$ might have been used to construct a diagonal matrix Ω^*, whose elements are $\hat{y}(1 - \hat{y})$, to re-estimate the β coefficients according to

$$\beta^* = (X'\Omega^{*-1}X)^{-1}(X'\Omega^{*-1}y),$$

e.g. Goldberger [1964], pp. 249–50. Since the heteroscedasticity does not introduce a bias in the estimates of the coefficients (although the estimates of the standard errors will be biased, e.g. Zellner and Lee [1965]), this alternative procedure was not considered to be worth the considerable extra computational costs of constructing the 1304 by 26 X matrix from the detailed survey data. The procedure used required only the 26 by 26 $X'X$ matrix showing the number of firms in each cross classification.

deviations from factor averages,[1] so that each industry, size class, or ownership element now shows the amount by which the probability for firms in, for example, mining, differs from the average probability for firms in all industries. The probability that a particular firm reacted in a certain way is found by taking the average probability for all firms, and adding or subtracting the industry, size group, and ownership deviations. These adjustments must be made for all firms except those in any sub-class for which, by chance, the probability is exactly equal to that for the entire group of 1221 or 1304 firms.

The second change was made because there appeared to be one major classification for which the additivity of size, industry, and ownership effects was implausible. The additivity assumption means that a single industry adjustment factor is used for all firms in, for example, the mining industry, regardless of their size and ownership. This makes it possible for an estimated probability to be negative. Suppose, for example, that no firms in the mining industry were affected, and neither were any foreign-controlled firms. If the number of firms which are both foreign-owned and in mining is small in relation to the numbers of foreign-owned firms, and of mining firms, the sum of the negative ownership and industry adjustment factors for the foreign-owned mining firms may be greater than the average probability for all firms. In these cases there are interaction effects between the major groupings which are ignored by the assumption that size, industry, and ownership effects are additive.

It appeared during the course of the R.C.B.F. survey that the insulation provided by foreign ownership has been relatively greater for small firms than for large ones, since many of the largest firms have access to foreign capital markets in any case. Thus it appeared that there was an interaction between size and ownership that made suspect the additivity assumption. The regressions were therefore run again using two size-ownership interaction terms. This was done by using two (rather than one) foreign-ownership categories, one for firms with assets of more than $5 million, and another for all foreign-controlled firms below that size. Although there was little or no increase in $\bar{R}^2$ (see Table 7.1 for a comparison of the two types of regression) it appeared from the difference between the two foreign-ownership adjustment factors that the interaction was a significant one, so all the regressions referring to the group of 1304 firms were re-run, taking account of the interaction term.

[1] See Feldstein [1966] for a detailed description of the procedure.

The regressions referring to the group of 1221 firms, which deal with sources of funds (Table 7.6) and reasons for not altering expenditures (Table 7.5), are presented on an unverified basis, and the answers reflect much higher probabilities, so that the effect of the size-ownership interaction was not as noticeable. There may, of course, be other interactions which might have been brought into the regressions, and their exclusion may have contributed to the low values of $\bar{R}^2$. This is another way of saying that our broad size, ownership, and industry classifications have only partly captured the inter-firm differences responsible for the differential effects of monetary policy. Unless the firms are divided into such small subgroups that the probability of being affected is very high (close to 1) for some groups and very low (close to 0) for others, the value of $\bar{R}^2$ will not be high.

The standard errors in brackets below the adjustment factors provide some indication of the relevance of each particular classification. The size of the standard errors is a function of the collinearity between the size, industry, and ownership variables, and of the variance of response unexplained by the regression. Needless to say, if any coefficient is not as large as its standard error, the regression provides little evidence that the ownership, size, or industry group in question has been affected more or less than the average firm.

D. Interpretation of the Survey Results

Tables 7.1 to 4 show the distribution of the expenditure effects of changes in credit conditions, Table 7.5 analyses the reasons given by firms for their reactions, Table 7.6 shows the sources of external funds used by the questionnaire responders, and Table 7.7 show the industry distribution of the aggregate expenditure effects of credit tightness. It is necessary to remember, when interpreting the tables, that Tables 7.2, 5, and 6, refer only to firms with assets under $90 million, while Tables 7.1, 3, 4, and 7 include as well the eighty-three large firms, and are on a 'verified' basis.

Table 7.1 contains estimates of the probability (in percentage terms) that firms in different industries and size groups altered their capital expenditures because of changes in credit conditions in 1956, 1959, or 1962. The evidence about each of the three periods is presented separately; thus we may look for differences between periods as well as among types of firm. In each of the periods the most substantial group difference was between firms controlled in Canada and those controlled abroad. The chief reason was that the firms controlled outside Canada, usually being subsidiaries of foreign firms, often use only retained earnings or funds from the parent company to finance their operations. (Note the $+11\cdot4$ per cent. foreign ownership adjustment factor in column 1 of Table 7.5.) There are some inter-industry differences, with utilities being more often affected in each period, textiles more in 1959, and construction in 1962. The proportion of firms affected does not vary substantially with size, once account has been taken of the industry and ownership characteristics of each size group. The following pages contain a separate analysis of the size, industry, and ownership factors, and a discussion of some other features of the survey evidence.

(1) *The size factor*

There are substantial differences in the effects of monetary policy on firms of different sizes, as the information in Table 7.5 quite clearly indicates. Firms of different sizes have different sources of finance, and also have investment programmes with distinctive characteristics. Although small firms (under $5 million in assets) were just as likely as were larger firms to have issued share capital during the 1954–62 period, they were much less likely to have issued bonds or debentures. (See the size class adjustment factors in columns 1 and 2 of Table 7.6.) They were not more likely to have used bank credit, although among those firms which did use bank credit, it provided a larger part of the external funds of small firms than of large firms. Thus we might expect, on the basis of the model of Chapter 1, that the discount rates used by small firms would be less affected by market rates of interest on long-term bonds, but perhaps more affected by changes in the availability of credit. It has already been suggested, in Section A of this chapter, that limitations on the amounts of funds restrict the number of feasible programmes to those whose requirements for funds satisfy the availability constraint.

What of size-group variations in the nature of investment programmes? Table 7.5 shows the answers given to question 3, which asked those firms whose expenditures were not affected in 1956, 1959, or 1962 to give reasons. The most striking difference between small and large firms was that small firms more often answered that they 'were not planning or making capital expenditures during the periods of credit restriction', while the large firms much more frequently answered that 'the increases in the cost of funds or restrictions on the amounts available were not great enough to affect [their] capital expenditures'. (See the size class adjustment factors in columns 2 and 4 of Table 7.5.) These answers, supported by interview data, suggest that the investment programmes of small firms are much lumpier, containing substantial outlays in some years and little or no investment in the intervening periods. The small firms therefore require new external funds only in those years when the programmes with the highest PV's all contain large capital outlays in the current period. The large firms are more regularly in the market for external funds, but their borrowings from any one market in any one year are not usually as large in relation to their average annual investment outlays.

Since the indivisibility of many fixed assets puts lumps in the capital expenditure programmes of small firms, and the small firms are more subject to large changes in budget constraints caused by the availability effects of a credit tightening, we would expect that when small firms are affected, the expenditures in question would be large in relation to average annual investment for firms of that size. On the basis of interviews with 80 of the 83 large firms, as well as with 50 of the 62 firms reporting in the mail questionnaire that their expenditures had been affected in 1956, 1959, or 1962, estimates were prepared of the amount of capital expenditure postponed or cancelled during the nine-month periods from August 1959 and from June 1962. The estimates are intended to be of the capital outlays that would have taken place during those periods had it not been for the tightening of credit conditions. The dummy variable regression technique already described was used to establish the expected amount of postponement by a firm in each sub-class. To find the estimate of expenditure reduction by any particular firm, adjustment factors for industry, size, and ownership are added to or subtracted from the average postponement by all firms. Note that the estimate is of the expected value of postponement by any firm in the group, and not just those whose expenditures were altered. If an estimate is wished of the amount of investment postponed by each firm which altered planned expenditures, it can be easily obtained by dividing the estimate from Table 7.3 by 1/100th of the percentage probability of response, derived from Table 7.1. The size-group adjustment factors in Table 7.3 indicate that, except for firms with assets over $150 million, the estimated absolute amount of postponed expenditure is not clearly related to size. This means that the postponements by smaller firms are much larger than those of bigger firms, if the expenditure changes are measured as proportions of the average annual capital expenditures by the firm.

(2) *The industry factor*

Industries differ in their sources of finance, the types of assets purchased, and the amount of expenditure affected by monetary policy. It is not easy to distinguish the influence of the pattern of finance from that of the types of asset purchased, as certain types of industry have traditionally been associated with certain types of finance. In these cases it perhaps does not matter whether we attribute the effects of monetary policy to reliance on a type of finance most sensitive to monetary policy, or to the purchase of assets which are usually financed in that way. For example, most utilities rely considerably on borrowed funds, both short and long term, use capital intensive methods employing assets with long lives, and are often affected by monetary policy. An exception is provided by the privately owned railways, which make relatively minor expenditures except in the initial development stages, and seldom obtain new external financing. The other utilities, mainly electric power, telephones, and pipelines, have relied extensively on all forms of external finance in the past decade (see Table 7.6), especially debt finance. The analysis of Chapter 1 implies that firms are concerned with the 'mix' of yield and risk that their shares provide, without stating definitely that there appears to be an optimum range within which the risk and yield characteristics of shares may be established. The substantial gearing undertaken by almost all the utilities suggests that there is such a range, at least in the opinion of those establishing financial policy for the utilities.[1] Whether or not the gearing of the utilities is deliberately intended to increase the yield and risk of an otherwise more stable income stream, the large and sustained capital expenditures of the utilities put them frequently in the market for external funds. Despite their generally powerful borrowing positions, the utilities have been fairly often influenced, by high interest rates, to alter their spending. Although the amounts have usually been moderate, there have been one or two very large postponements, and these are primarily

---

[1] The provincially owned utilities obtain all their funds from retained earnings, borrowing, or government subventions, so that their reliance on borrowing is not so much a matter of policy as is that of the utilities with individuals as shareholders.

responsible for the high estimates to be found in Table 7.3. The pipe-lines have not been affected in the same way, for although their expenditure programmes are very lumpy, the expected revenue loss from postponing an approved pipeline project is usually great enough to offset any interest rate incentive to postpone.

In the textile industry, also, the structure of assets and patterns of finance together suggest that monetary policy will have certain effects. Perhaps it is more important that we realize the joint importance of the assets and their financing, even though we cannot be sure what the relevance of a certain asset structure would be in the absence of the usual pattern of finance. Textile firms are usually reliant on bank loans which fluctuate seasonally with the level of inventories. Since short-term rates are generally lower than long-term rates, this pattern of finance is less expensive than obtaining long-term finance and lending out the idle funds when inventories are low. Textile firms were not very profitable during the 1954–62 period, so that new equity funds were not easily available. On the other hand, profit expecta-tions were not high either, so that there was not a great deal of pres-sure on funds for capital expenditures. When credit conditions tightened, there were not many investment plans at the new financing stage, so that there was not a large amount of capital expenditure reduction. Despite some pressure on bank lines of credit, the frequency of verified expenditure reductions was lower for in-ventories than for capital expenditures in this industry. (See Tables 7.2 and 7.4, and also p. 372 of *The Effects of Monetary Policy*.)

The mining and petroleum industries rely mainly on equity financing, and seldom borrow. (See Table 7.6.) Their operations often involve an initial mine development which usually 'cannot'[1] be financed by borrowing. The oil firms in general obtained their initial financing from parent companies outside Canada, while the mining firms have relied much more on share issues in Canada. If a mining firm is successful in its initial venture, the resulting cash flow is fre-quently large enough to finance subsequent developments without additional financing from outside the firm. Thus it was that many mining firms answered that they were not affected because they relied only on internal sources of finance. (See the industry adjust-

---

[1] This is the terminology used in the industry. To be more explicit, it is commonly believed that the available sets of projects all have such high dis-persions of returns as pure equity streams that they would be out of the 'accept-able' risk range if gearing were used in the early stages of development.

ment factors in column 1 of Table 7.5.) Both mining and petroleum firms often answered (column 5 of Table 7.5) that they were unconcerned with credit conditions, since their external funds were of a more speculative type, whose supply was unrelated to credit conditions. It is not easy to establish clearly the extent to which the ease of floating speculative share issues was correlated during 1954–62 with ease of credit conditions. Although we cannot use the same measures of the cost and availability of funds in both markets, it is likely that the co-movements in the two markets (as shown in Figure 8 in Section B) were slight enough to mask the impact of credit conditions on the prices of new mining shares.

The effects of credit conditions on capital expenditures in the construction industry were not above the average for all industries except in 1962, when they were greater than in any non-utility industry. This information is somewhat difficult to interpret, as the question referred to the capital expenditures by the firms themselves, which would include only their own facilities unless they were undertaking speculative building projects as principals. There were some of these latter ventures among the postponed projects, although most of the cutbacks in speculative building projects were apparently by the relatively small number of property development concerns (most of which were not surveyed by questionnaire). In these projects the rate of discount applied is very closely related to the rate at which long-term funds can be obtained, as well as the availability of temporary bank loans during the construction period. Since the revenues are spread over a considerable period of time, the present value of a project is quite sensitive to changes in the discount rates. Since these projects are often financed on an *ad hoc* basis, it is not surprising that there have been postponements at times when credit has been tight, nor that it is often difficult to tell what ventures of this kind might have taken place had interest rates been lower.

Examination of other industry coefficients does not disclose other remarkable inter-industry differences; which is in part a consequence of the very wide definitions of some of the industry groupings.

(3) *The foreign-ownership factor*

At one stage in the survey it seemed that foreign subsidiaries were likely to be affected by credit conditions in the same way as large domestic firms with international sources of finance. Simultaneous analysis of industry, size, and ownership factors shows that foreign ownership has rather more influence than can be so simply explained. As might be expected in any case, Table 7.5, column 1 shows how much more the foreign-controlled firms are reliant on parental and internally generated funds than are firms controlled in Canada. Table 7.6 shows the same, while Tables 7.1 to 4 indicate the smaller effects of credit conditions on expenditures. Interviews suggest that the discount rates implicitly employed by foreign-controlled firms are not as affected by Canadian credit conditions as are the discount rates used by domestically owned firms, even those with free access to capital markets outside Canada. As noted in Section C, foreign ownership is much more important for small firms than for large ones, since large firms often have reasonably easy access to foreign capital markets in any case. In all the tables where the size-ownership interaction terms have been introduced, it can be seen that foreign ownership has much more influence on the effects of monetary policy on small firms (assets under $5 million) than on larger ones.

(4) *Differences over time*

There are difficulties involved in using the survey evidence as a guide to differences over time in the use and effectiveness of monetary policy. For one thing, the circumstances in the three periods differed in several respects, so that it is not easy to determine their individual importance. In addition, the validity of questionnaire and interview data is related to the amount of time that has passed since the relevant event took place. Thus it was often found that memories were dim of the 1956–7 financial conditions; and the turnover of senior officials is fast enough that many of the persons interviewed had not been in a position to assess the effects of changes in credit conditions during the 1950s.

Although the evidence for the 1956–7 period is less reliable than that for 1959 or 1962, there are nevertheless some features worth mentioning. As might be expected, the capital expenditures by firms in the four smallest size classes were more affected by credit conditions in 1956 than in 1959 or 1962; for in the two latter periods the instructions to chartered bank branch managers requested them to take care of the needs of the smaller firms. (See the size class adjustment factors in Table 7.1.) The interview evidence from firms affected in 1956 was not adequate to allow estimates to be made like those for 1959 and 1962 in Table 7.3. What evidence there is indicates that the total expenditure effects during the three-quarters chosen as the period for measuring expenditure shifts were less in 1956 than in the other two periods, and greater in 1959 than 1962.

There are three plausible reasons for the expenditure effects being greater in 1959 than in 1962. First, the bank credit squeeze in the summer of 1959 coincided with high interest rates, both short and long term. As can be seen in Figure 9, long-term interest rates did not rise as far or as fast in 1962. Second, the credit restriction of 1962 was announced, along with a package of import surcharges, as a cure for a short term balance of payments problem, and firms were told that the government had no desire that they should cut back their capital spending. The 1959 measures were more directly concerned with restricting the aggregate level of domestic demand. Third, the Canadian dollar was at a substantial premium in 1959, reducing the attraction of foreign borrowing on short or long term. In 1962, on the other hand, the value of the Canadian dollar was pegged at a price of 92·5 cents U.S., and there was official encouragement of private borrowing abroad. Thus the effective international interest differential was larger in 1962 than in 1959, and recourse was more easily gained to foreign funds. For all these reasons it is not surprising that the effects of the 1959 credit conditions on capital expenditures were greater than the effects of the 1962 credit conditions. The difference might have been more substantial had the 1962 credit restriction not been accompanied by the import surcharges, which altered the cash-flow distributions for a number of alternative programmes, favouring the delay of projects involving a substantial import component. The very brevity (*ex ante* as well as *ex post*) of the 1962 measures may have increased their effects, taken as a package, on the timing of investment, since there was an incentive to postpone projects with a high import content, while the positive incentive effects for the provision of import-competitive capacity were limited by the short expected duration of the surcharges.

(5) *Tightness* vs. *ease*

The survey results reported in this chapter deal exclusively with the effects of three successive bouts of tight money, while no evidence has been presented of the expansionary effects of the intervening periods of relatively easier credit conditions. The R.C.B.F. questionnaire did include a question on the effects of the lower interest rates and increased availability of funds during 1961 and early 1962. Fewer firms gave affirmative answers to this question than to the

ones dealing with tighter credit conditions.[1] The question was a
difficult one to answer, and to interpret. If most of the effects of credit
restraint are felt through credit rationing, to what extent is the availability of funds to be thought of as being responsible for any increases in capital spending? The problem of discovering the effects
of credit ease are made more difficult, in the 1954–63 period, by the
general upward trend in long-term interest rates shown in Figure 9.
Thus firms often answered the question about credit ease to the effect
that they had not noticed any change; in fact, the total drop in industrial bond yields between their highest level in 1960 and their
lowest level in 1961 was less than 0·4 per cent. The modest decline in
interest rates, and the fact, mentioned in Section A, that credit
availability is expected by most firms as a matter of course, make it
unsurprising that the directly recognized effects of credit ease have
been so small.

(6) *Rates* vs. *availability*

When firms were interviewed about the effects of credit conditions,
attempts were made to find out what aspect of credit conditions was
most relevant to the alteration of capital expenditures. In about 75
per cent. of the verified cases (in both 1959 and 1962) of postponement by firms with assets under $5 million, restrictions on bank
lending were responsible. In the other cases, the small firms postponed projects because they thought that the demand for their products would be adversely affected by the credit restrictions. The postponements by larger firms were less often attributed to the unavailability of bank credit. Unavailability of bank credit was cited in
50 per cent. of the verified postponements by firms with assets between $5 and 25 million, but in less than 10 per cent. of the post-
ponements by firms with assets greater than 25 million. The large
utilities most often gave high interest rates as the reason for postponement, being anxious to avoid floating bond issues at unattractive
rates. Other large firms were influenced by interest rates, and also by
the expectation that credit restrictions would lead to reductions in
demand. As has already been noted in Subsection (1) above, the postponements by large firms were usually a much smaller proportion of
the annual capital expenditures of the firm than were those of the
small firms. Thus when the large firms adjusted their expenditures so
as to reduce or avoid borrowing at high rates, the adjustments were

[1] See pages 349 and 366 of *The Effects of Monetary Policy.*

usually marginal, while the rationing of bank credit caused small firms to postpone projects which were often much larger than the firm's average annual capital expenditures.

(7) *Lags*

The questionnaire and interview evidence, as presented, provides no clues as to the timing of the expenditure response to monetary policy. The quantitative estimates in Tables 7.3 and 7 refer to the amount of expenditure that would have taken place in the nine months following a specified date; August 1959, in the one case, and June 1962, in the other. To get estimates of these amounts it was necessary to analyse all the evidence of expenditure changes, and to estimate how much of the total change related to the particular nine-month periods. In some cases, prominent among which are the major postponements by utilities, only a small fraction of the postponed expenditure would have taken place in the specified periods. Since it is often difficult to establish what would have been the time pattern of outlays on projects that in fact were never undertaken, the estimates in Tables 7.3 and 7 should be treated with care. Since the interview and questionnaire evidence is not strong in this respect, the most useful evidence may be of the time pattern of outlays on different types of investment project.[1] By applying this kind of information to survey data indicating the number and nature of postponed projects, some idea can be obtained of the time profile of the direct expenditure effects of monetary policy. The evidence from the R.C.B.F. survey does not permit quantitative conclusions more ambitious than the following:

'For some categories of expenditure such as residential construction, the lags are variable but fairly short and fairly easy to predict. In other sectors of the economy, the lags depend on the nature of the expenditure, but a major proportion of the direct effects on employment and output may come within a period ranging from a few weeks to 6-9 months, although other effects—both direct and indirect—will extend into later periods. Our evidence suggests, moreover, that these lags can be shortened considerably by fairly dramatic changes in credit conditions, especially if the climate of business opinion and expectations is significantly affected by the policy measures themselves or by other events in the economy.'[2]

[1] Evidence of this kind may be found in Chapter IX of *The Effects of Monetary Policy*, and Chapter IV of *Taxation and Investment*.
[2] R.C.B.F. *Report*, p. 438.

TABLE 7.1

CAPITAL EXPENDITURES POSTPONED OR ABANDONED,
1956, 1959, 1961 (VERIFIED BASIS)

Percentage probability that a surveyed firm postponed capital expenditure because of tighter credit in 1956, 1959, or 1962. Percentage probability = average probability in all 1304 firms, plus or minus industry, size class, and ownership adjustment factors.

The regressions have been run both with and without a size-ownership interaction term. The adjustment factors in columns 1, 3, and 5 are from a regression which assumes that the size and ownership influences are additive. The adjustment factors in columns 2, 4, and 6 are based on a regression in which foreign-controlled firms are divided into two size classes to test for a size-ownership interaction.

Average percentage probability of postponement or adjustment (total no. of postponements divided by 1304)	0·97%		2·99%		2·38%	
Industry adjustment factors						
	1956		*1959*		*1962*	
	(1)	(2)	(3)	(4)	(5)	(6)
1. Food and beverages	−0·75	−0·73	−0·52	−0·44	+0·73	+0·81
	(1·25)	(1·21)	(2·09)	(2·03)	(1·89)	(1·83)
2. Wood products	+1·92	+1·89	+1·53	+1·41	+2·31	+2·20
	(1·24)	(1·20)	(2·08)	(2·01)	(1·88)	(1·82)
3. Textiles	−0·03	−0·02	+4·36	+4·34	−1·16	−1·18
	(1·33)	(1·30)	(2·23)	(2·18)	(2·01)	(1·97)
4. Mining, iron, and steel	+0·48	+0·25	−1·48	−1·82	−0·68	−0·90
	(0·98)	(0·81)	(1·65)	(1·36)	(1·49)	(1·22)
5. Other manufacturing	−0·65	−0·65	+0·63	+0·69	−0·71	−0·67
	(0·94)	(0·90)	(1·57)	(1·50)	(1·42)	(1·36)
6. Petroleum	+2·63	+2·55	+1·19	+1·04	+1·03	+0·89
	(1·48)	(1·45)	(2·48)	(2·42)	(2·24)	(2·18)
7. Electric power	+3·13	+3·33	+20·96	+21·64	+6·63	+7·32
	(2·20)	(2·23)	(3·69)	(3·73)	(3·33)	(3·37)
8. Railways	+13·42	+13·37	+11·74	+11·67	+13·74	+13·68
	(3·89)	(3·88)	(6·51)	(6·49)	(5·88)	(5·86)
9. Pipelines	+3·41	+3·47	−2·99	−2·79	−1·89	−1·67
	(2·16)	(2·15)	(3·62)	(3·59)	(3·27)	(3·24)
10. Telephones	−0·86	−0·80	+23·18	+23·39	+24·59	+24·83
	(3·15)	(3·14)	(5·27)	(5·25)	(4·76)	(4·74)
11. Other utilities	−1·08	−1·08	−3·82	−3·87	−1·30	−1·33
	(1·54)	(1·51)	(2·57)	(2·53)	(2·32)	(2·28)
12. Commercial services	−1·20	−1·23	−1·38	−1·52	−2·51	−2·65
	(1·61)	(1·58)	(2·69)	(2·65)	(2·43)	(2·39)
13. Construction	−1·45	−1·47	−0·84	−0·94	+4·60	+4·50
	(1·43)	(1·40)	(2·39)	(2·34)	(2·16)	(2·12)
14. Wholesale and retail trade	−1·18	−0·91	−4·12	−3·80	−2·59	−2·37
	(0)	(0)	(0)	(0)	(0)	(0)

TABLE 7.1—*continued*

Size-class adjustment factors Asset size (millions of dollars)	1956 (1)	(2)	1959 (3)	(4)	1962 (5)	(6)
1. Under 0·1	−0·36	−0·31	−0·78	−0·61	−2·30	−2·12
	(2·82)	(2·87)	(4·73)	(4·81)	(4·27)	(4·34)
2. 0·1–0·25	+1·48	+1·49	+1·45	+1·53	−0·28	−0·18
	(2·70)	(2·74)	(4·52)	(4·59)	(4·08)	(4·14)
3. 0·25–1	+0·60	+0·68	−0·13	+0·14	−0·54	−0·25
	(2·57)	(2·63)	(4·29)	(4·40)	(3·88)	(3·97)
4. 1–5	−0·28	+0·42	+0·93	+1·41	+0·89	+1·39
	(2·55)	(2·65)	(4·26)	(4·43)	(3·85)	(4·00)
5. 5–10	−0·46	−0·53	−0·70	−0·93	+0·04	−0·20
	(2·54)	(2·56)	(4·26)	(4·28)	(3·84)	(3·86)
6. 10–15	0·05	−0·05	−0·75	−1·08	−2·10	−2·44
	(2·65)	(2·66)	(4·43)	(4·44)	(4·00)	(4·01)
7. 15–25	−1·18	−1·27	+0·34	+0·03	+4·00	+3·67
	(2·62)	(2·63)	(4·39)	(4·40)	(3·96)	(3·97)
8. 25–50	−0·81	−0·91	−1·93	−2·27	−1·00	−1·36
	(2·61)	(2·62)	(4·37)	(4·38)	(3·94)	(3·95)
9. 50–90	+0·40	+0·36	+1·50	+1·28	+3·69	+3·43
	(2·82)	(2·83)	(4·72)	(4·73)	(4·26)	(4·27)
10. 90–150	−1·85	−1·95	−3·42	−3·78	−2·78	−3·18
	(3·06)	(3·06)	(5·12)	(5·13)	(4·62)	(4·63)
11. Over 150	+0·66	+0·57	+2·62	+2·30	−2·25	−2·59
	(2·79)	(2·80)	(4·68)	(4·69)	(4·22)	(4·23)
12. Size unknown	−2·53	−2·72	−0·29	−0·83	+0·80	+0·20
	(0)	(0)	(0)	(0)	(0)	(0)

Ownership adjustment factors	1956 (1)	(2)	1959 (3)	(4)	1962 (5)	(6)
1. Firms controlled outside Canada	0·00 (0·66)		−1·76 (1·11)		−1·22 (1·00)	
2. Firms with assets less than 5 million and controlled outside Canada		−0·50 (1·11)		−3·39 (1·86)		−2·81 (1·68)
3. Firms with assets more than 5 million and controlled outside Canada		0·28 (0·81)		−1·05 (1·37)		−0·48 (1·24)
4. Firms controlled within Canada	0·00 (0)	0·03 (0)	0·85 (0)	0·81 (0)	0·59 (0)	0·53 (0)
$\bar{R}^2$	0·029	0·029	0·075	0·075	0·058	0·058

Table 7.3 shows the number of firms in each industry, size, and ownership group of the 1304 firms.

The question read, in part: '. . . Were changes in the cost or availability of credit in whole or in part responsible for leading your firm to: . . . (e) Postpone any capital expenditures? . . . (f) Abandon plans for capital expenditures?' A verified 'yes' answer to either (e) or (f) was sufficient for a firm to be included in the above table.

In all Tables 7.1 to 6 the figures in brackets below the adjustment factors are their standard errors. The larger is the adjustment factor in relation to its standard error, the more strongly does the survey evidence indicate that the behaviour of the particular ownership, size, or industry group has been materially different from the average.

TABLE 7.2

CAPITAL EXPENDITURES POSTPONED OR ABANDONED, 1959—
VERIFIED AND UNVERIFIED PERCENTAGE PROBABILITY

	Verified	Unverified
Average percentage probability of postponement (for all 1221 surveyed firms with assets less than $90 million)	2·70%	8·02%

Industry adjustment factors	Number of surveyed firms in industry	Verified	Unverified
1. Food and beverages	93	−0·21% (2·03)	−0·39% (3·47)
2. Wood products	86	+2·61 (2·05)	+1·65 (3·50)
3. Textiles	77	+4·75 (2·13)	+4·84 (3·63)
4. Mining, iron, and steel	211	−1·16 (1·60)	+1·52 (2·73)
5. Other manufacturing	291	+1·01 (1·51)	−1·38 (2·58)
6. Petroleum	55	−1·89 (2·54)	−0·80 (4·34)
7. Electric power	15	+10·76 (4·32)	+8·36 (7·37)
8. Railways	4	−0·02 (8·10)	−1·63 (13·83)
9. Pipelines	18	−2·86 (3·97)	−0·44 (6·78)
10. Telephones	6	+46·42 (6·63)	+44·51 (11·31)
11. Other utilities	52	−3·48 (2·47)	+0·32 (4·22)
12. Commercial services	47	−0·98 (2·57)	−0·86 (4·38)
13. Construction	68	−0·34 (2·23)	−2·69 (3·81)
14. Wholesale and retail trade	198	−3·29 (0)	−2·65 (0)
	1221		

TABLE 7.2—*continued*

Size class adjustment factors

Asset size (millions of dollars)	Number of surveyed firms in size class	Verified	Unverified
1. Under 0·1	58	−0·91% (4·43)	+0·60% (7·55)
2. 0·1–0·25	96	+1·22 (4·24)	+7·12 (7·25)
3. 0·25–1	251	−0·33 (4·03)	+0·25 (6·87)
4. 1–5	230	+0·70 (4·01)	+1·89 (6·85)
5. 5–10	223	−0·55 (3·97)	+0·08 (6·78)
6. 10–15	90	−0·41 (4·15)	−2·13 (7·09)
7. 15–25	95	+0·36 (4·12)	−1·83 (7·04)
8. 25–50	109	−0·99 (4·11)	−5·18 (7·02)
9. 50–90	51	+1·78 (4·40)	−3·80 (7·52)
10. Size unknown	18	−0·09 (0)	−6·09 (0)
	1221		

Ownership adjustment factor

	Number of surveyed firms	Verified	Unverified
1. Firms controlled outside Canada	387	−1·18% (1·11)	−2·53% (1·89)
2. Firms controlled within Canada	834	+0·84 (0)	+1·17 (0)
$\bar{R}^2$		0·072	0·037

To find the percentage probability of response for any particular size and industry grouping, take the figure for average probability for all firms and add or subtract the appropriate industry, size-group, and ownership adjustment factors. Where the adjustment factor is small in relation to its standard error (in brackets below the adjustment factor) the survey evidence does not indicate that the probability of response for firms in that industry or size-group is materially different from the average.

M

TABLE 7.3

ESTIMATE OF THE ABSOLUTE VALUE OF EXPENDITURES POSTPONED
OR ABANDONED BY INDIVIDUAL FIRMS, 1959, 1962 DURING THE
NINE-MONTH PERIODS FOLLOWING AUGUST 1959 AND JUNE 1962
(All amounts are in thousands of dollars)

		1959	1962
Average amount of postponement or abandoned expenditure by each firm (i.e. total value of postponed expenditures/1304)		24·5	19·2

Industry adjustment factors	Number of surveyed firms in industry	1959	1962
1. Food and beverages	98	−13·7	−17·5
		(6·2)	(14·6)
2. Wood products	97	−41·3	−13·5
		(6·2)	(14·5)
3. Textiles	77	+0·71	−8·6
		(6·6)	(15·6)
4. Mining, iron, and steel	227	−19·2	−11·8
		(4·1)	(9·7)
5. Other manufacturing	301	+0·7	−4·3
		(4·6)	(10·7)
6. Petroleum	67	−22·3	−27·5
		(7·4)	(17·4)
7. Electric power	25	+859·7	+441·6
		(11·4)	(26·7)
8. Railways	7	−7·1	−11·8
		(19·8)	(46·5)
9. Pipelines	25	−65·9	−51·2
		(11·0)	(25·8)
10. Telephones	11	−91·7	−70·6
		(16·0)	(37·7)
11. Other utilities	53	−31·4	+86·0
		(7·7)	(18·1)
12. Commercial services	47	−23·2	−11·0
		(8·1)	(19·0)
13. Construction	68	−18·5	−6·7
		(7·2)	(16·8)
14. Wholesale and retail trade	201	−19·1	−14·9
		(0)	(0)
	1304		

TABLE 7.3—*continued*

Size-class adjustment factors

Asset size (millions of dollars)	Number of surveyed firms in group	1959	1962
1. Under 0·1	58	−19·8 (14·7)	−26·2 (34·5)
2. 0·1–0·25	96	−20·8 (14·0)	−27·0 (32·9)
3. 0·25–1	251	−14·0 (13·4)	−21·9 (31·6)
4. 1–5	230	−0·1 (13·5)	−14·2 (31·8)
5. 5–10	223	−3·8 (13·1)	−6·1 (30·7)
6. 10–15	90	−22·3 (13·6)	−11·4 (31·8)
7. 15–25	95	−11·0 (13·4)	+18·9 (31·6)
8. 25–50	109	−47·7 (13·4)	+32·1 (31·4)
9. 50–90	51	−22·9 (14·4)	+15·5 (33·9)
10. 90–150	27	+10·5 (15·7)	+24·5 (36·8)
11. Over 150	56	+291·0 (14·3)	+143·2 (33·6)
12. Size unknown	18	+20·9 (0)	+28·3 (0)
	1304		

Ownership adjustment factors

		1959	1962
Firms with assets less than 5 million and controlled outside Canada	113	−63·6 (5·7)	−22·2 (13·4)
Firms with assets more than 5 million and controlled outside Canada	311	−24·7 (4·2)	−30·9 (9·8)
Firms controlled inside Canada	880	+16·9 (0)	+13·8 (0)
$\bar{R}^2$		0·895	0·320

The estimate for any particular firm is found by taking the average for all firms and adding or subtracting industry, size, and ownership adjustment factors.

To find the estimate of the average amount of postponement by affected firms, divide the estimate from this table by 1/100th of the percentage probability derived from Table 7.1.

TABLE 7.4

INVENTORY REDUCTIONS, 1956, 1959, 1962 (VERIFIED BASIS)

	1956	1959	1962
Average percentage probability of inventory reduction (i.e. total number of firms reducing inventories/1304)	1·84%	2·68%	3·45%

Industry adjustment factors	1956	1959	1962
1. Food and beverages	−0·24 (1·62)	+0·04 (1·95)	+4·51 (2·20)
2. Wood products	+2·95 (1·61)	+3·52 (1·93)	+4·56 (2·19)
3. Textiles	+0·22 (1·74)	+1·01 (2·09)	+1·00 (2·37)
4. Mining, iron, and steel	−0·98 (1·08)	−1·04 (1·30)	−2·56 (1·47)
5. Other manufacturing	+2·68 (1·93)	+3·04 (1·44)	+3·66 (1·63)
6. Petroleum	−1·22 (1·93)	−2·48 (2·32)	−2·49 (2·63)
7. Electric power	−0·98 (2·98)	+7·57 (3·57)	+6·96 (4·05)
8. Railways	−0·44 (5·18)	−0·75 (6·22)	−1·22 (7·04)
9. Pipelines	−0·88 (2·87)	−1·91 (3·45)	−2·26 (3·90)
10. Telephones	+6·82 (4·19)	+5·19 (5·03)	+5·92 (5·69)
11. Other utilities	−2·29 (2·01)	−1·80 (2·42)	−2·27 (2·74)
12. Commercial services	−2·56 (2·11)	−3·52 (2·54)	−4·84 (2·87)
13. Construction	−2·99 (1·87)	−4·27 (2·25)	−4·01 (2·54)
14. Wholesale and retail trade	−1·80 (0)	−2·88 (0)	−4·31 (0)

TABLE 7.4—*continued*

Size-class adjustment factors Asset size (millions of dollars)	1956	1959	1962
1. Under 0·1	+5·42 (3·84)	+4·83 (4·61)	+2·51 (5·22)
2. 0·1–0·25	+0·34 (3·66)	−0·54 (4·40)	−0·98 (4·98)
3. 0·25–1	+2·58 (3·51)	+0·10 (4·22)	+1·76 (4·78)
4. 1–5	−1·62 (3·53)	+2·21 (4·24)	+2·60 (4·80)
5. 5–10	−1·87 (3·41)	−1·77 (4·10)	−2·58 (4·64)
6. 10–15	−1·90 (3·55)	−3·20 (4·26)	+0·64 (4·82)
7. 15–25	+0·03 (3·51)	−1·23 (4·22)	+2·29 (4·78)
8. 25–50	−1·98 (3·50)	−3·58 (4·20)	−4·78 (4·75)
9. 50–90	+5·58 (3·77)	+8·05 (4·53)	−4·63 (5·13)
10. 90–150	−1·86 (4·09)	+4·41 (4·91)	+0·14 (5·56)
11. Over 150	−0·54 (3·74)	−1·11 (4·49)	+0·02 (5·08)
12. Size unknown	−1·41 (0)	−2·23 (0)	−1·90 (0)

Ownership adjustment factors	1956	1959	1962
Firms with assets less than 5 million and controlled outside Canada	−0·97 (1·48)	−5·72 (1·78)	−4·61 (2·02)
Firms with assets more than 5 million and controlled outside Canada	−0·25 (1·09)	+0·04 (1·31)	−0·17 (1·48)
Firms controlled within Canada	+0·21 (0)	+0·72 (0)	+0·65 (0)
$\bar{R}^2$		0·054	0·056	0·053

The question read: '. . . were changes in the availability or cost of credit in whole or in part responsible for leading your firm to . . . (*d*) Deliberately reduce the size of your raw materials, work-in-progress, or finished goods inventories?'

Table 7.2 shows the number of firms in each industry, size, and ownership group of the 1221 firms.

TABLE 7.5

Reasons for not Altering Capital Expenditures in Response to Changes in Credit Conditions

1. Firm relies only on internal sources of finance or advances from associated companies.
2. Changes not great enough to affect planning.
3. Firm was committed to expenditures underway.
4. Not planning or making capital expenditures during period of credit restriction.
5. Other reasons.
6. One or more reasons given.

	(1)	(2)	(3)	(4)	(5)	(6)
Average percentage probability for 1221 firms	44·64%	24·90%	12·53%	17·94%	8·11%	85·01%

Industry adjustment factors

	(1)	(2)	(3)	(4)	(5)	(6)
1. Food and beverages	+2·38 (6·18)	+4·03 (5·47)	+4·31 (4·20)	−13·99 (4·72)	+2·37 (3·50)	−2·30 (4·50)
2. Wood products	+2·73 (6·24)	+1·60 (5·47)	−3·40 (4·24)	−9·08 (4·76)	+2·52 (3·53)	−0·18 (4·54)
3. Textiles	+9·22 (6·47)	+7·08 (5·73)	−3·67 (4·40)	−2·35 (4·94)	+0·90 (3·66)	+4·73 (4·71)
4. Mining, iron, and steel	+7·10 (4·86)	−2·22 (4·31)	+5·86 (3·31)	−8·15 (3·71)	+1·75 (2·75)	+2·03 (3·54)
5. Other manufacturing	+2·60 (4·60)	+4·59 (4·07)	−1·13 (3·13)	−1·93 (3·51)	−1·73 (2·60)	+3·26 (3·34)
6. Petroleum	+0·20 (7·72)	−7·72 (6·84)	+1·86 (5·25)	−0·24 (5·90)	+9·60 (4·37)	+1·12 (5·62)
7. Electric power	−35·75 (13·12)	−8·70 (11·63)	−0·62 (8·93)	+2·87 (10·02)	+3·91 (7·43)	−12·42 (9·54)
8. Railways	+35·61 (24·61)	+1·00 (21·81)	−14·58 (16·75)	+17·34 (18·80)	−8·11 (13·94)	+7·05 (17·91)
9. Pipelines	−24·72 (12·07)	−6·91 (10·70)	+1·81 (8·21)	+4·25 (9·22)	+12·78 (6·83)	−2·05 (8·78)
10. Telephones	−44·28 (20·13)	−38·12 (17·84)	−5·24 (13·70)	−10·41 (15·38)	−10·00 (11·40)	−75·57 (14·65)
11. Other utilities	−0·75 (7·51)	−4·57 (6·66)	+1·18 (5·11)	+0·79 (5·74)	+2·59 (4·25)	+2·59 (5·46)
12. Commercial services	4·10 (7·80)	−10·04 (6·92)	−0·22 (5·31)	−4·46 (5·96)	−3·75 (4·42)	−5·76 (5·68)
13. Construction	−4·14 (6·79)	−1·00 (6·02)	−0·43 (4·62)	+5·82 (5·19)	−1·95 (3·84)	−2·66 (4·94)
14. Wholesale and retail trade	−3·93 (0)	−1·23 (0)	−3·99 (0)	+3·21 (0)	−4·66 (0)	−3·06 (0)

TABLE 7.5—*continued*

Size-class adjustment factors *Asset size* *(millions of dollars)*	*(1)*	*(2)*	*(3)*	*(4)*	*(5)*	*(6)*
1. Under 0·1	−13·21	−13·70	−10·60	+8·85	−5·68	−8·88
	(13·44)	(11·92)	(9·15)	(10·27)	(7·61)	(9·78)
2. 0·1–0·25	−23·78	−13·80	−6·53	+14·79	−1·51	−12·93
	(12·89)	(11·43)	(8·77)	(9·85)	(7·30)	(9·38)
3. 0·25–1	+68·83	−9·63	−3·59	+12·20	−1·70	−3·99
	(12·23)	(10·84)	(8·32)	(9·34)	(6·93)	(8·90)
4. 1–5	−24·66	+0·84	−3·75	+0·45	+4·12	−2·52
	(12·19)	(10·80)	(8·29)	(9·30)	(6·90)	(8·87)
5. 5–10	−17·04	+2·58	+1·05	−5·82	−1·08	+1·67
	(12·07)	(10·69)	(8·21)	(9·22)	(6·83)	(8·78)
6. 10–15	−13·67	+16·51	+7·33	−9·97	−0·65	+9·66
	(12·61)	(11·18)	(8·58)	(9·64)	(7·14)	(9·18)
7. 15–25	−24·15	+13·11	+6·11	−5·80	−0·38	+5·11
	(12·53)	(11·10)	(8·53)	(9·57)	(7·09)	(9·12)
8. 25–50	−8·20	+7·92	+10·25	−11·95	+2·43	+8·99
	(12·49)	(11·07)	(8·50)	(9·54)	(7·07)	(9·09)
9. 50–90	−14·76	+8·76	+10·02	−15·81	+4·14	+7·74
	(13·38)	(11·86)	(9·10)	(10·22)	(7·58)	(9·74)
10. Size unknown	+23·19	−15·19	−5·33	−13·56	−10·52	+13·15
	(0)	(0)	(0)	(0)	(0)	(0)

Ownership adjustment factors	*(1)*	*(2)*	*(3)*	*(4)*	*(5)*	*(6)*
1. Firms controlled outside Canada	+11·40	−7·67	−5·71	−2·62	−1·55	+0·78
	(3·36)	(2·98)	(2·29)	(2·57)	(1·90)	(2·45)
2. Firms controlled within Canada	−5·29	+3·56	+2·65	+1·22	+0·72	−0·36
	(0)	(0)	(0)	(0)	(0)	(0)
$\bar{R}^2$	0·087	0·054	0·049	0·107	0·031	0·064

Question 2 on the mail questionnaire read as follows: 'If increases in the cost of external funds or restrictions on their availability have not led you to decrease your planned capital expenditures, is this because: (please check)'

'(a) Your firm relies only on internal sources of finance or advances from associated companies?' (No. of checks, as a percentage of the 1221 questionnaires, is shown in column 1 above.)

'(b) The increases in the cost of funds or restrictions on amounts available were not great enough to affect your planning of capital expenditures?' (column 2).

'(c) You were committed to expenditure programmes already underway?' (column 3).

'(d) Your firm was not planning or making capital expenditures during the periods of credit restriction?' (column 4).

'(e) Of other reasons?' (column 5).

Column 6 shows the percentage probability that a firm checked one or more of the five choices offered.

The information in this table has been taken directly from the questionnaires without systematic interview verification. The data refer to the 1221 firms, all with assets under $90 million in 1961, whose mail questionnaires were analysed.

TABLE 7.6

SOURCES OF FUNDS USED ONCE OR MORE DURING THE
PERIOD 1955-1962

	(1)	(2)	(3)	(4)
Average percentage probability for all 1221 firms	27·03	17·28	50·53	71·99

Industry adjustment factors	(1)	(2)	(3)	(4)
1. Food and beverages	−2·55	−2·67	+0·38	+3·87
	(4·56)	(4·50)	(6·19)	(5·57)
2. Wood products	−6·72	−4·25	−1·16	−9·51
	(4·61)	(4·55)	(6·25)	(5·62)
3. Textiles	−5·59	+0·85	+21·78	+7·67
	(4·78)	(4·72)	(6·48)	(5·83)
4. Mining, iron, and steel	5·37	−4·21	−8·39	−4·92
	(3·59)	(3·55)	(4·87)	(4·38)
5. Other manufacturing	−3·07	+0·73	+4·20	−0·29
	(3·40)	(3·35)	(4·60)	(4·14)
6. Petroleum	+24·75	−3·02	−14·23	+11·02
	(5·71)	(5·63)	(7·38)	(6·96)
7. Electric power	+18·40	+34·40	−13·12	−5·40
	(9·69)	(9·57)	(13·14)	(11·83)
8. Railways	−30·65	−22·49	−46·68	−69·31
	(18·18)	(17·95)	(24·66)	(22·19)
9. Pipelines	+31·60	+40·72	−11·00	+3·19
	(8·92)	(8·80)	(12·09)	(10·88)
10. Telephones	+46·28	+46·47	−9·85	+4·98
	(14·87)	(14·68)	(20·17)	(18·15)
11. Other utilities	−4·22	+4·42	−8·34	−5·81
	(5·55)	(5·48)	(7·52)	(6·77)
12. Commercial services	−1·62	+1·54	−12·99	−19·05
	(5·77)	(5·69)	(7·82)	(7·04)
13. Construction	−3·86	−5·68	+6·43	+7·81
	(5·02)	(4·95)	(6·80)	(6·12)
14. Wholesale and retail trade	−4·03	+0·17	+4·87	+6·68
	(0)	(0)	(0)	(0)

Column 1. Share capital issued at least once during the period 1955–62.
Column 2. Bonds or debentures issued at least once during the period 1955–62.
Column 3. Bank loans (non-term) used at least once between 1955 and 1962.
Column 4. Any external funds.

Percentage probability that a firm used external funds of a particular type is found by taking the mean percentage probability for all firms and then adding or subtracting the appropriate industry, size class, and ownership adjustment factors.

Information in this table has been taken directly from the question-

TABLE 7.6—*continued*

Size-class adjustment factors Asset size (in millions of dollars)	(1)	(2)	(3)	(4)
1. Under 0·1	+18·20	−15·94	−21·20	−5·95
	(9·93)	(9·81)	(13·47)	(12·12)
2. 0·1–0·25	+1·61	−17·20	−19·90	−3·70
	(9·52)	(9·41)	(12·92)	(11·63)
3. 0·25–1	−5·79	−11·46	−4·34	−4·27
	(9·04)	(8·92)	(12·26)	(11·03)
4. 1–5	−11·15	−4·52	+0·33	−1·44
	(9·00)	(8·89)	(12·21)	(10·99)
5. 5–10	+2·32	+6·24	+9·40	+5·64
	(8·92)	(8·80)	(12·09)	(10·88)
6. 10–15	+2·85	+6·26	+0·00	+1·69
	(9·32)	(9·20)	(12·64)	(11·38)
7. 15–25	+9·14	+16·43	+8·16	+5·49
	(9·26)	(9·14)	(12·55)	(11·30)
8. 25–50	+9·81	+16·80	+13·52	+10·18
	(9·23)	(9·11)	(12·52)	(11·26)
9. 50–90	+11·74	+24·88	+2·25	−0·05
	(9·89)	(9·76)	(13·40)	(12·06)
10. Size unknown	−27·92	−6·92	−17·03	−51·67
	(0)	(0)	(0)	(0)

Ownership adjustment factors	(1)	(2)	(3)	(4)
1. Firms controlled out- side Canada	−4·31 (2·48)	−8·96 (2·45)	−16·35 (3·37)	−11·73 (3·03)
2. Firms controlled with- in Canada	+2·00 (0)	+4·16 (0)	+7·59 (0)	+5·44 (0)
$\bar{R}^2$	0·093	0·163	0·095	0·092

naires without systematic verification. The data refer to the 1221 firms (all under $90 million in asset size) whose mail questionnaires were analysed.

The firms responding to the questionnaire were asked to indicate their sources of external funds during the period 1955–62. They were asked to show the amounts raised during each year from each of the following sources: '(a) Share capital issued' (column 1). '(b) bonds or debentures issued' (column 2). '(c) Term loans (i) from chartered banks, (ii) from other institutions (specify).' '(d) Bank loans (non-term)' (column 3). '(e) Commercial paper.' '(f) Other non-bank short-term borrowing.' The answers to (c), (e), and (f) are not shown in this table. Virtually all of the Canadian firms issuing commercial paper were covered by the survey, and a record of their borrowings may be found in the *Appendix Volume* to the R.C.B.F. *Report*. Column 4 of the table shows the percentage probability that a firm used external funds of one or more of the types (a) to (f) once or more between 1955 and 1962.

TABLE 7.7

Estimates of Aggregate Reductions in Investment Outlays During the Nine Months Following:

Industry	August 1959				June 1962			
	By firms with assets over $5 million	By all smaller firms[1]	Total for the industry	Total postponements as a percentage of total annual capital expenditures in the industry[2]	By firms with assets over $5 million	By all smaller firms[2]	Total for the industry	Total postponements as a percentage of total annual capital expenditures in the industry[2]
	Amounts in millions of dollars			%	Amounts in millions of dollars			%
1. Food and beverages	0·2	1·5	1·7	1·15	0·1	1·3	1·4	0·95
2. Wood products	0·2	3·7	3·9	1·54	1·5	2·3	3·8	1·50
3. Textiles	1·4	1·6	3·0	7·50	0·1	1·2	1·3	3·25
4. Mining, iron, and steel	0·6	1·8	2·4	0·48	2·3	1·2	3·5	0·70
5. Other manufacturing	0·8	2·2	3·0	1·04	0·7	1·9	2·6	0·90
6. Petroleum	0·4	1·0	1·4	0·36	0·1	0·8	0·9	0·23
7. Electric power	24·0	3·1	27·1	4·69	13·0	2·4	15·4	2·66
8. Railways	0·8	—	0·8	0·21	0·5	—	0·5	0·13
9. Oil and gas pipelines	0·2	0·7	0·9	0·60	0·3	0·5	0·8	0·53
10. Telephones	0·4	—	0·4	0·12	0·2	—	0·2	0·06
11. Other utilities	—	1·3	1·3	0·39	6·0	4·9	10·9	3·27
12. Commercial services	—	10·1	10·1	9·62	—	9·3	9·3	8·85
13. Construction	0·3	4·7	5·0	3·52	0·5	6·3	6·8	4·68
14. Wholesale and retail trade	1·6	3·8	5·4	1·86	0·3	3·4	3·7	1·27
Total for all industries	30·9	35·5	66·4	1·70	23·6	35·5	59·1	1·52

[1] The estimates for small firms were obtained by grossing up the postponements by the sample firms (done separately for each size class) to get a single estimate for all small firms. This was then allocated among industries on the basis of the 1961 capital expenditures by industry (from Department of Trade and Commerce [1963], pp. 11–12) less the expenditures reported by firms with assets over $5 million (obtained from the R.C.B.F. survey).

[2] The total expenditures by industry are from Department of Trade and Commerce [1963], pp. 11–12, for 1963, and Department of Trade and Commerce [1961], pp. 11–12, for 1959.

E. Conclusion

The R.C.B.F. survey results indicate that during the period 1954–62, monetary policy has not acted on investment solely, or even primarily, by changes in current and expected future market interest rates, but has been based more on credit rationing and the effects of credit restraint on subjective cash-flow distributions. The dummy variable multiple regressions also indicate that the size, industry, and ownership factors have all had some separate importance in determining which firms are likely to be affected. What is perhaps more important, the evidence shows that the choice of the monetary policy *mix* (i.e. the relative reliance on open-market operations, direct control over bank lending, and attempts to influence sales expectations) affects not only the total amount of investment altered but also its distribution among firms of different sizes and industries. Thus the extent to which monetary policy has differential effects on various types of investment depends to a considerable extent on the particular aspects of credit conditions on which the authorities choose to operate.

8

FISCAL MEASURES INFLUENCING RESEARCH AND DEVELOPMENT EXPENDITURES

A. INTRODUCTION

IN this chapter we shall discuss the tax treatment of research and development expenditures, and direct subsidies for approved research projects. The special tax treatment of R. & D. will be discussed with reference to the 1962 changes in the Canadian Income Tax Act.[1] The subsidies discussed are those which have been provided by the National Research Council (hereinafter N.R.C.) and the Defence Research Board (D.R.B.) since 1962.

From Chapter 4 we recall that the strategy of a firm's investment in research and development depends significantly on the technology and structure of the industry, and the advantages possessed by existing firms over outsiders. We saw examples of international and industry-wide co-operation, and others of research more closely guarded by individual firms. It was suggested that the larger groups of co-operating firms are more likely to arise where there are substantial economies of scale in research, or where for other reasons the members of the group may expect co-operation to increase their advantage over firms outside the group. The economic rationale behind special tax and subsidy treatment of research expenditures is that, whatever the size of the already co-operating group, many of the direct and indirect benefits of the research leak quickly outside, so that the total benefits to society from a given level of research are understated by the appropriate measures of the private rate of return to the firms doing research.

Research and development outlays are undertaken on the expectation that they will help in the discovery of new techniques, products, or processes so as either to increase the value of output for a given factor cost, or to decrease the required factor inputs for a given level

[1] Sections 72 and 72A, Income Tax Act, R.S.C., 1962–3, c.8, enacted 29 November 1962.

of output. Although the definition is not entirely satisfactory, we shall define technical progress as an outward movement in the production possibilities frontier for any combination of factors.[1] For the purposes of analysing investment behaviour it may be useful to classify technical progress on two different bases. The first distinction is between embodied and disembodied technical progress. Embodied technical progress can be utilized only by building machinery and equipment specifically designed to embody the new techniques. This is to be contrasted with disembodied technical progress, which changes the production possibilities curve for all capital stock regardless of age.

There is a second basis for the classification of technical progress which is essential to the discussion of externalities.[2] We shall analyse two extreme types of R. & D. outputs; knowledge which is the exclusive property of the finder, and that which is freely available to all (though, of course, not of equal value to all).

Cross-classifying, we have four limiting types of output from R. & D. activity. Although the actual results of any particular research effort will typically be some mixture of the four types, we shall analyse separately only the four extreme categories.

(1) *Embodied technical progress, being the exclusive property of the finder*

In this case, by definition, the firm, industry, or research association making the discovery receives the entire discovery value. Since the progress is of the embodied type there is an incentive to replace the existing capacity with equipment embodying the new techniques. The strength of the inducement to invest will depend on the relationship between the direct and overhead costs, the alternative uses, and the age, of the old equipment. If the discovering firm or organization is the only organization actually, or potentially, in the industry, then the distribution of the discovery value between the firm, factor suppliers, and product users will depend on the market structure and

---

[1] Since nothing is said about the relative sizes of the movement for various factor proportions or scales of output we are not necessarily assuming either homogeneity of production functions or any type of neutrality of technical progress.

[2] The definition of externality implied in the following discussion is equivalent to that set out by Buchanan and Stubblebine [1962]. The externalities to which we refer may be either 'potentially irrelevant' or 'irrelevant', since they may balance out in a particular case so as to leave the externally affected parties with no desire to alter the level of R. & D. activity performed by the inventing firm (ibid., p. 374).

cross-elasticities of demand. If the discovering firm is only one of a number of producers, and has sole control of the innovation through ownership of patent rights, then a market is likely to develop for the rights to use the new process, and/or the firm will expand to take a larger share of the market. Whether the other firms in the industry suffer capital losses because of the invention will depend on the nature of the market,[1] as well as on the extent to which technical progress had been expected to occur at that time. If an industry has regular, relatively predictable, technological advances of the embodied type, then firms presumably plan their investment on the expectation of obsolescence within a certain period. If assets are valued by the share market on the same expectation, there need be no market capital gains or losses when the expected event occurs. If neither the exact nature nor the timing of the invention had been expected with a high degree of certainty, there will be a pattern of capital gains and losses associated with the discovery when it occurs. Whether there are net external economies or diseconomies arising from greater expenditures on R. & D. will depend on the accuracy and variability of firms' and share markets' expectations about the direction and speed of technical progress. If the greater flow of embodied technical progress is consistently underestimated by those making investment decisions, then assets will in general be purchased on the assumption of a longer revenue life than will in fact be achieved, and the achieved social and private rate of return in the rest of the industry may be lowered by a faster technical advance of the inventing firm. Similarly, if the flow of new techniques is, or is thought to be, extremely variable in its nature and timing, the greater research activity may so increase the dispersion of the cash-flow distributions available to the non-inventing firms as to swamp the possible increases in the expected value (before risk adjustment) of their cash-flow distributions.[2]

[1] In the rest of the analysis we shall be assuming some inelasticity of demand for the output of any producer, and a considerable inelasticity for the industry as a whole. If the market price were fixed, and demand were completely elastic (production for the world market?), then no existing asset's PV would be affected by embodied technical progress (assuming complete elasticity of supply of the factors used by both old and new processes).

[2] Higher expected values of cash flow may exist if the patent rights are likely to be available at a price low enough to produce a net PV residue (before risk standardization) for the purchaser.

(2) *Disembodied technical progress, being the exclusive property of the finder*

As in the last case, there are potential capital losses,[1] the magnitude of which would depend on the extent to which the exact nature and timing of the breakthrough were forecast. In this case it begins to matter whether the discovering group is the whole industry, or a single participant whose discovery is guarded by patent privileges. In the latter case there is every likelihood that a market will develop for the rights to use the new technique, since by definition it can be used, without further capital expenditures, in all existing plants.

Since this type of technical progress does not destroy the use value of the existing capital stock, a faster rate of technical progress is less likely to produce net external diseconomies. The monopoly position of the discovering firm suggests that all the discovery value will in fact accrue to that firm. The existence of net external economies or diseconomies will then depend on the extent to which the progress (and the price of the right to use it) is anticipated by other inventing firms and by share buyers.

(3) *Embodied technical progress, freely available to all*

In this case there are capital gains and losses on all assets whose obsolescence had not been accurately anticipated. The advantages of the technical progress accrue to all those in a position to make new investments. If there is not free disposal of existing assets, or if the holders of existing assets which have suffered capital losses are not able to raise additional funds on good terms ('once bitten, twice shy'), the new entrant might have an advantage over the existing firm. If experience in the industry still conferred market power or technical superiority on a firm, then the existing firms might retain an advantage over outsiders.

Unless the inventing firm were better able to predict the date and exact nature of the discovery, it would be in no better position than any other firm to take advantage of the resulting investment opportunities. If the technical progress is not consistently under (or over-) estimated, or responsible for greater risk, all the potential entrants to the industry will receive PV increments from a faster rate of technical progress.[2] The inventing firm gets a larger share of the total benefits

---

[1] And possible capital gains for the firms whose assets were purchased, and valued by shareholders, on the assumption of earlier or more drastic obsolescence.

[2] The more so, the more elastic the demand for total industry output.

only if there are substantial time-lags in the transmission of knowledge among firms, or if firms are so specialized that other firms are less able than the inventing firm to take advantage of the new process, even though the techniques themselves are freely available to all.

(4) *Disembodied technical progress, freely available to all*

In this case there are fewer advantages possible for the inventing firm, since the disembodied character of the techniques makes it less important to predict the time of their arrival. Although the progress will increase the PV of the programmes of all the producing firms,[1] there will be no special gains for the firm doing the research. In this case (and in (3) above) the forces leading to merger or co-operation of interested firms are considerable. In the absence of such co-operation,[2] the undertaking of R. & D. will lead to external economies. The extent of the external economies, as in case (3) above, will depend on the ease with which the total market can be expanded, and the forces determining the size and number of non-co-operating groups.

The general case for research subsidies appears to rest on technical progress of types (3) and (4), especially the latter. If evidence (which should be of better quality than that found in this chapter and in Chapter 4) indicates that R. & D. efforts are producing many results possessing these characteristics to a considerable degree, there still remains the problem of choosing the most appropriate amount and form of subsidy. One basic difficulty is that the externalities are not 'separable',[3] i.e. the PV increments accruing to each of the firms, including the inventing firm, depend on the reactions of all the other firms to the results of the research. In addition, since R. & D. produces results whose characteristics are blends of the characteristics of the four extreme types discussed above, it is not clear what basis should be chosen for the subsidy payments. We may conclude from the analysis above that the externalities are likely to increase with the number of other firms in a position to take advantage of the results.

---

[1] This assumes, of course, that the elasticity of demand for the output of the industry is greater than one.

[2] To form what Davis and Whinston [1962], refer to as the 'natural unit': that unit which is large enough to internalize all the benefits from the R. & D. If such co-operation takes place (at no extra cost), the distinction vanishes between technical progress of types (3) and (4) (and so, for the same reason, does the distinction between types (1) and (2)).

[3] Davis and Whinston, op. cit., p. 244.

This suggests that expenditures which are particular to a firm's private process or product might produce smaller external effects than expenditures on basic research[1] whose results were published for general use, but there is no obvious way of dividing R. & D. expenditures according to the amount of external economies or diseconomies they are likely to produce.

B. THE DISTRIBUTION OF RESEARCH AND DEVELOPMENT EXPENDITURES

An analysis of the distribution of Canadian industrial research and development expenditures in 1961 might help to set the stage for study of the fiscal measures introduced in 1962. Bearing in mind that firms (and governments) differ in what they classify in their accounts as research and development expenditures, the efforts of the Business Finance Division of the Dominion Bureau of Statistics to obtain statistics on a comparable basis have made at least rough comparisons possible.

Table 8.1 shows the 1961 R. & D. expenditures (excluding capital expenditures) in Canada by industrial firms.

To find total outlays on research and development it is necessary to add payments made to organizations outside Canada, for which an industrial breakdown is unfortunately not available. These payments totalled $31·2 million in 1961, 87 per cent. of which went to parent, affiliate, or subsidiary firms in other countries.[2] Of the total of research expenditures undertaken within the reporting Canadian firms in 1961, 77 per cent. were financed by the reporting firms or their affiliates, and 16 per cent. were undertaken on government contracts.[3]

Tentative analysis of time-series data suggests that, for industry groups, R. & D. outlays have been more stable as a fraction of sales revenue than in absolute terms or as a function of time. Some regressions were run using 1955, 1957, 1959, and 1961 data for thirteen industries.[4] Experiments were run using pooled time-series

[1] Nelson [1959] uses this argument as the basis for his recommendation that basic research should be subsidized more than other forms of R. & D.

[2] Dominion Bureau of Statistics [1963], p. 8.

[3] The chief contractors were the Department of National Defence, Defence Production, and Atomic Energy of Canada. The Defence Research Board was a lesser contractor, responsible for approximately 10 per cent. of the total. For an analysis of these contracts, see Dominion Bureau of Statistics [1961a], p. 20.

[4] Surveys of R. & D. outlays in 1955, 1957, 1959, and 1961 have been made by the Dominion Bureau of Statistics, and published in four reports, of which the most recent is Dominion Bureau of Statistics [1963].

N

TABLE 8.1

Industry	R. & D. expenditures per $100 of sales[1]	R. & D. expenditures in millions of dollars
	$	$
Electrical products	2·67	21·76
Chemicals and chemical products	1·49	20·97
Transportation equipment	1·47	19·86
Machinery	1·10	4·90
Rubber	1·08	1·37
Textiles	1·01	1·13
Other manufacturing	0·98	5·20
Mines, quarries, and oil wells	0·91	7·06
Non-metallic mineral products	0·75	1·37
Metal fabricating	0·69	2·18
Furniture and fixtures	0·67	0·13
Paper and allied industries	0·45	7·07
Primary metals	0·44	7·59
Petroleum and coal products	0·35	5·10
Food and beverages	0·16	2·88
Transportation, storage, communication, and other utilities	0·14	3·14
Wood	0·07	0·08
Total, all industries	0·74	115·16

[1] The denominator is the total value of sales for all firms (in the industry) reporting R. & D. expenditures. The figures are derived from Dominion Bureau of Statistics [1963], Tables 1 and 12, pp. 11 and 18.

and cross-section data, allowing for time effects, industry effects, and interaction terms. The best regressions were:

$$\text{R. \& D.} = 2500 + 0.0122\,P + 0.179\,PE + 0.120\,PT + 42932\,T57$$
$$\phantom{\text{R. \& D.} = 2500 + } (0.007) \quad (0.039) \quad (0.020) \quad (5454)$$
$$\bar{R}^2 = 0.796.$$

$$\text{R. \& D.} = 1950 + 0.0011\,S + 0.0096\,SE + 0.0077\,ST + 42575\,T57$$
$$\phantom{\text{R. \& D.} = 1950 + } (0.0005) \quad (0.0018) \quad (0.0012) \quad (5234)$$
$$\bar{R}^2 = 0.816.$$

Where

R. & D. = R. & D. expenditures for the industry-year in thousands of dollars, being the sum of expenditures by firms reporting to the D.B.S. survey.

$P =$ Current annual profits of the whole industry (which presumably includes some firms doing R. & D. but not reporting to the survey).

$S =$ Current year sales of the industry (both sales and profits in thousands of dollars).

$E =$ Dummy variable taking the value 1 for each observation of the electrical apparatus and supplies industry, and 0 elsewhere.

$T =$ Dummy variable taking the value 1 for each observation of the transportation equipment industry, and 0 elsewhere.

$T57 =$ Dummy variable taking the value 1 for the 1957 observation of the transportation equipment industry.

The compound variables are the products of their components, e.g. $PE = P$ times E. The standard errors are in brackets below the estimated coefficients.

The equations suggest that R. & D. expenditures are slightly more closely related to current year sales than to current year profits, and are significantly higher in the transportation equipment and electrical apparatus industries. The R. & D. expenditures in the transportation industry were especially high in 1957, when major military aircraft projects were in the development stage. The two industries have been the prime recipients of Defence Research Board contracts and subsidies. The regression results tend to support the qualitative evidence of Chapter 4 that the level of sales is a benchmark frequently used when budget decisions are made about the appropriate level of research and development expenditures.

Evidence from a 1959 survey indicates that large firms are much more likely than small firms to support a research programme, but that for those small firms which do research, it is a larger fraction of their sales revenue.[1] Interview evidence suggests that there are substantial economies of scale in the operation of a research department and in the use of research results. Officials frequently emphasized that the hiring of senior scientific staff must be regarded as a fixed investment, and that frequent increases and decreases in the size of a research department would be sure to damage its productivity. A large firm is more likely to be able to support a continuing research

[1] Dominion Bureau of Statistics [1961b]. There is an obvious parallel with the distribution of capital expenditures (and the effects of monetary policy) among firms of different sizes. See Chapter 7.

programme of any given size,[1] as only with a substantial flow of research projects is a firm likely to be able to interleave the demands on the various research facilities.[2] The economies of scale are even more obvious in the case of specialized scientific equipment, which a small research department is not likely to be able to use to capacity. Large scale also permits parallel approaches to the same research problem, a feature which may be especially relevant where time is important, and the results of research unpredictable.[3]

Economies of scale in the use of research results may exist where the process or product discovered requires a certain scale of operation to be feasible. This is particularly so where the rights to the use of the research results can be closely controlled by patents or licences.[4] The special advantages to the large firm are limited by the fact that the small firm is always able to sell research results to another firm with adequate size to employ them.[5] It has also been argued that the institutional nature of research laboratories in large firms makes them well suited for development research, but less likely to produce major inventions.[6]

C. Description of Incentive Measures

Three separate research incentive schemes were adopted in 1962.

(1) *Additional tax deduction*

A tax measure in the April 1962 budget recommended that corporations be allowed to deduct all current and capital expenditures made in Canada on scientific research, when computing taxable income, and in addition to deduct from taxable income 50 per cent. of the excess of expenditures made in the current year over those made

---

[1] Evidence indicates, but not strongly, that the R. & D./sales ratio is higher for larger than for smaller firms within an industry. See Hamberg [1964]. No such relation was found by Worley [1961].

[2] This is a separate point from the risk-pooling aspect of a large research programme, which has been used as a basis for a defence of high industrial concentration, e.g. Baldwin [1962].

[3] This point is considered in more detail by Nelson [1961].

[4] Thus Griliches and Schmookler [1963], have found that patented inventions are distributed among firms of different sizes and industries in relation to the value added by the firm.

[5] Evidence that large firms are in a better position to employ the research results is provided by E. Mansfield's results [1963a, 1963b], that larger firms are quicker to adopt new techniques once they have been discovered.

[6] On both points, see Ames [1961], and on the latter point especially, Hamberg [1963].

during the base year.[1] As noted previously the definition of research adopted in the legislation specifically excludes several important types of information gathering activity.[2]

In 1965 the Finance Minister announced[3] that new legislation would be introduced to carry on the tax incentive for research after the expiry of the existing provision at the end of 1966. The new legislation increases the scope of the incentive by making it available as either a direct grant or a reduction of taxes (the 1962 incentive was not available until the firm was actually paying taxes). Instead of being an extra tax deduction of 50 per cent., the new incentive is a grant equal to 25 per cent. of all capital expenditures on R. & D. With a 50 per cent. tax rate the two measures provide an equivalent incentive for capital expenditures, except that there are no base year provisions for capital expenditures under the new incentive. There is a base year provision for R. & D. current outlays, however, as the 25 per cent. grant is available only for the excess of a particular year's R. & D. current outlays over the average current outlays for the three preceding years. The new measure thereby increases the value of the incentive for firms not currently earning profits, provides more incentive for R. & D. capital expenditures, and, in most cases, less for R. & D. current expenditures. Since the evidence presented in Section D below was collected in 1963, it does not deal at all with the legislation introduced in 1965, although, as has been noted elsewhere,[4] corporate officials making research decisions in 1965 usually assumed that some form of research incentive would be provided after 1966.

[1] The base year is the last taxation year ending before 11 April 1962.

[2] An Order-in-Council passed 1 March 1963, defines scientific research as 'a systematic investigation . . . in the field of science

   (a) to acquire new knowledge,
   (b) to devise or develop new products or processes, or
   (c) to apply newly acquired knowledge in making improvements to existing products or processes.

including expenditures for the development and testing of prototypes of new products or processes, but not to include:

   (a) market research,
   (b) sales promotion,
   (c) quality control of products or routine product testing,
   (d) research in social sciences,
   (e) prospecting, exploring, or drilling for minerals, petroleum, or natural gas, including geological, geophysical or related studies,
   (f) preparation of specifications . . . for commercial production'.

[3] Canada, House of Commons [1965], pp. 436-7.

[4] *Taxation and Investment*, p. 262.

(2) *Defence industrial research programme of the Defence Research Board*

The D.R.B. scheme is intended to cover half the cost of research projects chosen so as to further technological advance in defence-oriented industries.

(3) *Industrial research assistance programme of the National Research Council*

The N.R.C. assistance provides the salaries of personnel hired to undertake approved research projects. (The salaries are usually about one-half the total cost of the research programme.) The most important difference between the N.R.C. and D.R.B. schemes is that a firm which hopes to get an N.R.C. grant must show that the grant will lead to a (continuing) net increase in the company's research staff, while the D.R.B. is more interested in subsidizing projects which are likely to have a short- or long-term defence potential, and is less concerned that there should be a net increase in research activity.[1]

D. EFFECTS OF THE MEASURES

(1) *Additional tax deduction*

The coincidence of the tax change with the N.R.C. and D.R.B. schemes makes it difficult to analyse separately the effects of the 150 per cent. write-off. The effects of the tax incentive on present value calculations demonstrate its considerable impact on the return on research outlays. Appropriate points of comparison might be the tax treatment of research in other countries, and the Canadian treatment of other kinds of information-gathering expenditure. In 1961 firms spent $115 million on the current costs of research and development in Canada. Capital expenditures for research facilities were $12·5 million. If we assume that the capital expenditures for research facilities were 25 per cent. for buildings and 75 per cent. for machinery and equipment,[2] we can assess the present value of tax deductions under alternative tax systems. Table 8.2 shows the present

---

[1] The D.R.B. Research Committee estimate that perhaps half the personnel subsidized under their programme are additional staff hired to undertake the approved projects.

[2] This was the 1961 distribution between construction and machinery of all capital expenditures in manufacturing industries. Department of Trade and Commerce [1961].

TABLE 8.2
PRESENT VALUES OF TAX DEDUCTIONS FOR R. & D. CAPITAL EXPENDITURES
(As a percentage of the initial cost of the assets)

	Column 1 Pre-1962 Canadian treatment of all capital expenditures[1] (%)	Column 2 1963–5 Canadian treatment of capital expenditures of specified firms[2] (%)	Column 3 U.S. treatment[3] (but assuming a 50% tax rate for comparison purposes) (%)	Column 4 1962–6 Canadian treatment of R. & D. capital expenditures[4] (%)
(a) If deductions are available after 1 year	29·2	32·6	45·4	68·2
(b) If deductions are available immediately	32·1	35·9	50·0	75·0

PRESENT VALUES OF TAX DEDUCTIONS FOR R. & D. CURRENT OUTLAYS

	Pre-1962 Canadian treatment (%)	U.S. treatment (%)	1962–6 Canadian treatment (%)
(c) If deductions are available after 1 year	45·4	45·4	68·2
(d) If deductions are available immediately	50·0	50·0	75·0

All PV's are calculated using 10 per cent. as a representative standard-risk discount rate.

[1] I.e. 5 per cent. declining balance on buildings, and 20 per cent. declining balance on machinery. These rates still apply to non-R. & D. expenditures of firms not qualifying for special treatment under the 1963 amendments. See Chapter 6.

[2] This takes account of the 1963 accelerated depreciation (50 per cent. straight line) on Class 8 assets purchased by firms with the required degree of Canadian ownership and control. See Chapter 6 for details.

[3] As described in Van Hoorn [1962], p. 272. Corporations are allowed to write off all research and development expenditures, capital and current, against current income for tax purposes.

[4] Within the fiscal years 1962–6 inclusive, firms were able to write off 150 per cent. of current and capital R. & D. expenditures (in excess of those in the base year) against taxable income. The 1965 Budget Speech proposed that in 1967 and thereafter the 150 per cent. write-off be replaced by a grant equal to 25 per cent. of all R. & D. capital expenditures, and 75 per cent. of the increase in current R. & D. outlays over the average of the three preceding years. Canada, House of Commons [1965], pp. 436–7.

TABLE 8.3
ADDITIONAL DEDUCTION FOR SCIENTIFIC RESEARCH—SECTION 72A (1962)
(Summary of questionnaire responses)

Number of companies reporting: 115
Companies to which Section 72A does not apply: 18
Companies with tax saving: 28
Companies with no tax saving: 69

Total tax saving for 1962 fiscal year, by size and industry groups

	Total	Companies with tax saving	Companies with no tax saving	Incentive not applicable	Amount of saving	Per cent. of saving to taxable income
By size						
1. Large companies (with assets over $90 million)	51	19	25	7	958,068	0·47[2]
2. Medium size companies (with assets between $25–90 million)	38	8	23[1]	7	366,950	2·54[3]
3. Small companies (with assets less than $25 million)	26	1	21	4	1,927	6·7
Total	115	28	69	18	$1,327,000	0·6
By industry						
1. Mining and quarrying	11	4	6	1	127,818	0·38
2. Pulp and paper mills	12	6	6	—	129,044	0·18
3. Primary metal manufacturing	8	3	5	—	160,303	0·42
4. Petroleum, oil and gas wells and products	12	1	8	3	125,000	—
5. Other manufacturing	45	14	31	—	784,680	1·02
6. Transport, communication, utilities	21	—	12	9	—	—
7. Trade	6	—	1	5	—	—
Total	115	28	69	18	$1,327,000	0·6

TABLE 8.3—continued

		Total	Yes	No	No answer
Question 3: Was the saving (if any) the result of a planned change in the activities of the firm designed to take advantage of the provision?	*Answers to Question 3*				
	1. Large companies	19	3	15	1
	2. Medium size companies	8	3	5	—
	3. Small companies	1	1	—	—
	Total	28	7	20	1

(See Appendix I of *Taxation and Investment* for a copy of the questionnaire, and for an analysis of sampling procedures and response rates for the questionnaire.)

[1] One company which had a tax saving of $484 is included here because most of its research is carried out by an Association; therefore, this amount is not comparable to taxable income.

[2] Includes one company with saving but no taxable income.

[3] Includes two companies with tax saving but no taxable income.

value, at a 10 per cent. rate of discount, and with a 50 per cent. rate of corporate income tax, of the pre-1962 Canadian depreciation allowances for R. & D. capital expenditures, the Canadian allowances for non-R. & D. capital expenditures, the U.S. treatment, and the Canadian treatment under Sections 72 and 72A. The present values of tax deductions are calculated as percentages of the initial capital expenditures.[1]

Table 8.2 shows that both capital and current outlays for R. & D. are allowed substantially more tax deduction in Canada than they are in the United States. The tax advantages of approved R. & D. expenditures over expenditure on market research or other non-approved forms of information gathering are even more marked.

The Taxation Commission's mail questionnaire in the spring of 1963 included several questions about the impact of Sections 72 and 72A on 1962 tax payments. Of all the incentive measures dealt with in the questionnaire,[2] the R. & D. incentive was the only one which was considered by any substantial number of the respondents to have had any effects on their decisions. Although unverified responses to mail questionnaires are not reliable, they at least help to indicate the public reaction to a tax measure and give some idea of the number of firms affected. Table 8.3 shows the amounts of additional deduction claimed in 1962 by the Commission's sample of firms.

The calculations in Table 8.2 assume that the firm has sufficient taxable income to absorb all the allowed deductions. New or rapidly growing firms may not have currently taxable income, and the present value of the tax deductions is for them correspondingly reduced.

Interview evidence indicates that several firms with established research facilities have advanced by several years their planned expansion of R. & D. staff and facilities. Most of the large firms interviewed have also taken part in the N.R.C. or D.R.B. assistance programmes, so that it is difficult to isolate the effects of the tax incentive. Others noted that the effective size of the incentive depended on whether the firm's base year expenditures had been above or below their trend values.

[1] The calculations in rows (a) and (c) of Table 8.2 assume that all tax deductions reduce tax payments one year after the expenditures have been undertaken. This is an exaggeration of the usual lag in payments. If tax reductions were available immediately, the *PV* of each type of tax credit would rise by 10 per cent., as is shown by the calculations in rows (b) and (d).

[2] The other incentives are discussed fully in Chapters VII and X of *Taxation and Investment*. Those chapters include tabulations of the questionnaire responses.

(2) *The N.R.C. and D.R.B. support schemes*

Table 8.4 shows the amounts and industrial distribution of present and future funds allocated by mid 1964 under the N.R.C. assistance programme. A similar analysis of the D.R.B. grants is not available, but a list of the projects and firms indicates much greater concentration of support in the electrical equipment and electronics industries. Table 8.4 shows that several industries had a larger share of the N.R.C. support in 1964 than they had of the 1961 total of R. & D. outlays. In part, this is due to changes between 1961 and 1964 in the pattern of R. & D. expenditures, in part to the activities of a few large firms, and in part to the special features of the scheme. Several proposals have been turned down by the N.R.C. either because they did not represent an equivalent net increase in the firm's research activity, or because the project was thought by the N.R.C. committee to be development rather than research. This direction of support towards firms expanding their research activities in the search for entirely new products and processes naturally leads to a greater amount of support to those industries with rapidly changing products and technology, and also industries where at least some firms are capable of rapid growth. Both the N.R.C. and D.R.B. grants are available for new firms or small firms with little or no taxable income. This contrasts with the 1962 tax incentive, which had full value only for an established firm with enough currently taxable income to absorb the allowed deductions. In fact, a considerable number of the N.R.C. grants have gone to new firms or associations set up primarily in order to undertake the N.R.C.-sponsored research, and others to research-oriented firms without enough current profits to use the deductions allowed by the tax incentive.

(3) *Conclusion*

Can it be said that the three schemes we have examined have achieved the presumed purpose—to eliminate differences between social and private rates of return on research expenditures? This is not an easy question to answer, as the private returns to research are difficult to establish either *ex ante* or *ex post*. In computing the social rate of return, these problems are compounded by the addition of uncertainty about the appropriate size of the social group to be considered. In the modern world, technology crosses provincial and national borders almost as easily as it travels from firm to firm, or

TABLE 8.4

NATIONAL RESEARCH COUNCIL—INDUSTRIAL RESEARCH ASSISTANCE PROGRAMME
SUMMARY OF PROJECTS APPROVED MARCH 1962 TO AUGUST 1964 IN $'000 OF DOLLARS

Industry	Number of projects	Number of firms	(1) N.R.C. support 1962/3	(2) Ex-pended 1962/3	(3) N.R.C. support 1963/4	(4) Ex-pended 1963/4	(5) N.R.C. support 1964/5	(6) Average duration of projects	(7) For-ward support	(8) Total N.R.C. support	(9) Firms' share	(10) Total cost
Food and beverage	12	8	91	52	234	192	298	4·2	664	1,207	1,264	2,470
Rubber	2	1	49	25	140	81	215	5·5	880	1,200	908	2,108
Wood	3	2	—	—	63	26	112	4·3	208	346	454	800
Paper	6	4	45	33	74	66	83	3·1	67	250	388	638
Primary metals	6	5	40	40	162	128	277	3·3	270	715	979	1,695
Machinery	11	4	98	55	158	116	183	4·2	376	731	915	1,646
Electrical products	17	11	168	94	364	272	461	3·3	1291	2,118	2,824	4,942
Non-metallic minerals	7	4	45	21	109	88	113	3·8	304	526	469	994
Petroleum and coal products	3	2	8	8	47	45	76	3·3	95	223	224	447
Chemicals and chemical products	24	16	272	188	640	509	812	3·9	2044	3,554	3,873	7,427
Other	5	5	27	27	101	80	111	3·8	123	335	377	712
Totals	96	62	843	543	2092	1603	2741	3·8	6322	11,205	12,675	23,879

Columns (1) and (2) show the funds approved for grants during the specified years on projects approved.
Columns (3) and (4) show the amounts that the firms were able to spend; the discrepancy reflects delays, mostly caused by difficulties in hiring staff.
Column (6) shows the average expected duration of the approved projects, in years.
Column (7) shows the estimated N.R.C. outlays over the next five years on projects already approved.
Column (8) is the sum of Columns (1), (3), (5), and (7).
Column (9) shows the estimated expenditures by firms on plant, equipment, and materials for the approved projects.
Column (10) is the sum of Columns (8) and (9).

even from department to department within a firm. Should the technological advances in country B, based on country A's results, be given a positive or negative value, or ignored entirely, in A's calculations of the benefits flowing from research? Such technological aid to B may be considered as part of A's contribution to less developed economies, and be given a positive value in A's calculations. But it is also possible that it should have a negative value; for example, if the value to A of its research results depends on the margin of technological superiority over B that is gained thereby.

Some assumptions would have to be made about these central problems of measurement before the appropriateness of particular incentives could be assessed. This is particularly so if alternative measures differ in their balance of effects within and outside the borders of the country. For example, suppose that the PV of research results is directly related to the number of skilled scientists doing research and the size of the country using the results. Then if skilled scientists were fixed in supply in the short run, and if small countries adopted a scheme which caused scientists to immigrate, and then kept to themselves the results of the research, their actions would increase the PV of research in the small countries but reduce it for the world as a whole. This type of policy is to be contrasted with one which increases the total world supply of skilled scientists while not imposing a drain on the human resources of other countries.

If the goal of the Canadian tax and subsidy incentives has been solely to increase the amount of R. & D., without regard to the opportunity cost of the resources transferred from other industries or other countries, their success can be measured by reference solely to the expansion of R. & D. Both qualitative and quantitative evidence indicate that the 1962 tax and subsidy measures influenced a considerable number of decisions to expand R. & D. activity.

In assessing the overall suitability of the measures as features of public policy such a partial view is not appropriate. Even if narrowly nationalistic standards are used, whereby foreign resources are valued only at their foreign exchange cost, it is still necessary to establish the opportunity cost of domestic resources transferred, and compare the sum of the costs with some measure of the research results. Perhaps after the research projects have been completed, it will be possible, at least in the case of the N.R.C.–D.R.B. projects, to analyse the output, and to establish a *PV* for some of the results.[1] Many firms interviewed stated that past research activity has always been successful enough (taken as a whole) to encourage the adoption of an expanded programme, indicating that estimates of returns have tended to understate the expectation of even the private return.[2] But this fragmentary qualitative evidence is no substitute for detailed empirical study. The considerable fluctuations in the operative accounting definitions of research expenditures, and the fact that the direct results of the research are seldom explicitly valued, mean that statistical analysis of the yield on research expenditures may require study of specific research projects. An evaluation of the external economies, on which must depend any judgement about the value of the incentive measures, poses less tractable problems. It is possible that even the private return on research is enough above firms' estimates to justify the use of special measures,[3] but even then the choice of the appropriate degree of incentive requires the evaluation of external economies.

As in the case of other specific public policies dealt with in this book, final judgements about particular research incentives must not ignore macroeconomic balance and the general requirements of efficient resource allocation over time.

[1] The simplest measure, of course, would be the market value of the production rights, but this is inadequate for the same reason that the research incentives were originally introduced—because the total benefits of the research may be substantially greater than the discovery value under the control of the firm doing the research.

[2] Evidence from other countries tends to support this view. Mansfield [1965], has recently attempted to measure the *ex post* rate of return on R. & D., and found that his estimates of actual returns were higher than the firms' *ex ante* required rates of return.

[3] Assuming, of course, that rate of return calculations on other types of investment are not similarly biased downwards.

9

TAXATION AND RESOURCE DEVELOPMENT

THIS chapter describes the tax treatment of the petroleum and mining industries, assesses the special features of investment in these industries, and suggests how the pattern of investment outlays might be affected if there were no special tax provisions. These two industries are singled out for detailed study because of their substantial size, and because they have received special treatment under the corporation income tax. No explanation of the size and composition of investment outlays in Canada could be adequate unless account were taken of the factors governing investment in these two industries. The tax measures themselves are worth studying because of their substantial impact on investment incentives, and because even though they have been used as a part of the basic tax structure rather than as stabilization measures, their impact on resource allocation has brought them into many discussions of tax reform.

A. THE PRODUCTION OF OIL AND GAS

Investment programmes of firms operating in this industry may contain expenditures in four major areas:

    (i) exploration for oil and gas,
    (ii) production of crude oil and gas,
    (iii) refining of crude oil and processing of gas,
    (iv) marketing.

'Integrated' firms are those which undertake all four classes of expenditure, while the term 'producing' firms will be used to describe those which make expenditures only for exploration and production, Although the distinction cannot be made with great precision, exploratory drilling takes place 'outside the limits of known pools. either in search of a new field (a new field wildcat) or a new pool extending an existing field',[1] while production (development) drilling is for the extraction of oil or gas from known pools.

[1] Shearer [1964, p. 212].

Since the expected value and dispersion of the subjective probability distribution of returns from any drilling prospect is directly related to the proximity and nature of neighbouring wells, the amount of geophysical exploration that has been done, and the known characteristics of the region, not too much emphasis should be placed on the exact cut-off line between exploratory and development drilling. Nevertheless the distinction is a valuable one, as it is fairly consistently made throughout the industry and separates two classes of drilling for which the dispersion of rates of return is substantially different.[1]

Investment in refining and marketing (iii and iv above) has no special characteristics to distinguish it from investment in manufacturing and distribution generally. It is important for consideration in this chapter because a large proportion of investment in exploration and production is carried out by integrated firms also investing in refining and marketing. This vertical integration is especially important in the light of the tax measures to be considered below.

We shall compare the tax treatment of oil and gas production with that of manufacturing operations. The general reference will be to the treatment under the Canadian Income Tax Act and Regulations as they were in 1964. Detailed provisions will not be considered and the examples used are intended to illustrate the general pattern of tax provisions rather than to capture any precise circumstances. We shall deal with depletion allowances, the tax treatment of drilling and exploration expenses, provincial taxes and regulations, and the National Oil Policy.

(1) Depletion allowances[2]

The Canadian percentage depletion allowance permits $33\frac{1}{3}$ per cent. of a firm's net income from oil and gas production to be deducted

---

[1] Shearer [1964, p. 212] records that, in the period 1948–54, 90·5 per cent. of all development wells drilled in Western Canada were classified in the *Bulletin of the American Association of Petroleum Geologists* as successful, compared with success ratios of 18 per cent. for new field wildcats and 27 per cent. for all exploratory drilling. New field wildcats are a sub-class of exploratory drilling concerned with discovering a new field rather than a new pool extending an existing field. Whether or not preliminary geophysical costs are pro-rated as costs of drilling exploratory wells, the per-well cost is also greater for exploration than for development drilling. See M. W. Matthews [1963, p. 120].

[2] In this section we shall be concerned only with operators' depletion. To qualify as an operator, a corporation or individual must have an interest in profits net of operating costs. There are also non-operators and shareholder depletion provisions. Under Part XII, Section 1202 of the Income Tax Regula-

when computing income subject to tax. An alternative system,[1] similar to that used in the United States, would grant a certain percentage of the firm's gross income from oil and gas production as a depletion allowance. Both types of allowance were originally designed to compensate roughly for the fact that certain lease acquisition and discovery costs were not allowable expenses. In Canada, at least since 1962, there are now almost no expenditures which are not allowed as tax deductions, so that the depletion allowance is no longer intended as a device for allocating expenses against taxable income. The Canadian net depletion allowance can only be claimed on income net of all current and accumulated past drilling and exploration expenditures, so that firms must have some taxable income net of all allowable expenses before they can claim any depletion allowance.

We may illustrate the differences between the gross and net depletion allowances, and the general features of both, as follows:

(The definitions below are for this chapter alone.)

PV_T = present value of income tax payable by the firm over the n years within the investment horizon.

$R_{E \& P}$ = gross revenues from the firm's exploration and production activities during the year. These revenues may come from the sale of crude oil or unprocessed gas, or from the sale or farming out of drilling or production rights.

$R_{R \& M}$ = gross revenue from the firm's refining and marketing activities.

$C_{D \& E}$ = current outlays on drilling and exploration. These include all payments for drilling rights (see Subsection (2) below for details).

C_P = current costs of producing crude oil, including depreciation allowances on depreciable well equipment.

---

tions, non-operators who have a share or royalty based on the volume or gross value of mineral production may deduct as a depletion allowance 25 per cent. of the income so received. Under Part XIII, Section 1300 of the Income Tax Regulations, shareholders of Canadian corporations earning mineral profits may claim as a depletion allowance 10 per cent., 15 per cent., or 20 per cent. of dividends received, depending on whether mineral profits constitute more than 25 per cent., 50 per cent., or 75 per cent. of the corporation's income. The categories of operators, non-operators, and shareholder depletion apply with respect to income from metal mines as well as from oil and gas production.

[1] As recommended by the Royal Commission on Canada's Economic Prospects [1957, Appendix H].

$C_{R\ \&\ M}$ = current costs of refining and marketing, including depreciation allowances.

C^* = accumulated net excess of C items over R items. In any year t when the total of allowed costs (C items) is greater than total revenues, the net tax is zero, and the difference is added to $C_t{}^*_{-1}$ to obtain $C_t{}^*$. If in any year the R items total more than the C items, the difference is subtracted from $C_t{}^*_{-1}$ to obtain $C_t{}^*$. Tax is only paid in those years when $C_t{}^*_{-1}$ is not great enough to cover the excess of the current revenues over the current costs. C_P and $C_{R\ \&\ M}$ items can only be carried forward 5 years in C^*, after which time they are no longer deductible. $C_{D\ \&\ E}$ can be carried forward indefinitely. Subject to the limitations on the length of time for which C_P and $C_{R\ \&\ M}$ items can be carried forward, $C_t{}^*$, the value of C^* at the end of year t, is found as follows:

$$C_t{}^* = C_t{}^*_{-1} - \hat{C}_t{}^* - \tilde{C}_t{}^*$$

where $\hat{C}_t{}^*$ is the lesser of
(a) $C_t{}^*_{-1}$
(b) $R_{E\ \&\ P} - C_P - C_{D\ \&\ E}$
and $\tilde{C}_t{}^*$ is the lesser of
(a) $C_t{}^*_{-1} - \hat{C}_t{}^*$
(b) $R_{E\ \&\ P} + R_{R\ \&\ M} - C_P - C_{D\ \&\ E} - C_{R\ \&\ M} - \hat{C}_t{}^*$.

δ' = the expected percentage rate of net depletion allowance.
δ'' = the expected percentage rate of gross depletion allowance.
τ_t = the expected percentage rate of corporation income tax.
r = standard-risk annual rate of discount.

Although all of the variables may take different values for different years within the n-year horizon, the time subscripts are suppressed to simplify the notation.

(a) *Net depletion allowance*

$$PV_T = \sum_{t=1}^{n} [\tau_t(R_{E\ \&\ P} - C_{D\ \&\ E} - C_P - \hat{C}^*)(1 - \delta') +$$

$$\tau_t(R_{R\ \&\ M} - C_{R\ \&\ M} - \tilde{C}^*)](1 + r)^{-t}$$

$$\frac{\partial(PV_T)}{\partial\,(\delta')} = \sum_{t=1}^{n} \tau_t(-R_{E\ \&\ P} + C_{D\ \&\ E} + C_P + \hat{C}^*)(1 + r)^{-t}$$

(b) *Gross depletion allowance*

$$PV_T = \sum_{t=1}^{n} \tau_t [R_{E \& P} + R_{R \& M} - C_{D \& E} - C_P -$$

$$C_{R \& M} - \hat{C}^* - \tilde{C}^* - \delta''(R_{E \& P})](1 + r)^{-t}$$

$$\frac{\partial(PV_T)}{\partial(\delta'')} = \sum_{t=1}^{n} \tau_t (-R_{E \quad P})(1 + r)^{-t}$$

The values of the R's, C's, δ', δ'', τ_t, and r that are relevant in the calculation of the expected present value of tax payments are the best present estimates of the expected values in each of the years within the n-year investment horizon. Thus the effects, on the PV of tax payments, of any present or proposed future change in the rate of percentage depletion depends on decision-makers' subjective estimates of depletion rates in a number of future years.

We can see the relevant differences between gross and net depletion by looking at the partial derivatives of the tax payments with respect to changes in the rate of depletion. In the case of the net depletion allowance, the tax advantage of depletion increases with increases in the revenue from oil and gas production, or in the rate of depletion allowance, or in the number of years the increased rate is expected to be applicable, or in the rate of discount. The tax advantage provided by net depletion decreases with increases in drilling or exploration expenditures written off against production income. This latter relationship does not hold in the case of the gross depletion allowance, since the $C_{D \& E}$, C_P, and $\hat{C}^*$ and $\tilde{C}^*$ terms do not enter the derivative $\dfrac{\partial(PV_T)}{\partial(\delta')}$. It has therefore been argued, in favour of a gross allowance, that a net depletion allowance discourages exploration expenditure, and reduces the advantage of immediate deductibility of drilling and exploration expenditures.[1] In a similar way, the net depletion allowance increases the tax advantages conferred upon integrated firms. With respect to depletion allowances, the integrated firm has no advantage over the producing firm if there is a gross depletion allowance. If there is a net allowance, however, and integrated firms are able to offset drilling and exploration expenditures against refining and marketing income, then there is a corresponding increase in the amount of production income subject to the depletion allowance. Thus the present Canadian depletion allowance is of

[1] e.g. Royal Commission on Canada's Economic Prospects [1957, especially pp. 494–6].

greater advantage to integrated firms than to those whose only revenue is from the production of crude oil and gas.

The effects of the net depletion allowance on the rate of return on
new investment are illustrated at the end of the section, on the
assumption that the selling price of the output, and the direct operating costs, are unaffected by changes in the rate of depletion allowance.
The general arguments against the use of depletion allowances as a
part of taxation policy have used the same assumptions, and have
suggested that a distortion is thereby introduced in the allocation of
resources.[1] In defence of depletion allowances, it has been argued by
S. L. McDonald [1961] that a depletion allowance (referring to the
U.S. gross depletion allowance) offsets the discrimination otherwise
introduced by the corporation income tax against capital intensive
and risky ventures.[2] In cases where it is reasonable to assume, as
McDonald does, that capital earns only a required return, and profits
accruing to shareholders over time do not contain a pure rent element, it is true that a profits tax may be interpreted as a tax on the
use of a particular factor, if the point of reference is a tax system
where there is more favourable treatment of payments to that factor.
McDonald argues that rates of return in high risk industries are
higher than in low risk industries, by amounts just sufficient to compensate for the extra risk. This is, of course, entirely consistent with
investment behaviour as analysed in this study. McDonald concludes
that a flat-rate corporation tax will discourage investment in relatively
risky industries, among which he includes the oil and gas industry.
His conclusion only follows if the required payment for risk-bearing
is in terms of a rate of return differential measured in absolute rather
than proportional terms, or if the loss-offset provisions of the tax
are not complete and consistent. With full loss-offsets, only the absolute rate of profits is altered by the imposition of a tax (accepting
McDonald's assumption of full shifting), and the relative sizes of
rates of return and present values of risky and non-risky projects
remain unchanged. As pointed out in Section B of Chapter 6, even
the absolute rate of return (on new investment) would not be altered
by the imposition of a corporate income tax if all expenditures could
be charged off against taxable income.

Both of the arguments used by McDonald to defend the depletion

[1] e.g. Harberger [1955].
[2] See also subsequent contributions by Davidson [1963], Eldridge [1962],
Hause [1963], and Musgrave [1962].

allowance are general rather than particular to the oil and gas industry, and therefore, even to the extent that his assumptions might be satisfied, do not provide a rationale for special treatment of oil and gas production. Even if the corporation income tax does favour less capital intensive and less risky investments than do alternative tax systems, there is no reason to suppose that depletion allowances for certain industries, based neither on capital intensity nor on the degree of risk, are an appropriate means of adjustment.

If there is a case for special treatment of revenues from oil and gas production, it must rather be based on discrepancies between the social and private rate of return in the industry. In the United States it has been argued that the requirement for building up inventories of proven reserves for defence reasons[1] makes the social rate of return on investment in oil reserves greater than the private rate of return. In any event, a subsidy for current extraction of a resource is not the most efficient way of encouraging the creation of a larger stock of unused reserves. A more plausible reason in the Canadian situation would relate to the external economies accompanying research and exploration in areas where the total discovery value of resources does not accrue to the exploring firm. This argument is closely analogous to that underlying the special treatment of industrial research and development expenditures. It would seem more appropriate, if there are such external economies in exploration expenditures, to provide special tax treatment for them rather than for revenue from the sale of proven reserves.

Finally, we must not lose sight of the fact that government actions to affect the allocation of investment between industries and between countries comprise all the regulations, tariffs, royalties, taxes, and government expenditures that influence either selling prices or the costs of production. It would be a mistake to make a judgement on the allocation effects of the depletion allowance in abstraction from the other aspects of government policy affecting investment in oil and gas production.

(2) Drilling and exploration expenditures

The general definition of taxable income employed in the Income Tax Act allows expenditures to be deducted from income (rather than capitalized, or disallowed entirely) if they are incurred directly in the

---

[1] For the industry view, see Lambert [1955, pp. 449–61].

course of earning the income of the current year. Section 83A[1] of the Income Tax Act provides special treatment for drilling and exploration expenditures, as it allows certain classes of taxpayers to deduct drilling and exploration expenditures from income as soon as they are incurred, despite the fact that they are almost always undertaken in order to produce income in several subsequent periods. For firms whose principal business is mining, oil or gas exploration, or the production, distribution, refining or marketing of gas and petroleum products, the treatment of exploration and drilling is more favourable than that of ordinary business expenses in that they may be carried forward indefinitely and under certain circumstances may be passed on to another firm if the corporation is wound up. In the case of ordinary business expenses, the loss carry-forward for normal expenses is limited to five years, and unclaimed expenses cannot in general be transferred to another corporation.

The size of the tax advantage due to this special treatment depends on the availability of other income against which to offset the drilling and exploration expenditures, and, of course, upon the rate of corporation income tax. Integrated firms usually have a higher average ratio of taxable income to drilling and exploration expenses than do producing firms, and are therefore likely to be able to receive the tax deductions sooner. The unlimited carry-forward and possible transfer of unclaimed drilling expenditures to successor corporations reduces

---

[1] Prior to 1962 the Canadian Income Tax Act (Section 83A) defined these expenses to include all geophysical exploration and survey expenditures, all direct drilling costs, expenditures on non-depreciable assets, and lease rentals subject to an upper limit of one dollar per acre. The 1962 amendments extended the definition of allowable drilling and exploration expenditures to include payments made to acquire the right to drill. At the same time, revenues from the sale of such rights became subject to tax in the hands of the vendor. The 1962 Budget Resolutions also extended somewhat the rights of successor corporations to take over unclaimed drilling and exploration expenditures. Subsection 46 of Section 83A now allows a successor corporation which is itself wound up to pass on to a third corporation the yet unclaimed drilling and exploration expenditures acquired from a predecessor corporation. Prior to the change, the right to deduct any particular expenditure could only change hands once. Even after the 1962 changes the rights to deduct drilling and exploration expenditures from any income are restricted to expenditures in Canada by firms whose principal business is the mining of minerals, or the production, refining, and marketing of oil, gas, or petroleum products. (Clause 19 of the 1963 Income Tax Resolutions extended this right to companies whose principal business is the operation of oil or gas pipelines.) Other firms or individuals may deduct drilling and exploration expenditures only to the extent of their income from operating oil and gas wells in Canada.

the advantage of integration somewhat, as these provisions increase the probability that the producing firm will be able eventually to get the tax deduction.

The examples in Table 9.1 (p. 206) illustrate the extent to which the present value of the immediate write-off is dependent on the availability of other current income (as well as on the relevant rate of discount). The effective encouragement of drilling and exploration activity therefore depends on the financial history of the firm as well as the scope and attractiveness of available exploration possibilities. The larger, older, more integrated firms are more likely to be able to write off the expenditures immediately, and thus have a larger incentive to expand exploration activity. It would be inappropriate to attribute the greater exploration activity of the larger firms primarily to this influence, as there also appear to be economies of scale in exploration expenditures. Geophysical exploration in advance of wildcat drilling leads to a higher success ratio in exploratory drilling, and such research is not easily or economically undertaken on a small scale.[1] Furthermore, large firms are able to move in quickly to acquire a large fraction of the leases near a successful test well, and thus are able to gain for themselves a larger proportion of the discovery value of a new field. Interviews did disclose, however, that there have been cases where the small size of some producing firms actually gives them some advantages in speed of decision-making which allows them to move in quickly to promising areas and to take advantage of some of the external economies of exploration work by the larger firms. Furthermore, many small firms try to capture some of the advantages of size (although not of integration) by participation as partners in a far larger number and variety of drilling opportunities than they could discover or finance on their own.[2] This has the effect of decreasing the dispersion of the cash-flow distributions of these firms. Since these contracts allow a material improvement in the risk characteristics of the investment programmes of small firms, these firms are willing to accept a lower expected rate of return on partnership deals in order to gain participation in a larger number of projects with independent risks. The large firms can therefore increase the return on their shares of the wells, since the

[1] See Shearer [1964, especially pp. 218–26]. A more extended analysis, based on U.S. experience, is presented by McKie [1960].

[2] The trading processes by which these deals are made are fully described in Chapter 8 of Grayson [1960].

smaller firms are willing to enter deals with a lower present value (before risk standardization) than would be acceptable to the large firm. The large firms require a higher present value at any given discount rate (before risk adjustment), since fractional participation does not materially affect the risk characteristics of the drilling programme of a firm with a large number of wells spread throughout several different oil fields.

(3) *Provincial taxes and regulations*

There is no possibility of explaining adequately in a few paragraphs the complexities of the provincial regulations governing the production of oil and gas. All that we may hope to consider are some of the main taxes and regulations affecting drilling decisions, and to suggest their effects on the structure of investment programmes. We shall deal with drilling rights and leases, royalties, and regulations governing allowable rates of production and well spacing.

(a) *Drilling rights.* It was noted under (2) above that since 1962 all 'bonus payments' (payments for drilling rights) and lease payments have been deductible as drilling and exploration expenses for the purchasing firm (and classified as income for the vendor). In British Columbia and Alberta, the more recently settled provinces, almost all the mineral rights are in the hands of the Crown, while in Saskatchewan and Manitoba a large fraction of the original land grants included mineral rights. Most mineral rights are therefore leased from the Crown.[1] The leasing rights are one way in which the Crown might appropriate some of the rent on intra-marginal producing properties, since most Crown leases are issued by auction.

(b) *Royalties.* The main producing provinces charge royalties on oil and gas production. British Columbia and Alberta have sliding rates depending on the volume of output from the well in question. The rates of all the provinces (including the sliding scales of British Columbia and Alberta) fall between 5 and 16⅔ per cent., and are applied to the total well-head value of production. The sliding scales (higher rates for higher volume) are presumably intended to enlarge the proportion of the total economic rent coming to the provincial treasury. Inter-provincial and international competition set the chief limits on the extent to which the profits of the producer can be taxed without the location or amount of investment being altered.

---

[1] In Alberta, Saskatchewan, and Manitoba there are also annual property taxes on the value of oil reserves. For details, see Finnis [1963].

(c) *Allowable rates of production.* Since underground oil reservoirs can be tapped from a number of different lease sites, there is an incentive for extensive drilling and fast production rates if an oil field is covered by leases held by non-cooperating firms. In the absence of control, this would lead to over-drilling in areas covered by small leaseholds, and a reduction in total oil or gas recovery, due to over-fast extraction. Several different methods have been used by conservation authorities to combat these incentives. One obvious way, which has been used in all the western provinces, is to set minimum spacing requirements, making adjustments occasionally in the case of special field characteristics. In the light of the general incentive to over-drilling in Alberta (see (d) below), the minimum spacing requirements have often been effective constraints on the density of wells, although the density has still usually been greater than would be found in an unitized field. A second way of avoiding over-drilling is to encourage or enforce co-operation of all the lease holders drilling in the same pool or field, so that they restrict the amount of drilling in the interests of joint profit maximization. This unitization of fields has been carried furthest in Saskatchewan, although there has been some on a smaller scale in other provinces.

The tendency to over-fast extraction could presumably be eliminated by full unitization of all fields, as then the producers would have nothing to gain by producing at a rate so fast as to reduce the present value of the total output of the field. Since unitization is not general, the provinces each set maximum permitted rates (M.P.R.)[1] of extraction for each well, depending on the geological characteristics of the pool. The M.P.R.s are intended to be set so as to maximize the (undiscounted) total production from a field over its lifetime. Since an independent operator of a unitized field would presumably produce so as to maximize the net present value of production, the M.P.R.s are lower than the rates that would be chosen by an profit maximizing group, however large the area covered. The ignoring of the time discount factor in the calculation of the M.P.R.s therefore results in under-production from the most efficient wells, and thus leads to excessive production-spreading in developed fields,

[1] Sometimes this differs from the maximum economic rate (M.E.R.), so called because it is supposed to maximize the total of oil extracted from a field. The M.E.R. is based on the known characteristics of a pool, while the M.P.R. is the permitted rate. In new pools, the M.P.R. may have to be set before the pool's characteristics are known well enough for the M.E.R. to be established. See Matthews [1963, p. 109].

and to development drilling of new fields in advance of the date appropriate for maximizing the net present value of production.[1]

(d) *Pro-rationing*. Since the demand for crude oil in Alberta at the posted well-head price is less than the sum of the M.P.R.s of the producing wells, the conservation board sets economic allowance entitlements for each well, intended to be adequate to cover the costs of the well over the first seven years (the Initial Economic Allowance) and thereafter to cover only operating and maintenance costs (the Operating Economic Allowance). The excess of the market demand over the sum of the Economic Allowances is then pro-rated among wells in proportion to the excess of their M.P.R.s over their Economic Allowances. The pro-rationing scheme was designed to deal with an over-capacity situation, but obviously affects investment incentives in such a way as to perpetuate the situation it was intended to remedy. Since firms may draw their total allowed production from their most efficient wells, they are willing to drill other wells which if considered on their own would be sub-marginal, but which may be used to increase the firm's total production quota.[2] There is thus an incentive to drill wells whose M.P.R.s are not high enough to make the wells attractive if they were considered on their own merits. In addition, of course, there is the continued installation of excess capacity. Since the drilling in question is development drilling of proven reserves, there can be no argument that the pro-rationing system works so as to increase exploratory drilling and the volume of proven reserves. On the contrary, the pro-rationing province is likely to find that an ever smaller proportion of total exploration activity is carried out there. Certainly the net present value contribution of production from any given geological formation is less in the pro-rationing province, so that unless the crude oil from other provinces is very far from being substitutable for a firm's refining and marketing purposes, there will be a shift in exploratory activity away from the pro-rationing province.

---

[1] This is on the assumption, valid at present, that Canadian crude could not compete against Venezuelan or Middle East crude on world markets, and thus that Canadian crude is used primarily for the Canadian market. An alternative description of the same situation is that higher M.P.R.s would increase the total available economic rent from production, no matter how the rent might be distributed among provinces, producers, refiners, and consumers.

[2] A series of changes in the Alberta pro-rationing system in the four years preceding 1 May 1969, will remove some of the more wasteful features of the system described in the text. The Economic Allowances are to be reduced, and will provide only guaranteed minimum levels of production. For details, see Bucovetsky [1966, p. 68].

(4) *The national oil policy*

Because several of the large international oil companies have excess reserves and production capacity in each of the major producing countries, the choice of which oil to use to fill refinery requirements in any particular country comes to depend upon pumping, gathering, and shipping costs, and especially on political considerations.[1] Since the world crude price has been high enough in the past decade that the refining and marketing operations of the seven large world oil firms often do not show much profit,[2] countries with net crude imports may wish to enlarge the use of domestic crude so as to have the large firms earn taxable profits within the consuming country, as well as to aid the current account of their balance of payments. This wish is especially likely to be an active one if there are independent producers with spare capacity in the consuming country. In the United States, imports are controlled by means of import permits given to refinery operators in proportion to their refinery throughput.[3] In Canada, the desire to enlarge the Canadian share of crude oil production was expressed in the National Oil Policy in 1961. The goals set by the government were such as to encourage exports of Canadian crude to certain northern U.S. refineries, and to discourage the use of imported crude to fill the demands of the Ontario market. Thus there has been a considerable expansion of refinery capacity in Ontario to process western crude for the Ontario market. Given the way the National Oil Policy was presented, in terms of industry targets, it is not possible to measure precisely its effects on the return on investment in new oil production or refining capacity, especially as it is not known precisely how the large firms in the industry came to their decisions about the proportion of the quota that they would each plan to provide. Some firms, at least, considered the expansion of their own use of Canadian crude as a requirement of maintaining a strong representation in the Canadian market, and used rate of return calculations only in their choice of the preferred method of substituting domestic for imported crude. It is likely that the government let each large firm know what part it was expected to play in expanding the use of Canadian crude. The National Oil Policy is a clear example

---

[1] This matter is well dealt with, in some detail, by Adelman [1964].

[2] Adelman [1964, p. 115].

[3] These import permits are then traded among firms, at prices which Adelman [1964, p. 88] estimated to range in 1961–2 between $1 and $2 for the right to import one barrel.

of a government policy having substantial but not easily definable effects on the estimated cash-flow distributions of alternative investment programmes.

(5) *Example calculations*

Finally, it would be useful to show how some of the tax provisions affect the rates of return on typical drilling projects. The examples in

TABLE 9.1

		Column (1) D.C.F. rate of return under existing rules (including $33\frac{1}{3}\%$ net depletion allowance) (%)	Column (2) D.C.F. rate of return with no depletion allowance (%)	Column (3) D.C.F. rate of return with no depletion allowance, and drilling expenses written off over the life of the well (%)
(1) An oil well has an expected life of 14 years, with years 1–5 having the major flow. The cash flow payback period is 3·4 years. (Depreciable investment 15 per cent., drilling and exploration expense 85 per cent.)	(a) (b)	20·5 19·0	19·0 16·5	13 13
(2) A gas well has an expected life of 25 years with level annual production. The cash flow payback period is 8·3 years. (Depreciable investment 35 per cent., drilling and exploration expense 65 per cent.)	(a) (b)	13·0 11·2	12·3 10·2	9 9
(3) An oil well has an expected life of 32 years, with production 40 per cent. below peak during final 20 years. Cash flow payback period is 3·5 years. (Depreciable investment 15 per cent., drilling and exploration expense 85 per cent.)	(a) (b)	24·0 22·8	21·8 20·0	15 15

The calculations in the rows marked (*a*) assume that the firm has other income against which it can write-off all expenditures as soon as the law permits. In rows (*b*) the expenditures are only written off against the income from the well in question. The rates of return in column (1), rows (*b*), were those used by the firm from whose files the examples were chosen. The other calculations have been made using the same cost and revenue assumptions. The oil-well calculations assume a constant price for crude oil; while the gas-well calculations are based on an estimate that the price of the gas will rise by 30 per cent. during the first seven years of production, and thereafter remain constant.

Table 9.1 are chosen from the files of a producing firm to illustrate the type of development drilling opportunity that they face. The internal rates of return of the example projects are calculated on the basis of the present regulations (column (1)) and two alternative tax policies. Under the first alternative tax policy (column (2)), there is no depletion allowance, while all other tax provisions remain as at present. Under the second alternative (column (3)), drilling and exploration costs must be written off on a rate of production basis over the estimated total output of the well, rather than, as now, written off as soon as desired. Under all the alternative policies depreciable well assets are written off at 30 per cent. on the declining balance (as under the present depreciation rules).

The calculations are done on the basis of two different assumptions about the other costs and revenues of the firm. We assume in rows (*a*) that the firm has sufficient current income from other production (or from refining and marketing) to utilize all the allowed tax deductions as soon as they become available. The calculations in the rows marked (*b*) assume that the firm has no other taxable income, and can therefore use the allowed deduction only against the income from the present project. All the examples assume a corporation income-tax rate of 50 per cent.

B. TAXATION OF THE MINING INDUSTRY

The precise features of the taxation of mining in Canada have been set out elsewhere;[1] in this section we shall outline the special features only so far as is necessary to make intelligible the subsequent discussion of their effects on investment decisions.

(1) *Depletion*

The various kinds of depletion allowance, and the rates, are the same as those described in the last section. In the case of oil production, however, the allowance applies only to revenue from the sale of crude oil, while in mining the allowance covers income earned in concentrating and smelting the ore to the primary metal stage. The depletion allowance on profits from concentration and smelting is only available to a firm operating a mine, so that there are obvious tax advantages to vertical integration.

---

[1] Bucovetsky [1966], Cork [1962].

(2) *Exploration and development expenditures*

The tax treatment of these expenditures is very like the treatment of drilling and exploration expenses in the oil industry. All expenditures on exploration and development, right up to the date when regular production is started (except outlays on depreciable assets), may be written off whenever desired, against any income, or carried forward indefinitely. As in the oil industry, companies are only eligible for the immediate write-off of exploration and development expenses against any income if their principal business is mining or exploring for minerals of certain types (including the production, refining, and distribution of oil and gas). The chief difference between the treatment of exploration and development costs in the two industries is that since 1962 the sale of oil or gas drilling rights has been held to produce taxable income, and the purchaser can include the price as part of his drilling and exploration expense. In mining, on the other hand, income from the sale of mining properties is not taxable, and amounts paid for properties may not be treated as expenses except in those circumstances where the purchase includes some transfer of unclaimed exploration and development expenditures. Thus an exploration company may deduct its costs immediately from whatever income is available, yet there is no tax on the sales value of the mining properties discovered. This would represent a substantial incentive for the discovery and sale of mining properties (there is now no parallel situation in the oil industry) but for the fact that the sales price is not an allowable expense for the purchaser, thus lowering the scale of bid prices feasible for the producing firms.

(3) *Provincial taxes and regulations*

The royalties and property taxes applicable to mines and mineral production are more or less the same as those applicable to oil and gas. There are no regulations in mining parallel to those governing well spacing and allowable rates of production of oil and gas.

(4) *Tax exempt period for new mines*

The unique aspect of mining taxation in Canada is the three-year tax-exempt period for new mines. Since depreciation, as well as exploration and drilling expenditures, may be postponed until the tax-exempt period is over, the net reduction in tax due to the exemption may be considerable for any mine that can be brought to full output within three years of commencing production. The impact of the exempt period may be demonstrated as follows.

Definitions

δ_t' and r are, as before, the percentage rate of net depletion allowance in period t and a standard-risk rate of discount. In this example the time periods are one year in length.

$R_{pt} =$ revenue in period t from the sale of prime metal, ore, or concentrate.

$C_{pt} =$ period t costs of exploration and development, and of producing prime metal, ore, or concentrate. The costs of acquiring properties are not included, nor are depreciation allowances.

$C_t^* =$ The backlog of cost items (excluding depreciation) remaining unclaimed at the end of period t. C_0^*, the backlog of cost items at the time the mine first comes into production, will comprise mainly accumulated exploration and development costs.

$$C_t^* = C_{t-1}^* - \hat{C}_t^*$$

where $\hat{C}_t^*$ is the lesser of

    (a) C_{t-1}^*,
    (b) $R_{pt} - C_{pt}$.

$D_t^* =$ The backlog of unclaimed depreciation allowances at the end of period t. D_t is the current depreciation allowance in period t.

$$D_t^* = D_{t-1}^* + D_t - \hat{D}_t^*.$$

The value of $\hat{D}_t^*$ depends on whether or not there is a three-year tax-exempt period. If there is not a tax-free period, $\hat{D}_t^*$ is the lesser of

    (a) $D_{t-1}^* + D_t$,
    (b) $R_{pt} - C_{pt} - \hat{C}_t^*$.

If there is a three-year tax-exempt period, $\hat{D}_t^* = 0$ for $t = 1, 2, 3$, and thereafter is defined as above.

Using these definitions, we may evaluate the present value of tax payments on a new mine at the beginning of the period when the mine comes into production. If there is no tax free period, then

$$PV_T = \sum_{t=1}^{n} (R_{pt} - C_{pt} - \hat{C}_t^* - \hat{D}_t^*)(1 - \delta_t')(\tau_t)(1 + r)^{-t}.$$

If there is a three-year tax-exempt period, then the present value of the tax payments will be

$$PV_T = \sum_{t=4}^{n} (R_{pt} - C_{pt} - \hat{C}_t{}^* - \hat{D}_t{}^*)(1 - \delta_t')(\tau_t)(1 + r)^{-t}.$$

Since the sum of the terms inside the first bracket is in each period larger in the case where there is no tax-free period, the existence of a three-year tax-exempt period reduces the present-value impact of the other special tax provisions. Thus changes in the rate of allowance for either depreciation or depletion or changes in the corporation income tax have less impact on PV_T when there is a tax-free period.

The following example illustrates the relative importance of the various special tax provisions on a mine project with certain assumed production revenues.[1]

A mine is expected to cost \$10 million to develop and to produce ore valued at \$2·4 million annually (net of current operating costs) before taxation for the first three years of operation, and 2 million for each of the following seven years, at which time the ore-body is expected to be exhausted and the equipment without value. Assuming a 50 per cent. tax rate, $33\frac{1}{3}$ per cent. net depletion allowance, provincial mining taxes on the Quebec scale,[2] a three-year tax-free period, capital cost allowances of 30 per cent. on the declining balance for 5 million of the initial cost and unrestricted write-off of the other \$5 million (pre-production expenses), the expected discounted cash flow rate of return is 15·7 per cent.[3] If there were no depletion allowance the return would be 15·2 per cent.; if there were a depletion allowance but no tax-free period the anticipated return would be 12·8 per cent. If there were neither a tax-free period nor a depletion allowance, the anticipated return would be 10·5 per cent. If there were no tax-free period, no depletion allowance, and an average capital cost allowance of 20 per cent. on the declining balance of the cost of the fixed assets (unrestricted write-off of pre-production expenses

---

[1] This example is from *Taxation and Investment*, Chapter IX.

[2] Averaging \$70,000 annually over the life of the mine.

[3] These calculations treat the mine as a separate enterprise. The rate of return would be higher if the mine was developed by a firm with other income against which to write off the capital cost allowances and pre-production expenses. The advantages accruing to the large mining firm with mineral and non-mineral income are in this respect similar to those of the integrated oil firms. Expenditures may be more quickly charged against income, and the total depletable income may be greater for the integrated firms.

still being allowed), the anticipated return would be 10·0 per cent. If there were no tax-free period, no depletion allowance, a capital cost allowance of 20 per cent. on the declining balance of the fixed assets, and if the pre-production expenses had to be written off on a unit-of-production basis over the life of the mine, the rate of return would be 9·0 per cent.

The example indicates that for the sample project the tax-exempt period has a greater effect on rate of return than have the other special incentives at their existing levels. This is true over a fairly wide range of examples; in all cases except where the revenues from the mine are of long duration or are slow to build up, or where the firm's rates of discount are very low.

C. The Rationale and Effects of the Tax Treatment of the Mining and Petroleum Industries

In this section we shall analyse the reasons given for special tax treatment of the resource industries in the light of the observed characteristics of investment programmes in the two industries. Finally, we shall consider what types of investment have been influenced by the special measures, and what the pattern of expenditures might have been in their absence.

(1) Reasons for special treatment

We shall not deal with the history of the special treatment, but only with the reasons which have been used to justify it on the basis of the riskiness or national importance of the industries.

(a) Risk. In Section A (1) of the chapter we considered S. L. McDonald's argument about the depletion allowance, and saw that in order to have particular application to the mineral industries it had to assume unique risk characteristics of investment programmes in these industries. Most other analyses of the special measures have also assumed that the risks in question are substantially different from those in other industries. In the terms of our model, should we interpret the industry view as being that the cash-flow distributions of individual projects have a higher standard deviation than have the revenues from projects in other industries? Or is it suggested that firms in resource industries are denied the risk-spreading opportunities available in other industries? On the basis of our model, the riskiness of projects has no particular relevance for the riskiness of investment in a particular industry unless for some reason firms are

P

not able to construct (by means of risk-sharing, fractional participation, gearing, &c.) investment programmes of any desired risk characteristics. One reason might be provided by the special tax incentives themselves, whose availability is restricted to firms whose principal activities are within the industry. If a substantial part of the dispersion of the cash-flow distributions of mining and oil investment *programmes* is due to a high positive correlation of cash flows of all the available *projects*, then there may necessarily be higher dispersion associated with the cash-flow distributions of any mining or oil investment programme than would be found in another industry. Another reason might be that the specialized knowledge required to choose and manage investment projects in these industries is so little adaptable for use in other industries, and vice versa, that diversification across industry lines can only be achieved at a considerable loss in (both risk-standardized and non-risk-standardized) present value of the programmes. On the assumption that any possible programme in mining or oil has higher risk than any preferred programme in other industries, then the chosen programmes within mining and oil (after allowing for inter-industry diversification) will be riskier than the average programme outside the industry. Then if it is possible to show that the ordinary tax system discriminates against risk bearing, there is a *prima facie* case for special treatment, assuming that the market-established risk–yield trade-offs are thought to have some normative significance.

What is the evidence? The large scale of many mineral developments (as well as many other developments—pulp mills, chemical plants, steel rolling mills, &c.) means either that they must be undertaken by very large firms or that the firms or groups of firms involved are not able to balance their investment programmes by including many other projects. This has meant that small firms often are responsible for the early mine exploration, but either sell their interests or go into a joint venture with a large producing firm when the time comes to go into production. In oil the situation is slightly different, as there are rather more economies of scale in the exploration itself, and rather fewer in the drilling and production. Thus in the oil industry a small firm may be exclusively concerned with part interests in either wildcat or development drilling of leases owned by large firms. In part because of the special tax provisions relating to new mines, mining companies are far more frequently started for the purpose of developing a single prospect, while even the smaller oil firms have more widely spread interests and a longer expected life. It would not do to exaggerate the resultant riskiness of the small mining firms, as there is a considerable amount of risk-spreading done at a higher level. That is, there are extensive intercorporate shareholdings, and many of the individuals involved in mining have holdings in a large number of small mines.

Aside from this qualitative evidence of the types of risk pooling and project sharing that firms use to decrease the riskiness of their investment programmes, it is difficult to gather evidence about inter-industry risk differences, either in terms of projects or programmes. The mean size and variability of time series of accounting profits or cash flow are poor bases for inter-industry comparisons of subjective probability distributions of cash flow, since the special tax measures and the uneven time distribution of investment in the resource industries means that there are substantial inter-industry differences in the relationship between the cash-flow distributions within the investment horizon and the current values of accounting profits or cash flow. Interview evidence indicates that the greater efforts within the mining industry to diversify among minerals and to integrate vertically are reducing the expected standard deviation of receipts for at least some of the major firms. The smaller firms in both the mining and oil industries are continuing to increase their use of one or more types of joint venture, thus reducing the dispersion of the cash-flow distributions available for any particular amount of capital investment. Evidence about particular projects does not indicate that such pooling is not capable of reducing the dispersion of the cash-flow distributions of even a small firm close to that available to other industries.[1]

Supposing that the σ_t's of the investment programmes of mining and oil firms were inevitably above those of firms in other industries (although evidence is very difficult to obtain and interpret, the hypothesis is not a likely one)[2] is there therefore a case for special tax

[1] We should not forget that much depends on the precise nature of the firm's operations. The results of development drilling for oil are if anything more predictable than the results of typical industrial projects, while wildcat drilling and mine prospecting have cash-flow distributions with very large dispersions. The stability of receipts from an established mine depends primarily on the price movements of the mineral in question. See Chapter IX of *Taxation and Investment* for further analysis along these lines.

[2] Established rate of return standards (which have probably not been properly converted to a risk-standardized basis) in the seventy largest firms do not indicate that the required rate of return is higher in mining (see Chapter 3, Table 3.2).

treatment? McDonald has argued that there is, since the corporation income tax discriminates against the use of capital, and in particular against risky uses of capital. As we have noted before, his argument is true only if some expenditures (such as capital expenditures) cannot be charged off against taxable income, and the share market 'charges for' risk in terms of a certain percentage return on capital rather than some fraction of a risk-standardized return. Further empirical research may help to decide the latter question. The incompleteness of loss offsets and the deductability of interest but not dividend payments provide other reasons why the corporation tax may favour less risky industries, while the taxation of capital gains at a rate lower than that on income (or, especially, at a zero rate) favours firms whose risky ventures produce assets with a discovery value, as long as the sale of such assets is treated as a capital gain for tax purposes. If the net effect of these factors is to discourage risk-taking, then there appears to be a case for tax reform, based on the specific disadvantage of the existing system rather than on aid to certain of the industries whose growth is possibly discouraged by the present system. This assumes, of course, that fluctuating receipts have a social cost, and that share buyers establish the economically correct trade-off between risk and yield in their portfolio selection.

Although the paragraphs above use the standard deviations of cash-flow distributions as the prime measure of riskiness, other moments of cash-flow distributions may sometimes be so important as to dominate the standard deviation in share valuation. For example, the average dividend plus capital gain return to the buyer of a new share issue of a small mine has been shown to be considerably below that available elsewhere, over a considerable period, while the dispersion of returns has been higher than average. Interviews with industry and stock market specialists indicate that the glamour and known riskiness (especially the small chance of a very large gain) of mining ventures has attracted a class of share buyers who value very highly the positive skewness of the rate of return distribution of a mine prospect.

We should not ignore another possible explanation; that a certain portion of the share market, such as the market for penny mining

---

However, officials in mining firms often stressed that the great range of error in their predictions of costs and revenues made it dangerous to rely to any extent on formal rate of return rules.

shares, may attract buyers who attach positive utility to larger dispersion as well as to positive skewness. The existence of a substantial number of buyers willing to take a lower expected return in order to get a greater variablity of return would to some extent reduce, in the sub-markets ('gamblers' dens') to which these buyers were attracted, whatever bias the corporation income tax in its present form might impose against risky investments.

If a tentative policy judgement is to be made, it must be that if there are unique risk characteristics of investment programmes in the resource industries, and if the corporation income tax discriminates against risk, the appropriate remedy would seem to be changes in the provisions of the general corporate tax rather than special tax measures for particular industries.

(b) *Social rate of return greater than private.* It has been suggested that mining and oil resource development confers national advantages which are not taken account of in private rate of return calculations, and thus should be given special tax treatment. The national security argument has never been seriously put forward in Canada, and will not be dealt with here. In addition, there are two types of external economy which have been supposed to accompany investment in resource development. First, investment in exploration in most circumstances provides information about the mineral content of land other than that controlled by the exploring firm. Often this means that the discovery value of oil or ore reserves accrues to the state and a number of firms other than those doing the exploration. If this extra information has a value, then the calculations by the profit-maximizing explorer will understate the social return on the exploration activity. The argument was considered in detail in the preceding chapter.

Secondly, it has been suggested, especially with respect to mine development, that the firms opening mines must build town sites, provide transportation and schooling, and in general provide most of the infra-structure financed by the state in more developed regions of the country. If this town site development has a continuing value to the community, and is of a kind that is usually provided for out of tax revenues, there is a case for tax relief of the firms responsible. However, as in the case of the risk argument, it appears that specific support of community development expenditures (or charges levied on firms for facilities built by the state for the benefit of a temporary mining community) would provide a more accurate balancing of

social costs and benefits than is provided by a mixture of tax concessions not specifically related to the value or cost of community
development accompanying a mine project.

(2) *Effects on investment*

Whatever may be the justification for the special tax incentives for
resource industries, it is important to know their effects, and the
likely pattern of investment which would exist under alternative tax
policies. The special provisions increase the *PV* of investment in
mineral production, and increase the cash flows of producing firms.
What would the pattern of investment be like if the incentive did not
exist?

(a) *Oil and gas.* In view of the U.S. oil policy, and the massive
reserves of low cost crude in the Middle East, Libya, and Venezuela,
it is unlikely that Canadian crude oil would find large markets outside Canada.[1] At the same time, given the National Oil Policy, the
substantial proven reserves, and the probability of further discovery,
it is likely that Canadian crude oil and gas will provide a larger fraction of total Canadian requirements. Investment in the production of
crude oil for export is therefore likely to be submarginal in any case,
and investment to produce Canadian requirements safely intra-
marginal with or without special taxation measures. If Canadian fuel
oil prices are to be related closely to the landed price of foreign crude,
the taxation of domestic operations is not likely to affect the price of
the Canadian output, and neither, therefore, the amount of investment required to produce the output demanded. Changes in tax
incentives based on either the production or the profits of the firms
does affect the amount of pure rent accruing to the firms in the industry, as well as the return available to the marginal entrant. Where
there are no collusive arrangements to prevent the creation of excess
producing capacity, the tax incentives may be responsible for some
additional investment in proven reserves, and increases in bonus
payments and bid prices for leases. Tax incentives beyond a certain
level would cause the creation of enough excess capacity that the

---

[1] It is true that a major discovery, or much cheaper methods of utilizing the
Athabaska tar sands, might cause Canadian crude to penetrate further into the
United States, but the movement would surely be limited as long as there exists
substantial excess capacity in the southern U.S. fields. Natural gas has already
penetrated considerably, and might come to provide a major share of the North
American requirements, depending, of course, on the extent of new gas finds in
the United States.

well-head price of crude would be driven down, particularly in producing areas far from landing ports for foreign crude oil. If prices in Central and Western Canada thus reflect to some extent increases or decreases in taxation, then the removal of the present concessions might raise fuel and gas prices and thus increase the share of the energy market provided by coal and electricity. These shifts might be considerable in some areas, but not of great aggregate importance. Thus the production of Canadian oil and gas is not likely to be sensitive to increases or decreases in the existing tax concessions. The amount of exploration is not likely to be affected much by changes in the depletion allowances, but changes in the write-off provisions might easily affect the level of exploration, particularly that financed by firms not themselves producing oil or gas.

(b) Mining investment in Canada is less dominated by foreign controlled firms than is investment in oil and gas (about 77 per cent. controlled outside Canada, compared with over 90 per cent. for oil and gas), but in many ways the amount of investment in Canada is more sensitive to the nature of investment opportunities in other countries. There are many firms operating either in Canada or in a foreign country which are interested in developing reliable raw material sources (U.S., Japanese, and Canadian steel firms are examples) and will in general develop where the costs are lowest for a given security of ownership and continuity of supply. Even though the major ore developments sponsored by these firms are not screened by very precise rate of return rules, the considerable element of concession in Canadian mining taxation probably would make a difference to the location of some marginal projects.[1]

The continued operation of existing marginal mines (gold mines are the most likely examples) often depends on the extent of production subsidy or tax concession. In most of these cases the marginal revenues from operating the mine can be quite clearly defined and calculated, and the influence of the tax concessions is obvious.

There has already been some investment in other industries by uranium companies, and extension into fabrication and further stages of production by steel-, copper-, lead-, and zinc-producing firms. As

---

[1] In addition, the Canadian ore sources are frequently marginal to U.S. users. This has made Canadian production and employment very dependent on changes in the U.S. final demand. R. J. Wonnacott [1961, p. 83] estimates that 47 per cent. of the demand for the output of the metal mining and refining sector is generated by U.S. final demand.

the cash flow from recently established mines continue to grow, it is likely that the funds generated by mining operations will lead some mining firms to participate directly in other industries, and others to pay out a higher fraction of their earnings as dividends. The balance between the rates of return on mining and non-mining investment would be altered if the special concessions were changed, and this is a margin where considerable adjustments might be made.

Given that mining operations are currently generating funds (after tax) to the point where many Canadian-based firms are building up substantial cash reserves,[1] it is likely that the extra cash flow due to the tax concessions is responsible for downward pressure on the required rate of return on mining ventures. If the removal of the concessions put these firms in a position where they were no longer generating much surplus cash, the required rate of return might rise, especially for those firms which have been unwilling or unable to find alternative investments in other industries.

In sum, the main effect of the special measures in the oil industry is to alter the division of rent between the federal government, the provinces, and the firms, with some additional effects on the level of exploration. In mining the concessions are greater, and the effects on the direction and nature of investment much more significant. Without the incentives, mining firms would turn more to other countries and other industries, and there might easily be reductions both in the volume of exploration and the number of new mines reaching the development stage. This is more likely to be true of marginal additions to the national capacity for producing the standard base metals than for the major foreign financed iron ore mines, the uranium boom, or the Saskatchewan potash development.

We have considered several types of rationale for the special tax treatment of resource industries. Some of the discussion suggested the presence of external economies which might provide grounds for incentives specifically related to exploration expenditures, but none of the other arguments for favoured tax treatment stood up to analysis. There do not appear to be special characteristics of the resource industries that provide any obvious economic rationale for percentage depletion, or for tax-exempt periods for new mines.

[1] [See Cork 1962, pp. 66–7].

10

CONCLUSION

In the Introduction it was recognized that some idea of the objectives of economic policy was a precondition of any sensible attempt to describe the effects of particular monetary and fiscal policies. The basic problem of specifying a social preference function by which alternative economic outcomes could be evaluated was carefully skirted. It was adequate, at that stage, to conclude that investment expenditures are not only major determinants of the current level of income and employment but also establish the allocation of resources over time and among regions and industries. The analysis of specific instruments therefore required us to consider the timing and distribution of their effects on investment, and policies were given more credit if they were of a sort whose results could be relatively easily predicted. Whether or not it is important for policies to act quickly depends on how they are to be used; in general, it is useful to have at least some policies whose effects are not only predictable but also rapid. Given the relatively short duration of post-war business cycles, and the difficulties of forecasting the turning-points, a quick response has become a desirable characteristic for any of the policies described as stabilization policies. Chapters 5, 6, and 7 dealt with a number of these policies, and evaluated them with respect to the predictability, magnitude, and rapidity of their effects.

Chapter 8 considered the effects of taxation measures designed to influence the flow of information about new investment opportunities, while Chapter 9 dealt with the various taxation measures influencing investment in natural resource development. Both these measures were evaluated as longer-term structural measures justified (or not) on the basis of differences between social and private rates of return.

In all the chapters the analysis has been partial, in that particular measures were compared with others designed to do more or less the same job. Suppose that this sort of analysis had been carried out for a much wider range of potential policy instruments, and that the evaluation had been adequate to identify the most efficient instruments to do particular jobs. Would it then be possible to suggest how the best mix of policies should be chosen in order to achieve better overall results from economic management? After all, it is not much use having the best available set of policy instruments if there is no rational way of deciding how and when they should be used.

In the early chapters of the book, great emphasis was put on the fact that firms cannot act optimally (on anyone's behalf) unless they consider the joint effects of the various individual projects they may be considering. Just as it is only rational for firms to choose projects on the basis of their contribution to alternative investment programmes, so public policies must be chosen as a set, in recognition of their joint effects on the economic variables affecting social welfare. This prescription is acceptable but vague. How could it be made more precise?

If policies are to be chosen in the light of their joint effects on the economy, the choice must be made using a framework which allows their interactions to be assessed. At the level of the firm, the unifying feature is the investment programme. Policies were seen to influence behaviour by altering the present-value ranking of alternative investment programmes. If it were possible to find a similar unifying framework for the whole economy, the problems of policy choice could be dealt with in an analogous manner. It is possible to characterize each potential time path of national income in a way similar to the streams of cash-flow distributions of individual investment programmes. The distribution of income and employment among groups and individuals should also be specified, as it will affect the total utility attached to any given level of national income. The valuation problems are, of course, much less tractable for the aggregate economy than they are for individual firms. In the case of firms it is quite natural to evaluate the consequences of alternatives in financial terms, and the principles of optimal behaviour are quite clearly defined. The appropriate rate for trading-off risk against yield is dictated by the relative prices of securities bearing different amounts of risk, so that there is no need to resort to individual utility functions. The evaluation of alternative time streams of national income raises a whole host of additional problems. For the society as a whole there is no strong reason for valuing output in terms of its market prices, yet no clear way of showing how alternative distributions, among individuals, of the national income should be evaluated. Similarly it is difficult to know how much disutility ought to be attached to a greater probability that personal and/or aggregate incomes will differ from their expected values. Macro-economic policy models often make the computationally convenient assumption of a quadratic utility function, which then gives the variance of estimated income a direct role to play. The search must go on for more appropriate ways of characterizing alternative states of the economy (over time) and ranking them in preference. Given some sort of social preference ordering over alternative paths of development for the economy, the choice of optimum policies involves a set of economic relationships and a tool kit of economic policies. If the tool kit is a good one, and if the set of economic relationships (call the set a macro-model) has a sound structure, then the policy-maker chooses that set of economic policies which produces the preferred path of development for the economy. There is much to be done before we shall be close to having a macro-model with a sound enough structure and adequate detail to provide a reasonable basis for analysing a broad range of alternative sets of policy instruments. This book has attempted to contribute to this development by setting out some criteria for judging the efficiency of different types of taxation and monetary policies. Some rough attempts have also been made to judge the relative efficiency of a number of particular policies. A brief review of some of the tentative conclusions may help to provide some basis for suggestions about the appropriate nature of a macro-model adequate to picture the pattern of effects of the most efficient policies.

The chapters concerned primarily with stabilization policies found that the most important distinction between competing policies was the extent to which they influenced the timing of investment outlays. The temporary measures which affect the cash flows from all operations (such as a change in the depreciation allowances on all fixed assets) have a much smaller present value impact on investment programmes than do those measures (such as changes in the depreciation allowances available on fixed assets purchased during a specified period) specifically designed to influence the profitability of investment expenditures in a particular time period. Thus temporary changes in the corporation income tax have a much smaller present-value impact than do cyclical changes in investment allowances. The present-value impact, in these cases, is the difference between the present value of a programme with a lump of expenditures in the current period and a programme otherwise similar but with a large lump of expenditures either spread out evenly over time or postponed until the end of the temporary period of application of the special tax measures. There is nothing to be gained in rehearsing the rationale for this in any detail; it may be sufficient to remind the reader that the main reason for the difference is that cyclical changes in tax rates (or depreciation, or interest, &c.) may not influence the firm's expectations about the average rate likely to be applicable over the lives of the projects in the investment programme. Measures which are more time-specific, such as an investment reserve scheme, are much more likely to lead to a re-ranking of investment programmes with different time paths of investment expenditures. The various measures also differ in their impacts on the unpredictability of cash flows, although the evidence on this score was difficult to obtain, and the *a priori* arguments not conclusive.

The chapters dealing with taxation measures intended to influence the allocation of investment among industries or activities took a different slant than those dealing with stabilization policies. There was less concern about the timing of their effects, and more about their longer-term influence on the pattern of investment and industrial activity. The supposition was made that these policies are intended to compensate for differences between social and private rates of return on certain types of expenditure. The policies were then examined to see to what extent they have had the intended effects. Expenditures on research and development have been given special tax treatment because they are thought to confer benefits directly on firms other than those making the outlays. Various types of R. & D. activity were studied, and were seen to be likely to have different sorts of external effects. The incentive schemes have present value impacts great enough to have influenced expenditures, although there was no evidence that helped to decide whether the measures have been such as to account adequately for the external effects. The usual arguments on behalf of special taxation treatment of the extractive industries have made reference to the possible discrimination of the corporation income tax against risky ventures (such as the extractive industries) and also to the possibility of external economies from the exploration for and development of resource deposits. Neither argument was seen to provide an adequate rationale for incentives of the type and size examined, and more efficient means were suggested of accounting for possible divergences between social and private rates of return.

Would it be possible to develop a macro-model sufficiently realistic to allow both stabilization and resource allocation policies to be analysed within a comprehensive framework? The partial analysis in the earlier chapters suggests that such a model should attempt to capture the effects of policies on the risk-standardized present values of alternative investment programmes. It is not necessary, or even practicable, that a macro-model should be able to compare alternative policies at the level of detail of, say, the analysis in Chapters 5 to 7. That sort of detailed examination should serve to reveal the more efficient of the alternative instruments, and it must then be the job of the macro-model to illustrate the aggregate effects of alternative sets of values for the more efficient of the policy instruments.

This indicates that the macro-model should be dis-aggregated enough (at least in some of its versions) to show the distribution of activity among industries, and to have the investment opportunities in each sector specified in such a way that the various taxation measures assume their correct relative importance. The comparison of alternative measures also requires that their impact on the timing of investment be revealed. This is a formidable task, for the available investment expenditures data appear to be consistent with a number of alternative patterns of lagged response,[1] whatever level of aggregation is used. The main reason for this imprecision in the specification of investment equations is that there is no consistent relationship between the subjective cash-flow distributions and the various available *ex post* time series of cash flows. The key to better investment functions lies in the derivation of more appropriate proxy variables for the characteristics of the cash-flow distributions assumed to underlie investment decisions.

It would also be desirable for the flows of investment expenditures be related to the amount and nature of research and development effort, in such a way as to show the final impact of research and development expenditures, and to derive more meaningful indicators of the technological capacity of given stocks of fixed capital, knowledge, and skills. This is asking too much, for the processes by which useful techniques are discovered and dispersed have not yet revealed themselves in the data, and Chapter 8 suggested some of the reasons why this should continue to be so. But as long as the macro model is used with appropriate caution, it need not be expected to do everything at once. There will always be considerations involved in a

[1] For example, see Griliches and Wallace [1965].

policy choice that cannot be brought explicitly into a model of the economy, and different sorts of questions may be dealt with by different sorts of models. What is required is not that an identical framework be used on all occasions, but that the links between the alternative models should be made explicit. Only in this way can the chosen policies be made reasonably consistent with one another.

To explore the possibilities of establishing an appropriate framework within which to assess alternative sets of policies must be the task of another day. All that this concluding note has done is state the minimum requirements of an adequate framework, and to show how the partial analysis undertaken in this book should help in the selection of relatively efficient policy instruments. These policy instruments should then be assessed within a macro-economic framework taking direct account of the ultimate goals of economic management. Even if such a framework is not immediately available, analysis of public policies using methods such as those suggested in earlier chapters is essential, both for the departments responsible for designing the policies, and for the firms whose investment alternatives are influenced by them.

REFERENCES

This list of cited works is alphabetical by author and chronological for works by the same author.

ADELMAN, M. A. [1964], 'The World Oil Outlook' in M. CLAWSON (ed.), *Natural Resources and International Development*, Baltimore, Johns Hopkins.

AMES, EDWARD [1961], 'Research, Invention, Development, and Innovation', *American Economic Review* 51, 370–81.

ARROW, K. J. [1953], *The Role of Securities in the Optimal Allocation of Risk-Bearing* (Cowles Commission Papers, New Series, No. 77), Chicago, Ill., University of Chicago. (Also in *Review of Economic Studies*, 1964.)

BALDWIN, W. L. [1962], 'Contracted Research and the Case for Big Business', *Journal of Political Economy* 70, 294–8.

BANK OF CANADA [1962], *Submissions by the Bank of Canada to the Royal Commission on Banking and Finance*, Ottawa, Bank of Canada.

—— [1965], *Statistical Summary-Supplement* 1965, Ottawa, Bank of Canada.

BARRÈRE, ALAIN [1961], 'Capital Intensity and the Combination of the Factors of Production' in LUTZ, F. and HAGUE, D. C. (eds.), *The Theory of Capital*, pp. 143–60, London, Macmillan.

BAUMOL, WILLIAM J. [1959], *Business Behaviour, Value and Growth*, New York, Macmillan.

BAUMOL, W. J. [1962], 'On the Theory of the Expansion of the Firm', *American Economic Review* 52, 1078–87.

BIRD, RICHARD M. [1963a], 'Depreciation Allowances and Countercyclical Policy in the United Kingdom, 1945–1960', *Canadian Tax Journal* 11, 253–73 and 353–79.

—— [1963b], 'Countercyclical Variations in Depreciation Allowances in the U.K.', *National Tax Journal*, Vol. 17.

BLACK, J. [1959], 'Investment Allowances, Initial Allowances, and Cheap Loans as a Means of Encouraging Investment', *Review of Economic Studies* 27, 44–49.

BREWER, K. R. W. [1963], 'Decisions Under Uncertainty: Comment', *Quarterly Journal of Economics* 77, 159–61.

BROCKIE, M. D. and GREY, A. L. [1956], 'The Marginal Efficiency of Capital and Investment Programming', *Economic Journal* 66, 662–75.

BROWN, E. CARY [1962], 'Tax Credits as Investment Incentives', *National Tax Journal*, Vol. 15.

BUCHANAN, J. M. and STUBBLEBINE, W. C. [1962], 'Externality', *Economica* New Series, 29, 371–84.

226   REFERENCES

BUCOVETSKY, M. [1966], *The Taxation of Mineral Extraction* (a study prepared for the Royal Commission on Taxation), Ottawa, Queen's Printer.

CANADA, PARLIAMENT, HOUSE OF COMMONS, 1965, *Official Report of Debates*, Vol. 110, Ottawa, Queen's Printer.

CANARP, CURT [1963], 'Investment Funds—And How They Can Be Used to Combat Recession and Unemployment', *Skandinaviska Banken Quarterly Review* 44, 33–40.

CARTER, C. F. and WILLIAMS, B. R. [1959], *Science in Industry*, Oxford, Oxford University Press.

CLARKSON, GEOFFREY P. E. [1962], *Portfolio Selection: A Simulation of Trust Investment*, Englewood Cliffs, N.J., Prentice-Hall.

CORK, E. K. [1962], *Finance in the Mining Industry* (Staff Study for the Royal Commission on Banking and Finance), Ottawa, Queen's Printer.

CORNER, A. C. and WILLIAMS, ALAN [1965], 'The Sensitivity of Businesses to Initial and Investment Allowances', *Economica* 32, 32–47.

CYERT, R. M., DILL, W. R., and MARCH, J. G. [1958], 'The Role of Expectations in Business Decision-Making', *Administrative Science Quarterly* 3, 307–40.

—— and MARCH, JAMES G. [1960], 'Research into a Behavioural Theory of the Firm', Carnegie Institute of Technology, *Reprint* No. 49.

—— —— [1963], *A Behavioural Theory of the Firm*, Englewood Cliffs, N.J., Prentice-Hall.

DAVIDSON, PAUL [1963], 'Public Policy Problems of the Domestic Crude Oil Industry', *American Economic Review* 53, 85–108.

DAVIS, O. and WHINSTON, A. [1962], 'Externalities, Welfare and the Theory of Games', *Journal of Political Economy* 70, 241–62.

DEBREU, G. [1959], *Theory of Value*, Cowles Foundation Monograph 17, New York, Wiley.

DEPARTMENT OF TRADE AND COMMERCE [1961], *Public and Private Investment in Canada. Outlook* 1961, Ottawa, Queen's Printer.

—— [1963], *Public and Private Investment in Canada, Outlook 1963*, Ottawa, Queen's Printer.

DOMINION BUREAU OF STATISTICS [1961a], *Federal Government Expenditures on Scientific Activities, Fiscal Year 1960–61*, Ottawa, Queen's Printer.

—— [1961b], *Industrial Research-Development Expenditures in Canada 1959*, Ottawa, Queen's Printer.

—— [1963], *Industrial Research and Development Expenditures in Canada 1961*, Ottawa, Queen's Printer.

DOW, J. C. R. [1964], *The Management of the British Economy, 1945–1960* (National Institute of Economic and Social Studies, 22), Cambridge, Cambridge University Press.

EDWARDS, RONALD STANLEY [1950], *Co-operative Industrial Research: A Study of the Economic aspects of the Research Associations Grant-*

aided by the Department of Scientific and Industrial Research, London, Pitman.

EGERTON, R. A. D. [1960], *Investment Decisions Under Uncertainty*, Liverpool, Liverpool University Press.

EISNER, R. and STROTZ, R. H. [1963], 'Determinants of Business Investment', Research Study Two, Commission on Money and Credit, *Impacts of Monetary Policy*, Englewood Cliffs, Prentice-Hall.

ELDRIDGE, D. A. [1962], 'Rate of Return, Resource Allocation and Percentage Depletion', *National Tax Journal*, Vol. 15.

ELLSBERG, DANIEL [1961], 'Risk, Ambiguity, and the Savage Axioms', *Quarterly Journal of Economics* **75**, 642–69.

—— [1963], 'Risk, Ambiguity, and the Savage Axioms: Reply', *Quarterly Journal of Economics* **77**, 336–42.

FARRAR, D. E. [1962], *The Investment Decision Under Uncertainty*, Englewood Cliffs, Prentice-Hall.

FELDSTEIN, MARTIN S. [1966], 'A Binary Variable Multiple Regression Method of Analysing Factors affecting Peri-natal Mortality and other Outcomes of Pregnancy', *Journal of the Royal Statistical Society*, Series A, **129**, 61–73.

FELLNER, WILLIAM [1961], 'Distortion of Subjective Probabilities as a Reaction to Uncertainty, *Quarterly Journal of Economics* **75**, 670–89.

—— [1963], 'Slanted Subjective Probabilities and Randomization: Reply to Howard Raiffa and K. R. W. Brewer', *Quarterly Journal of Economics* **77**, 676–90.

FINNIS, F. H. [1963], 'Provincial and Municipal Taxation in Canada' in Canadian Tax Foundation *Oil and Gas Production and Taxes* (Canadian Tax Paper 33), Toronto.

GOLDBERGER, A. S. [1964], *Econometric Theory*, New York, Wiley.

GOODE, RICHARD [1957], 'Special Tax Measures to Restrain Investment', *International Monetary Fund Staff Papers* **5**, 434–48.

GORDON, MYRON J. [1962], *The Investment, Financing, and Valuation of the Corporation*, Homewood, Illinois, Richard Irwin.

GORDON, R. A. [1961], *Business Leadership in the Large Corporation* 2nd edn., Berkeley, Berkeley University Press.

GRAYSON, C. JACKSON, JR. [1960], *Decisions Under Uncertainty: Drilling Decisions by Oil and Gas Operators*, Boston, Harvard University, Division of Research, Graduate School of Business Administration.

GRILICHES, ZVI and SCHMOOKLER, JACOB [1963], 'Inventing and Maximizing', *American Economic Review* **53**, 725–9.

—— and WALLACE, N. [1965], 'The Determinants of Investment Revisited', *International Economic Review* **6**, 311–29.

HALL, CHALLIS A. [1960], *Fiscal Policy for Stable Growth: A Study in Dynamic Macroeconomics*, New York, Holt-Rinehart and Winston.

Q

HAMBERG, D. [1963], 'Invention in the Industrial Research Laboratory', *Journal of Political Economy* **71**, 95–115.

—— [1964], 'Size of Firm, Oligopoly, and Research: The Evidence', *Canadian Journal of Economics and Political Science* **30**, 62–75.

HARBERGER, A. C. [1955], 'The Taxation of Mineral Industries', *Federal Tax Policy for Economic Growth and Stability* (Papers submitted by Panelists Appearing Before the Subcommittee on Tax Policy), Joint Committee on the Economic Report, 84th Congress, 1st Session, Washington, U.S.G.P.O.

HARING, J. E. and SMITH, G. C. [1959], 'Utility Theory, Decision Theory, and Profit Maximization', *American Economic Review* **49**, 566–83.

HARING, J. E. [1961], 'The Investment Horizon', *Metroeconomica* **13**, 77–93.

HART, A. G. [1942], 'Risk, Uncertainty, and the Unprofitability of Compounding Probabilities' in Lange, McIntyre and Yntema (eds.), *Studies in Mathematical Economics and Econometrics in Memory of Henry Schultz*, pp. 110–18, Chicago, University of Chicago Press. (Reprinted in American Economic Association *Readings in the Theory of Income Distribution*, pp. 547–57, London, Allen and Unwin, 1950.)

HAUSE, JOHN C. [1963], 'The Economic Consequences of Percentage Depletion Allowances', *National Tax Journal*, Vol. 16.

HELLIWELL, J. F. [1966], *Taxation and Investment: A Study of Capital Expenditure Decisions in Large Corporations*, Ottawa, Queen's Printer.

HERTZ, D. B. [1961], 'La Recherche-développement considerée comme facteur de production', *Économie Appliquée* **14**, 425–44.

HICKS, SIR JOHN [1962], 'Liquidity', *Economic Journal* **72**, 787–803.

HIGGINS, BENJAMIN [1954], 'Government Measures to Regularize Private Investment in Other Countries Than the United States', Universities-National Bureau Committee for Economic Research, *Regularization of Business Investment*, pp. 459–81, Princeton, Princeton University Press.

HIRSCHLEIFER, J. [1965], 'Investment Decision Under Uncertainty: Choice-Theoretic Approaches', *Quarterly Journal of Economics* **79**, 509–36.

—— [1966], 'Investment Decision Under Uncertainty: Applications of the State-Preference Approach', *Quarterly Journal of Economics* **80**, 252–77.

JOHNSON, H. G. and WINDER, J. W. L. [1962], *Lags in the Effects of Monetary Policy* (Working Paper for the Royal Commission on Banking and Finance), Ottawa, Queen's Printer.

JORGENSON, D. W. [1963], 'Capital Theory and Investment Behaviour', *American Economic Review* **53**, 247–59.

KNIGHT, FRANK H. [1964], *Risk, Uncertainty and Profit*, New York, Augustus M. Kelley (reprint of 1921 edition).

LAMBERT, S. C. [1955], 'Percentage Depletion and the National Interest' in *Federal Tax Policy for Economic Growth and Stability* (Papers submitted by the Panelists Appearing before the Sub-committee on Tax Policy), Joint Committee on the Economic Report, 84th Congress, 1st Session, Washington, U.S.G.P.O.

LANGE, OSKAR [1944], *Price Flexibility and Employment*, Cowles Commission Monograph No. 8, Bloomington, Indiana, Principia Press.

LERNER, E. M. and CARLETON, W. T. [1964], 'The Integration of Capital Budgeting and Stock Valuation', *American Economic Review* 54, 683–702.

LINTNER, JOHN [1964], 'Optimal Dividends and Corporate Growth under Uncertainty', *Quarterly Journal of Economics* 78, 49–95.

LUCE, D. R. and RAIFFA, H. [1957], *Games and Decisions: Introduction and Critical Survey*, New York, Wiley.

LUNDBERG, ERIK [1959], 'The Profitability of Investment', *Economic Journal* 69, 653–77.

LUTZ, FRIEDRICH A. and LUTZ, VERA C. [1951], *The Theory of the Investment of the Firm*, Princeton, Princeton University Press.

MACHLUP, FRITZ [1962], 'The Supply of Inventors and Inventions' in *The Rate and Direction of Inventive Activity* (N.B.E.R. Conference Vol. 13), Princeton, Princeton University Press.

MANSFIELD, E. [1963a], 'The Speed of Response of Firms to New Techniques', *Quarterly Journal of Economics* 77, 290–311.

—— [1963b], 'Size of Firm, Market Structure, and Innovation', *Journal of Political Economy* 71, 556–76.

—— [1965], 'Rates of Return from Industrial Research and Development', *American Economic Review* 55, 310–22.

MARCH, J. G. and SIMON, H. A. [1958], *Organizations*, New York, Wiley.

MARKOWITZ, HARRY M. [1959], *Portfolio Selection: Efficient Diversification of Investments*, New York, Wiley.

MARRIS, ROBIN [1963], 'A Model of the "Managerial" Enterprise', *Quarterly Journal of Economics* 77, 185–209.

—— [1964], *The Economic Theory of 'Managerial' Capitalism*, London, Macmillan.

MATTHEWS, M. W. [1963], 'Operating Methods in the Oil and Gas Industry' in Canadian Tax Foundation, *Oil and Gas Production and Taxes* (Canadian Tax Paper 33), Toronto.

MCDONALD, STEPHEN L. [1961], 'Percentage Depletion and the Allocation of Resources: The Case of Oil and Gas', *National Tax Journal* 14, 323–6.

MCKIE, JAMES W. [1960], 'Market Structure and Uncertainty in Oil and Gas Exploration', *Quarterly Journal of Economics* 74, 543–71.

MILDNER, ERWIN and SCOTT, IRA [1962], 'An Innovation In Fiscal Policy: The Swedish Investment Reserve System', *National Tax Journal* 15, 276–80.

MODIGLIANI, F. and MILLER, MERTON H. [1958], 'The Cost of Capital, Corporation Finance and the Theory of Investment', *American Economic Review* **48**, 261–97.

MOORE, A. MILTON [1963], *Taxes and Exports* (Canadian Tax Paper 35), Toronto, Canadian Tax Foundation.

MUSGRAVE, R. A. [1962], 'Another Look at Depletion', *National Tax Journal* **15**, 205–8.

NATIONAL ECONOMIC DEVELOPMENT COUNCIL [1965a], *Investment Appraisal*, London, H.M.S.O.

—— [1965b], *Investment in Machine Tools*, London, H.M.S.O.

NELSON, R. R. [1959], 'The Simple Economics of Basic Scientific Research', *Journal of Political Economy* **67**, 297–306.

—— [1961], 'Uncertainty, Learning, and the Economics of Parallel Research and Development Efforts', *Review of Economics and Statistics* **43**, 351–64.

NORTCLIFFE, E. B. [1960], *Common Market Fiscal Systems*, London, Sweet and Maxwell.

RICHARDSON, G. B. [1960], *Information and Investment*, London, Oxford University Press.

RAIFFA, HOWARD [1961], 'Risk, Ambiguity, and the Savage Axioms: Comment', *Quarterly Journal of Economics* **75**, 690–4.

ROBERTS, HARRY V. [1963], 'Risk, Ambiguity, and the Savage Axioms: Comment', *Quarterly Journal of Economics* **77**, 327–35.

ROY, A. D. [1952], 'Safety First and the Holding of Assets', *Econometrica* **20**, 431–49.

ROYAL COMMISSION ON BANKING AND FINANCE [1964], *Report*. Ottawa, Queen's Printer.

ROYAL COMMISSION ON CANADA'S ECONOMIC PROSPECTS [1957], *Report*. Ottawa, Queen's Printer.

SANDBERG, LARS G. [1963], 'A Comment on "An Innovation in Fiscal Policy: The Swedish Investment Reserve System" ', *National Tax Journal*, Vol. 16.

SAVAGE, L. J. [1954], *The Foundations of Statistics*, New York, Wiley; London, Chapman and Hall.

SHACKLE, G. L. S. [1952], *Expectation in Economics*, 2nd ed., Cambridge, Cambridge University Press.

—— [1955], *Uncertainty in Economics, and Other Reflections*, Cambridge, Cambridge University Press.

—— [1961], *Decision, Order, and Time in Human Affairs*, Cambridge, Cambridge University Press.

—— [1965], 'The Interest Elasticity of Investment' in HAHN, F. H. and BRECHLING, F. P. R. (eds.), *The Theory of Interest Rates* (Proceedings of a Conference Held by the International Economic Association), London, Macmillan.

SHARP, M. W. [1953], 'Deferred Depreciation Reviewed', *Canadian Tax Journal* **1**, 277–86.

SHEARER, RONALD A. [1964], 'Nationality, Size of Firm, And Exploration for Petroleum in Western Canada, 1946–54', *Canadian Journal of Economics and Political Science* **30**, 211–27.

SHUBIK, MARTIN [1959], *Strategy and Market Structure: Competition, Oligopoly, and the Theory of Games*, New York, Wiley.

—— [1963], 'Simulation and Gaming: Their Value to the Study of Pricing and Other Market Variables' in A. R. OXENFELDT (ed.), *Models of Markets*, New York and London, Columbia University Press.

SIMON, H. A. [1959], 'Theories of Decision-Making in Economics and Behavioural Science', *American Economic Review* **49**, 253–83.

—— [1962], 'New Developments in the Theory of the Firm', *American Economic Review* **52**, 1–15.

TARSHIS, LORIE [1961], 'The Elasticity of the Marginal Efficiency Function', *American Economic Review* **51**, 958–85.

THEIL, H. [1961] *Economic Forecasts and Policy*, Amsterdam, North-Holland Publishing Company.

TOBIN, JAMES [1958], 'Liquidity Preference as Behaviour Towards Risk', *Review of Economic Studies* **25**, 65–86.

—— [1965], 'The Theory of Portfolio Selection' in HAHN and BRECHLING (eds.), *The Theory of Interest Rates*, London, Macmillan.

VAN HOORN, J., JR. [1962], *Tax Treatment of Research and Development*, Paris, O.E.C.D.

WAGNER, H. M. [1958], 'Advances in Game Theory: A Review Article', *American Economic Review* **48**, 368–87.

WHITE, W. H. [1958], 'The Rate of Interest, the Marginal Efficiency of Capital, and Investment Programming', *Economic Journal* **68**, 51–9.

—— [1962], 'Illusions in the Marginal Investment Subsidy', *National Tax Journal* **15**, 26–31.

—— [1966], 'The Stronger Effects of Monetary Policy on Corporations', in Economic Council of Canada, *Conference on Stabilization Policies*, Ottawa, Queen's Printer.

WICKMAN, KRISTER [1963], *The Swedish Investment Reserve System in Instrument of Contracyclical Policy*. Introductory Statement given before the President's Advisory Committee on Labour-Management Policy. Washington, published by the Swedish Institute, Stockholm.

WILLIAMSON, O. E. [1963], 'Managerial Discretion and Business Behaviour', *American Economic Review* **53**, 1032–57.

—— [1964], *The Economics of Discretionary Behavior: Managerial Objectives in a Theory of the Firm*, Englewood Cliffs, Prentice-Hall.

WONNACOTT, R. J. [1961], *Canadian–American Dependence, An Inter-industry Analysis of Production and Prices*, Amsterdam, North-Holland Publishing Company.

WORLEY, JAMES S. [1961], 'Industrial Research and the New Competition', *Journal of Political Economy* **69**, 183–6.

WRIGHT, ROBERT W. [1964], *Investment Decision in Industry*, London, Chapman and Hall.

YOUNG, J. H. and HELLIWELL, J. F., with the assistance of W. A. MCKAY, [1965], *The Effects of Monetary Policy on Corporations*, Ottawa, Queen's Printer.

ZELLNER, A. and LEE, T. H. [1965], 'Joint Estimation of Relationships Involving Discrete Random Variables', *Econometrica* **33**, 382–94.

AUTHOR INDEX

SUBJECT INDEX

Printed in Great Britain by Richard Clay (The Chaucer Press), Ltd., Bungay, Suffolk.